RUNAWAYS

PRIDE & JOY

Writer: Brian K. Vaughan
Pencils: Adrian Alphona
Inks: David Newbold and Craig Yeung
Colors: Brian Reber

Cover Art: Takeshi Miyazawa
Letters: Virtual Calligraphy
Assistant Editors: Stephanie Moore &
MacKenzie Cadenhead
Editor: C.B. Cebulski

Collections Editor: Jeff Youngquist
Assistant Editor: Jennifer Grünwald
Book Designer: Jeof Vita

Editor in Chief: Joe Quesada
Publisher: Dan Buckley

RUNAWAYS created by
Brian K. Vaughan and Adrian Alphona

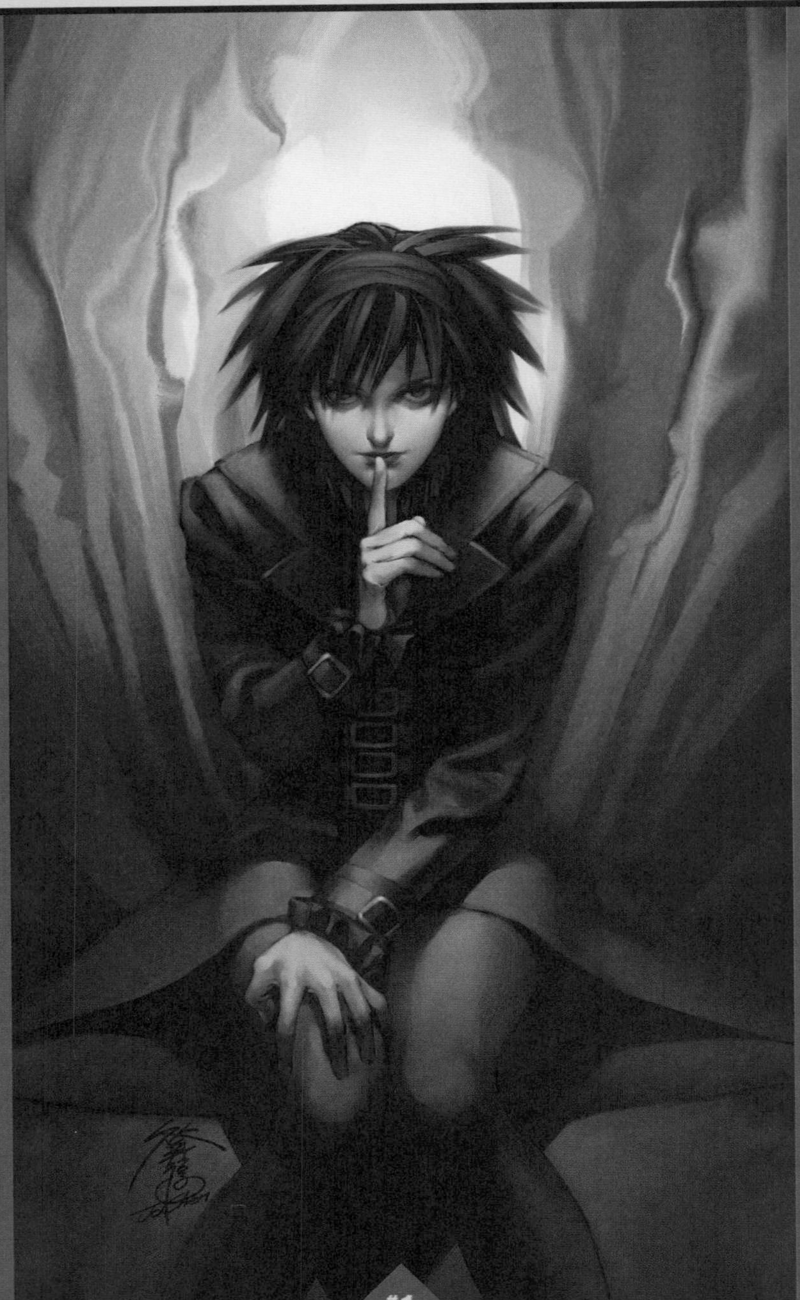
#1

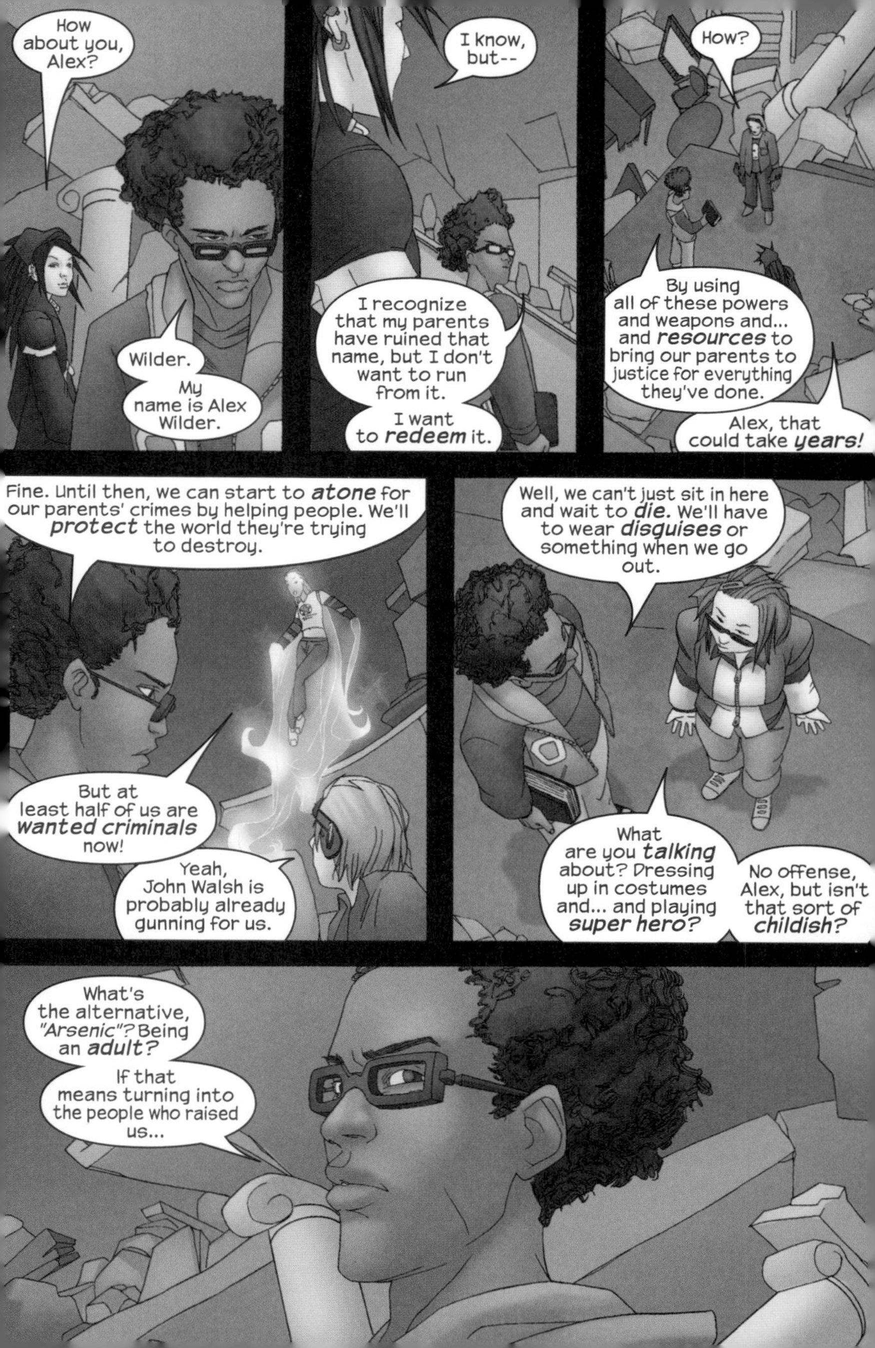
How about you, Alex?
Wilder.
My name is Alex Wilder.
I know, but--
I recognize that my parents have ruined that name, but I don't want to run from it.
I want to *redeem* it.
How?
By using all of these powers and weapons and... and *resources* to bring our parents to justice for everything they've done.
Alex, that could take *years!*
Fine. Until then, we can start to *atone* for our parents' crimes by helping people. We'll *protect* the world they're trying to destroy.
But at least half of us are *wanted criminals* now!
Yeah, John Walsh is probably already gunning for us.
Well, we can't just sit in here and wait to *die.* We'll have to wear *disguises* or something when we go out.
What are you *talking* about? Dressing up in costumes and... and playing *super hero?*
No offense, Alex, but isn't that sort of *childish?*
What's the alternative, "Arsenic"? Being an *adult?*
If that means turning into the people who raised us...

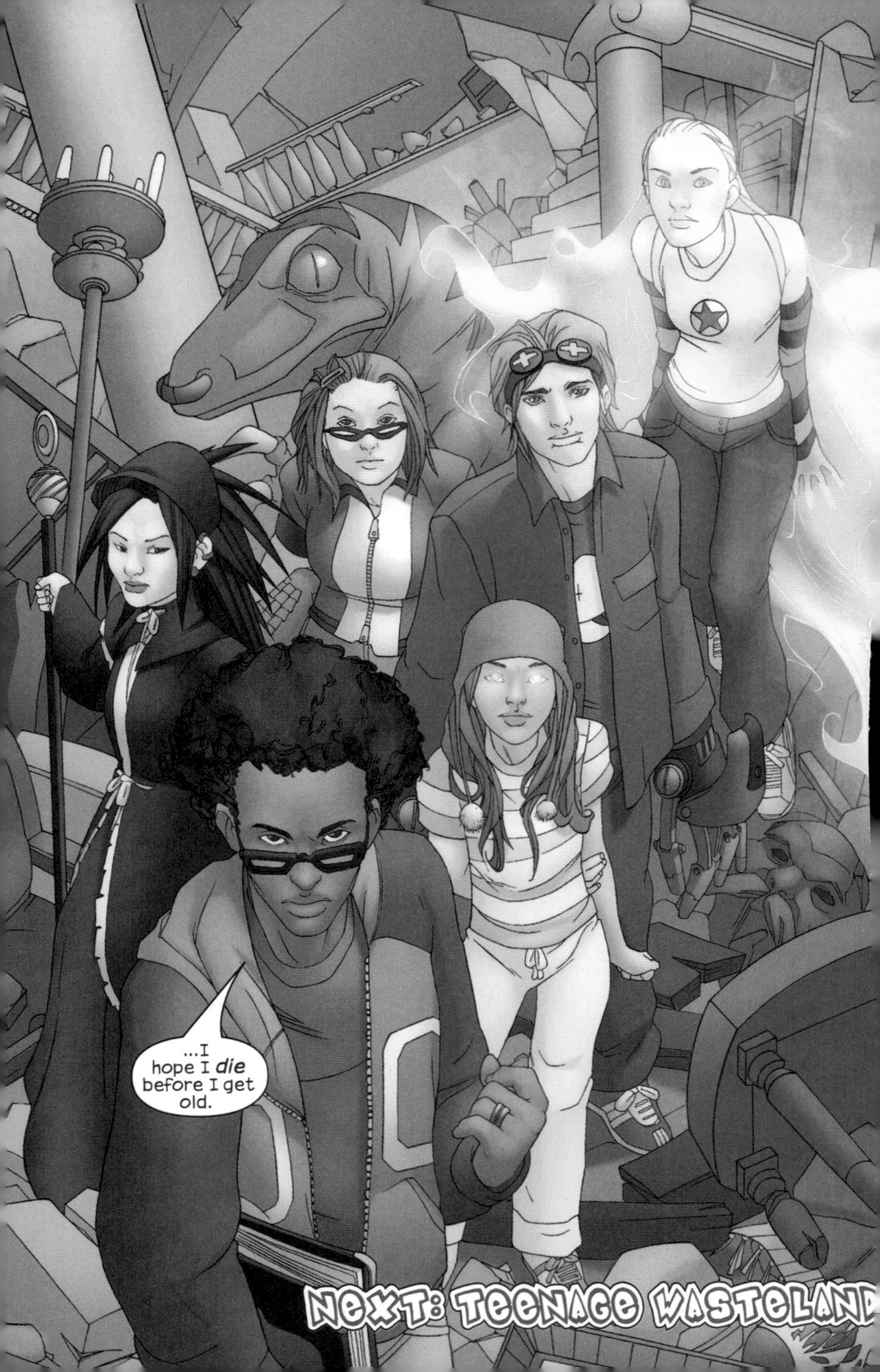

...I hope I *die* before I get old.
NEXT: TEENAGE WASTELAND

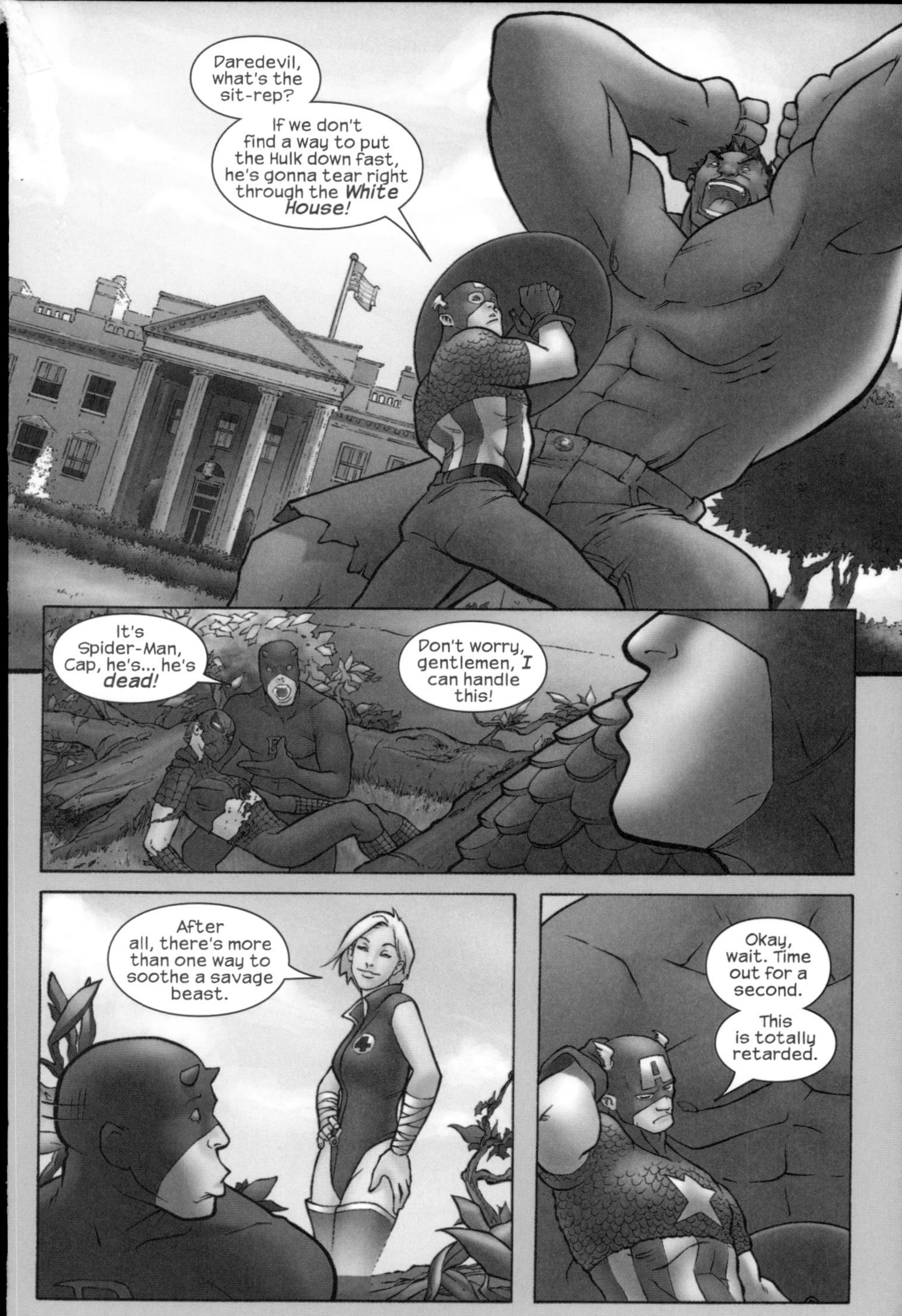
Daredevil, what's the sit-rep?
If we don't find a way to put the Hulk down fast, he's gonna tear right through the *White House!*
It's Spider-Man, Cap, he's... he's *dead!*
Don't worry, gentlemen, *I* can handle this!
After all, there's more than one way to soothe a savage beast.
Okay, wait. Time out for a second.
This is totally retarded.

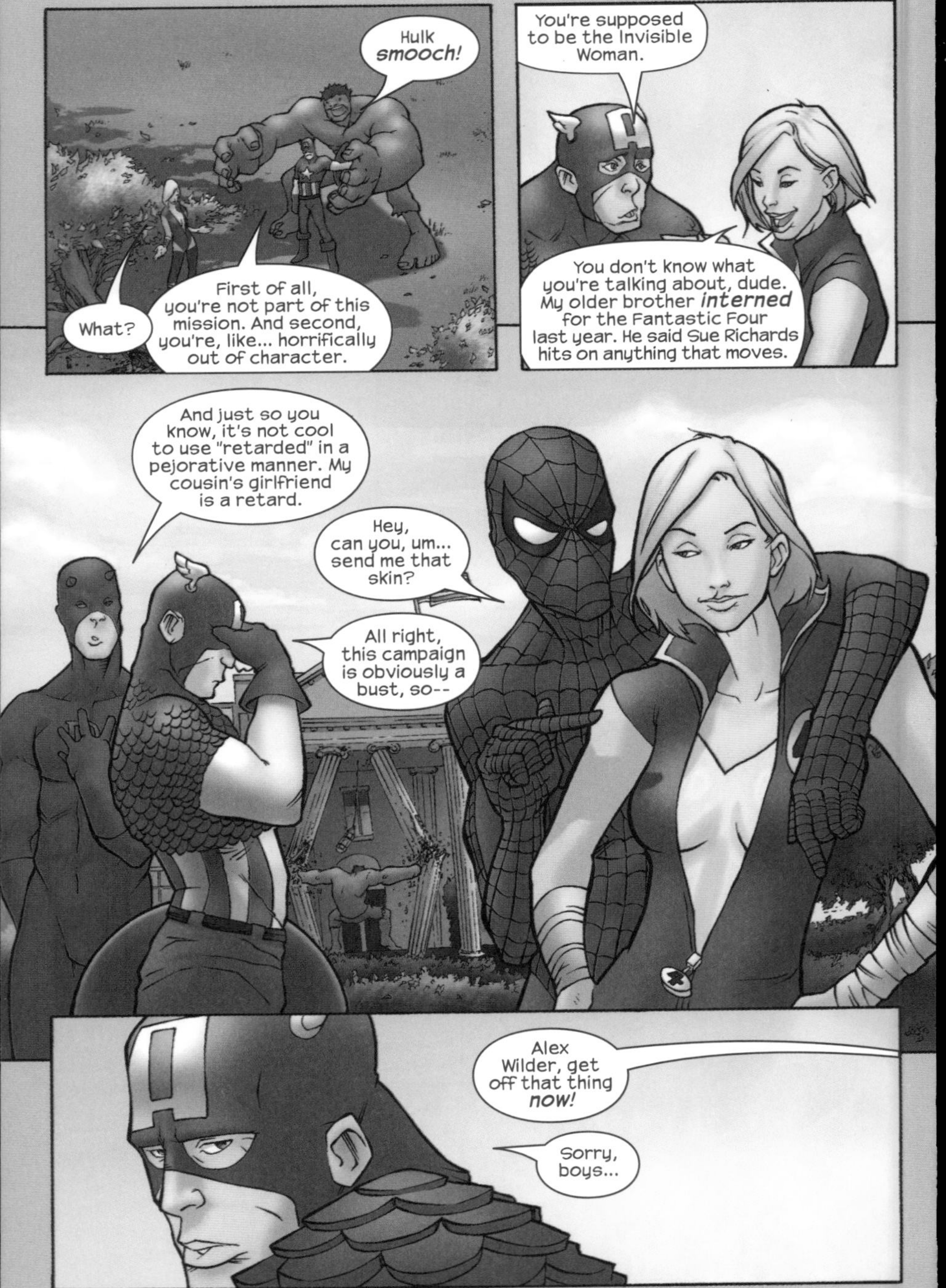
Hulk smooch!
What?
First of all, you're not part of this mission. And second, you're, like... horrifically out of character.
You're supposed to be the Invisible Woman.
You don't know what you're talking about, dude. My older brother *interned* for the Fantastic Four last year. He said Sue Richards hits on anything that moves.
And just so you know, it's not cool to use "retarded" in a pejorative manner. My cousin's girlfriend is a retard.
Hey, can you, um... send me that skin?
All right, this campaign is obviously a bust, so--
Alex Wilder, get off that thing *now!*
Sorry, boys...

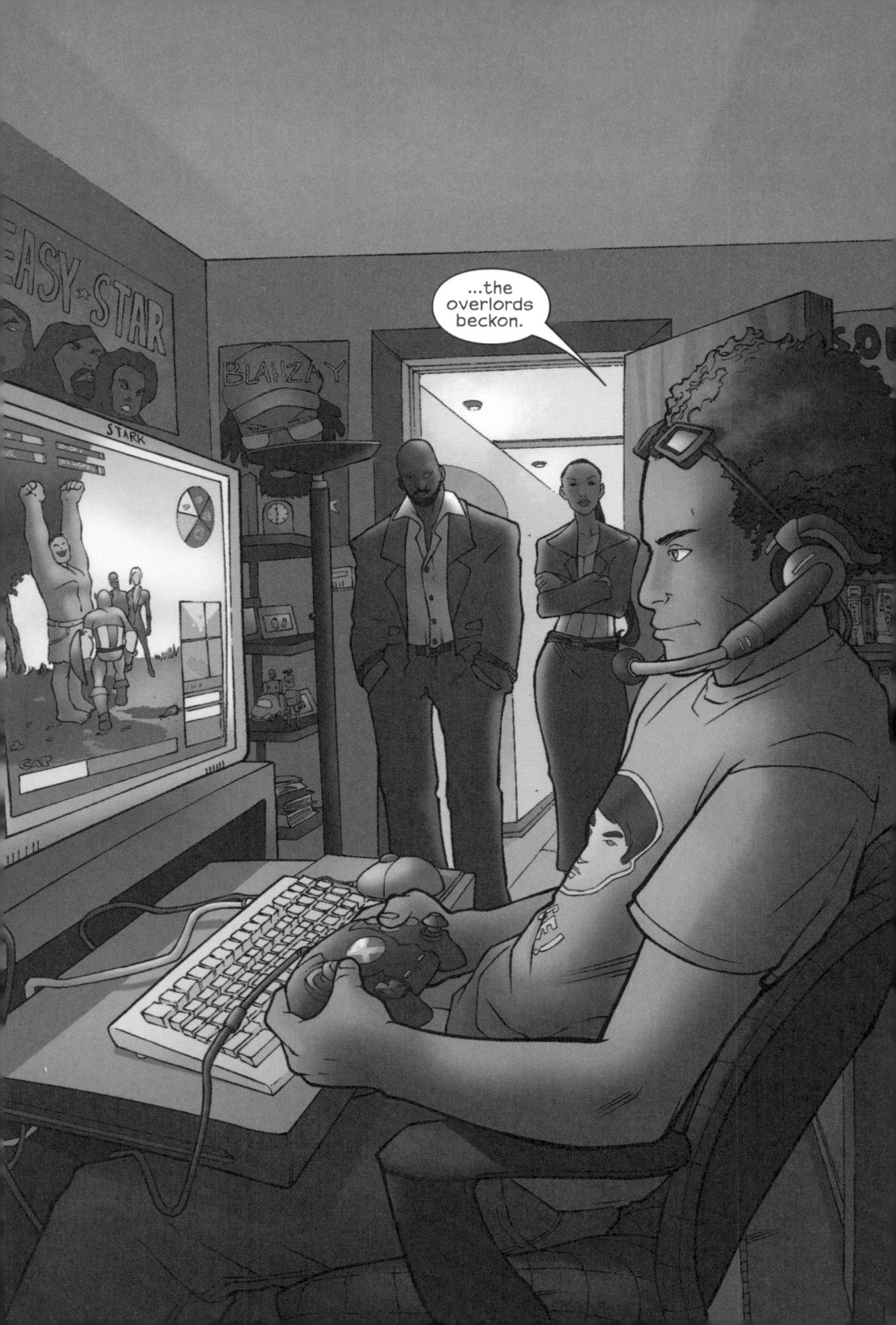
...the overlords beckon.
EASY STAR
BLAHZAY
STARK
CAP

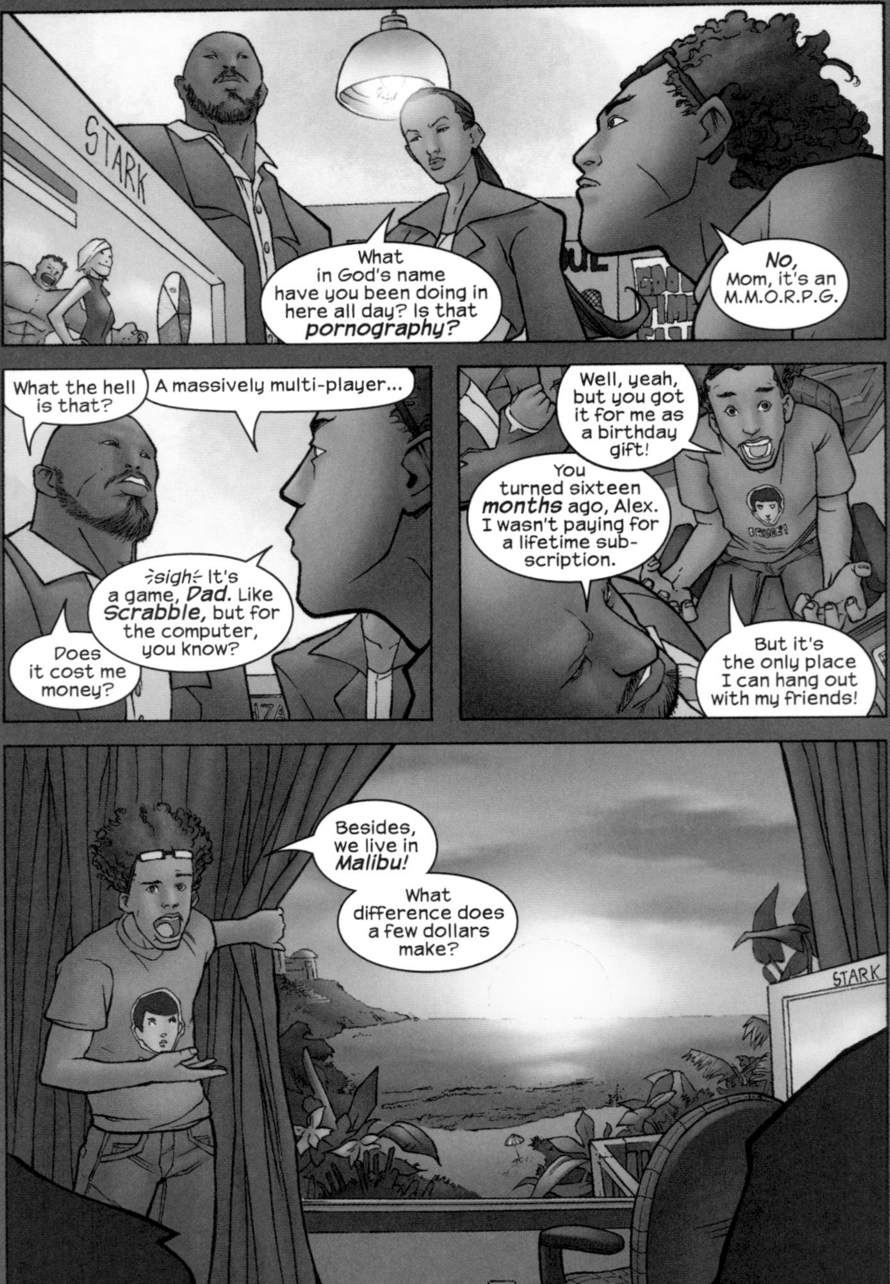
STARK
What in God's name have you been doing in here all day? Is that *pornography?*
No, Mom, it's an M.M.O.R.P.G.
What the hell is that?
A massively multi-player...
sigh It's a game, *Dad.* Like *Scrabble,* but for the computer, you know?
Does it cost me money?
Well, yeah, but you got it for me as a birthday gift!
You turned sixteen *months* ago, Alex. I wasn't paying for a lifetime sub-scription.
But it's the only place I can hang out with my friends!
Besides, we live in *Malibu!*
What difference does a few dollars make?
STARK

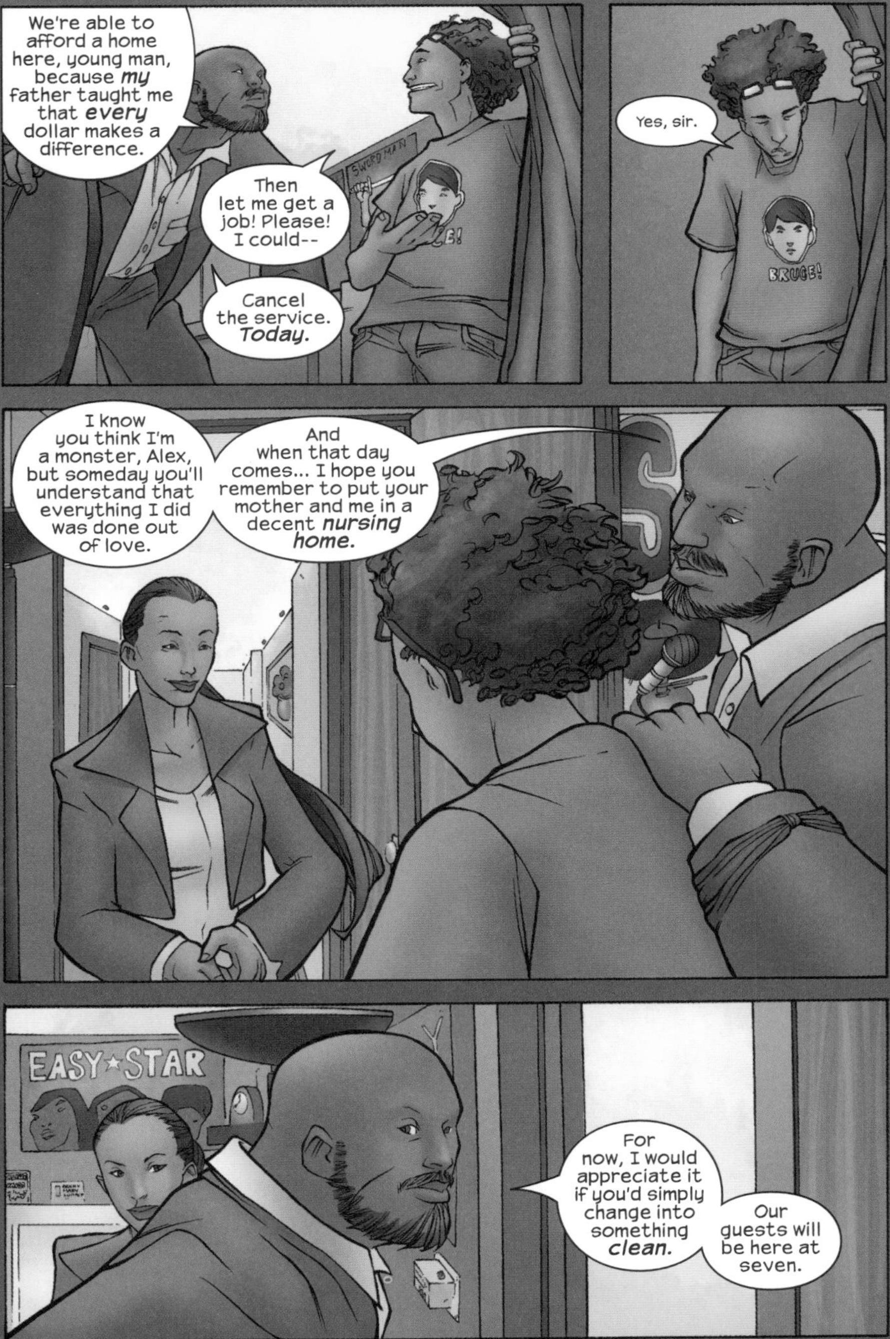
We're able to afford a home here, young man, because *my* father taught me that *every* dollar makes a difference.
SWORD MAN
Then let me get a job! Please! I could--
Cancel the service. *Today.*
Yes, sir.
BRUCE!
I know you think I'm a monster, Alex, but someday you'll understand that everything I did was done out of love.
And when that day comes... I hope you remember to put your mother and me in a decent *nursing home.*
EASY★STAR
For now, I would appreciate it if you'd simply change into something *clean.*
Our guests will be here at seven.

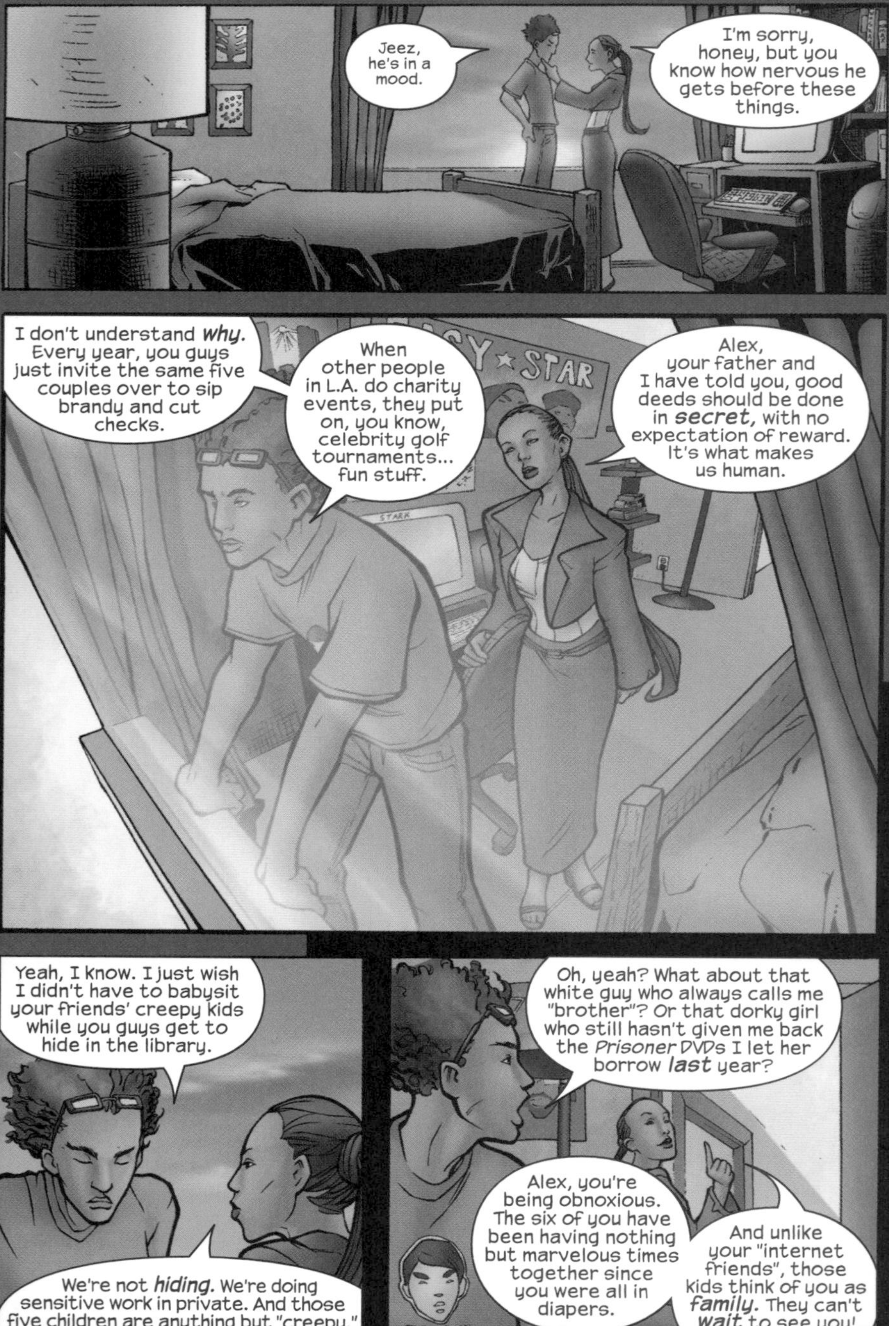

Jeez, he's in a mood.
I'm sorry, honey, but you know how nervous he gets before these things.
I don't understand *why.* Every year, you guys just invite the same five couples over to sip brandy and cut checks.
When other people in L.A. do charity events, they put on, you know, celebrity golf tournaments... fun stuff.
Alex, your father and I have told you, good deeds should be done in *secret,* with no expectation of reward. It's what makes us human.
Yeah, I know. I just wish I didn't have to babysit your friends' creepy kids while you guys get to hide in the library.
We're not *hiding.* We're doing sensitive work in private. And those five children are anything but "creepy."
Oh, yeah? What about that white guy who always calls me "brother"? Or that dorky girl who still hasn't given me back the *Prisoner* DVDs I let her borrow *last* year?
Alex, you're being obnoxious. The six of you have been having nothing but marvelous times together since you were all in diapers.
And unlike your "internet friends", those kids think of you as *family.* They can't *wait* to see you!

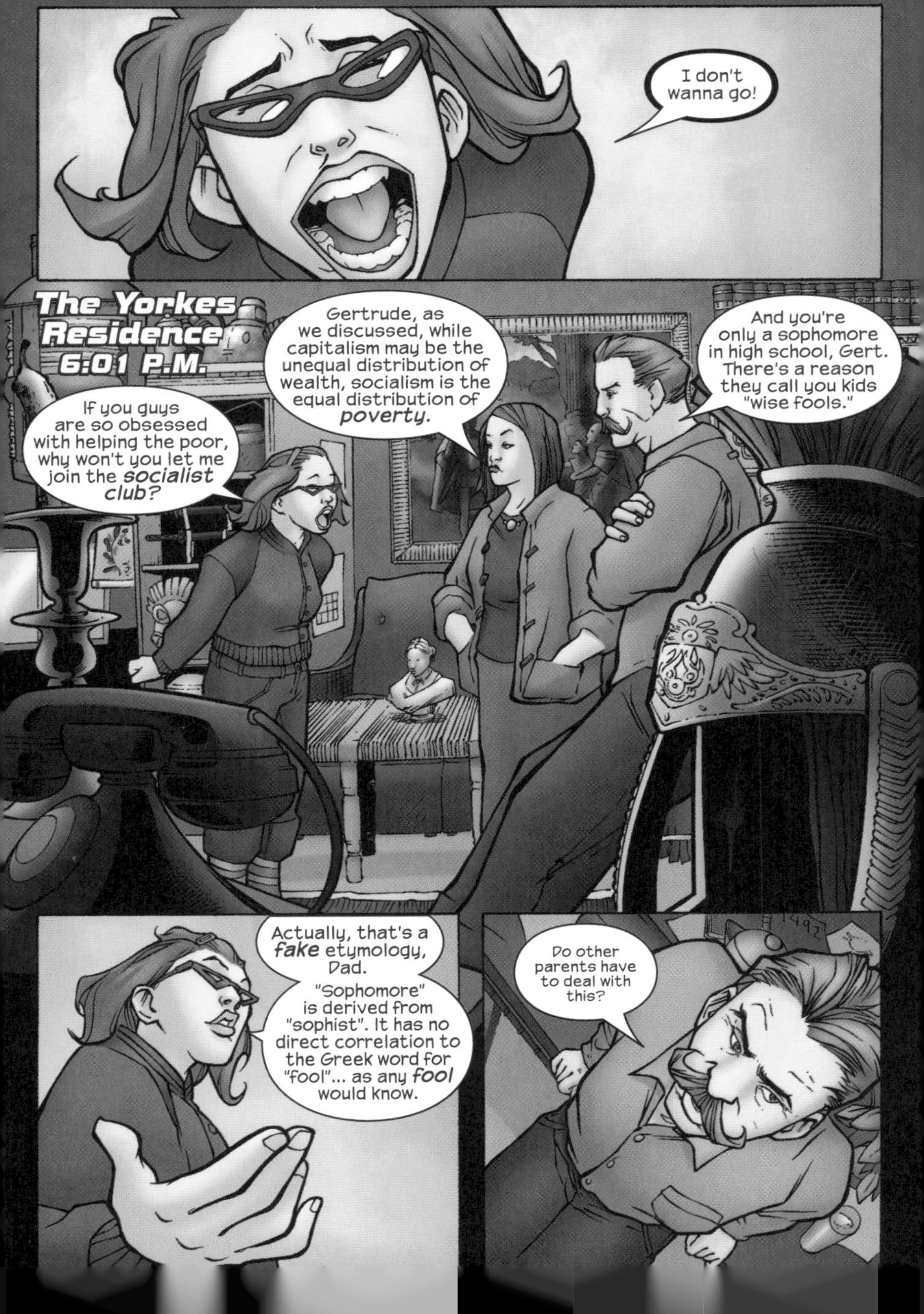
I don't wanna go!
The Yorkes Residence 6:01 P.M.
If you guys are so obsessed with helping the poor, why won't you let me join the *socialist club?*
Gertrude, as we discussed, while capitalism may be the unequal distribution of wealth, socialism is the equal distribution of *poverty.*
And you're only a sophomore in high school, Gert. There's a reason they call you kids "wise fools."
Actually, that's a *fake* etymology, Dad.
"Sophomore" is derived from "sophist". It has no direct correlation to the Greek word for "fool"... as any *fool* would know.
Do other parents have to deal with this?

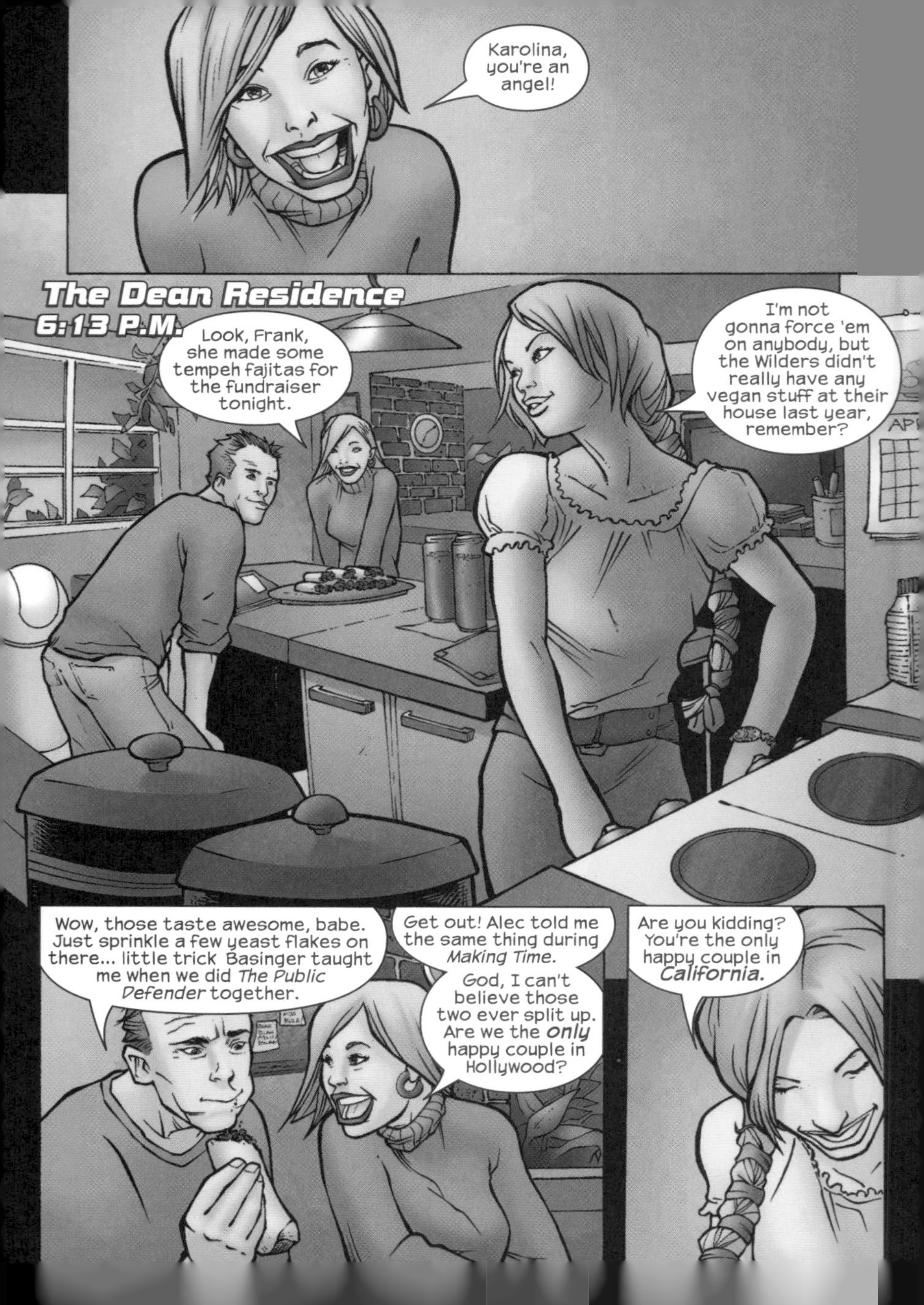
Karolina, you're an angel!
The Dean Residence
6:13 P.M.
Look, Frank, she made some tempeh fajitas for the fundraiser tonight.
I'm not gonna force 'em on anybody, but the Wilders didn't really have any vegan stuff at their house last year, remember?
Wow, those taste awesome, babe. Just sprinkle a few yeast flakes on there... little trick Basinger taught me when we did *The Public Defender* together.
Get out! Alec told me the same thing during *Making Time.*
God, I can't believe those two ever split up. Are we the *only* happy couple in Hollywood?
Are you kidding? You're the only happy couple in *California.*

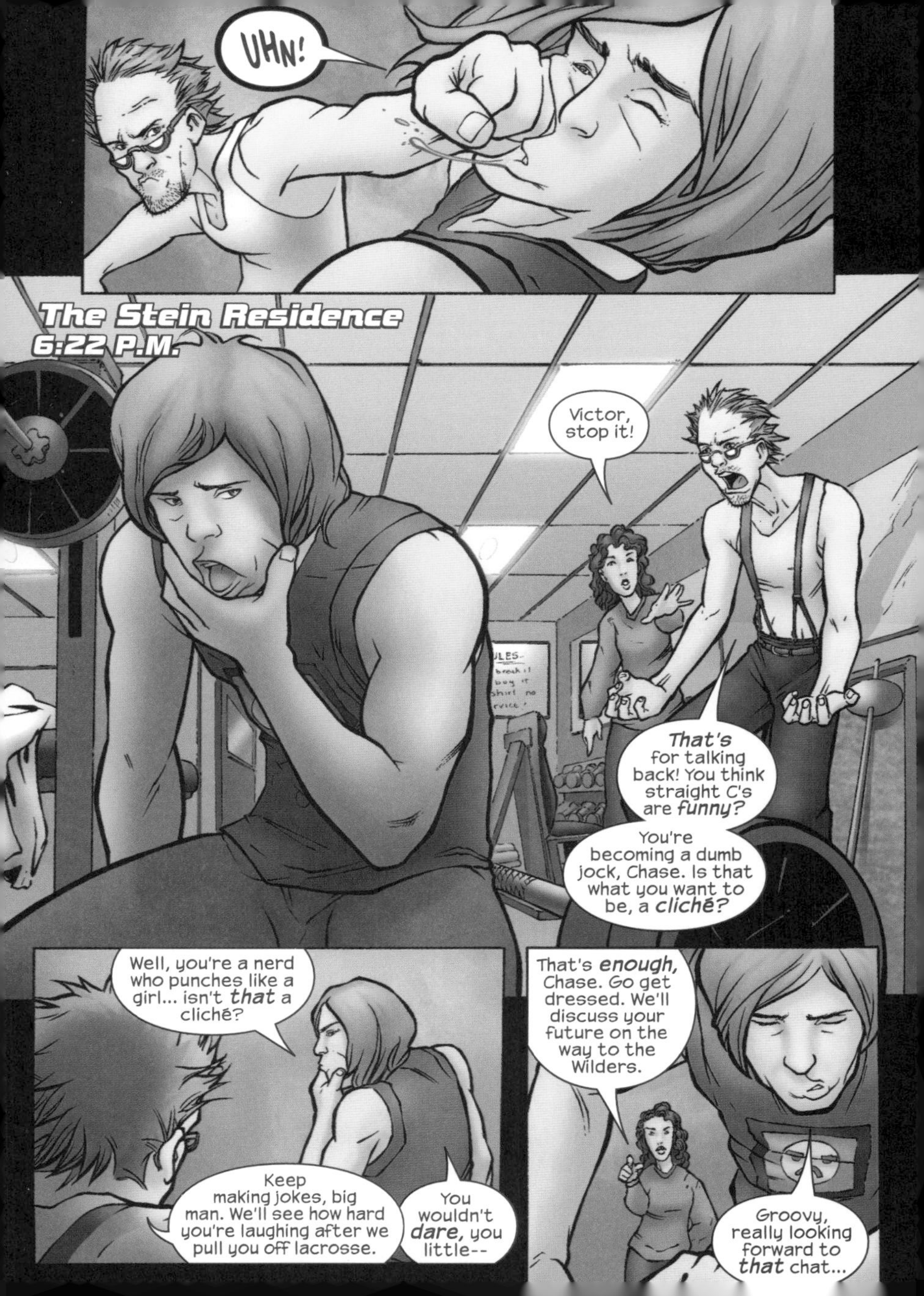
UHN!
The Stein Residence 6:22 P.M.
Victor, stop it!
That's for talking back! You think straight C's are funny?
You're becoming a dumb jock, Chase. Is that what you want to be, a cliché?
Well, you're a nerd who punches like a girl... isn't that a cliché?
Keep making jokes, big man. We'll see how hard you're laughing after we pull you off lacrosse.
You wouldn't dare, you little--
That's enough, Chase. Go get dressed. We'll discuss your future on the way to the Wilders.
Groovy, really looking forward to that chat...

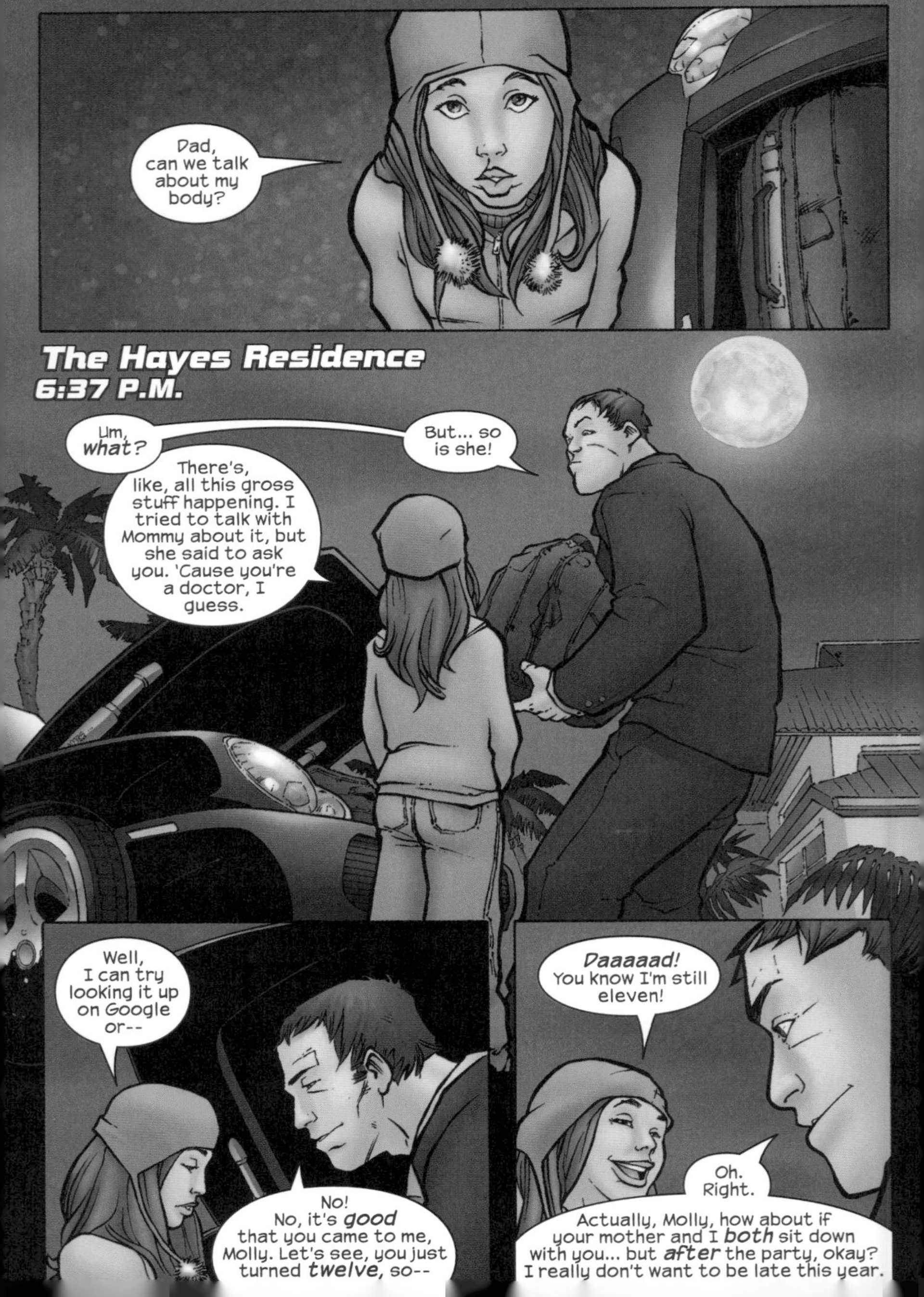

Dad, can we talk about my body?
The Hayes Residence
6:37 P.M.
Um, *what?*
There's, like, all this gross stuff happening. I tried to talk with Mommy about it, but she said to ask you. 'Cause you're a doctor, I guess.
But... so is she!
Well, I can try looking it up on Google or--
No! No, it's **good** that you came to me, Molly. Let's see, you just turned **twelve,** so--
Daaaaad! You know I'm still eleven!
Oh. Right.
Actually, Molly, how about if your mother and I **both** sit down with you... but **after** the party, okay? I really don't want to be late this year.

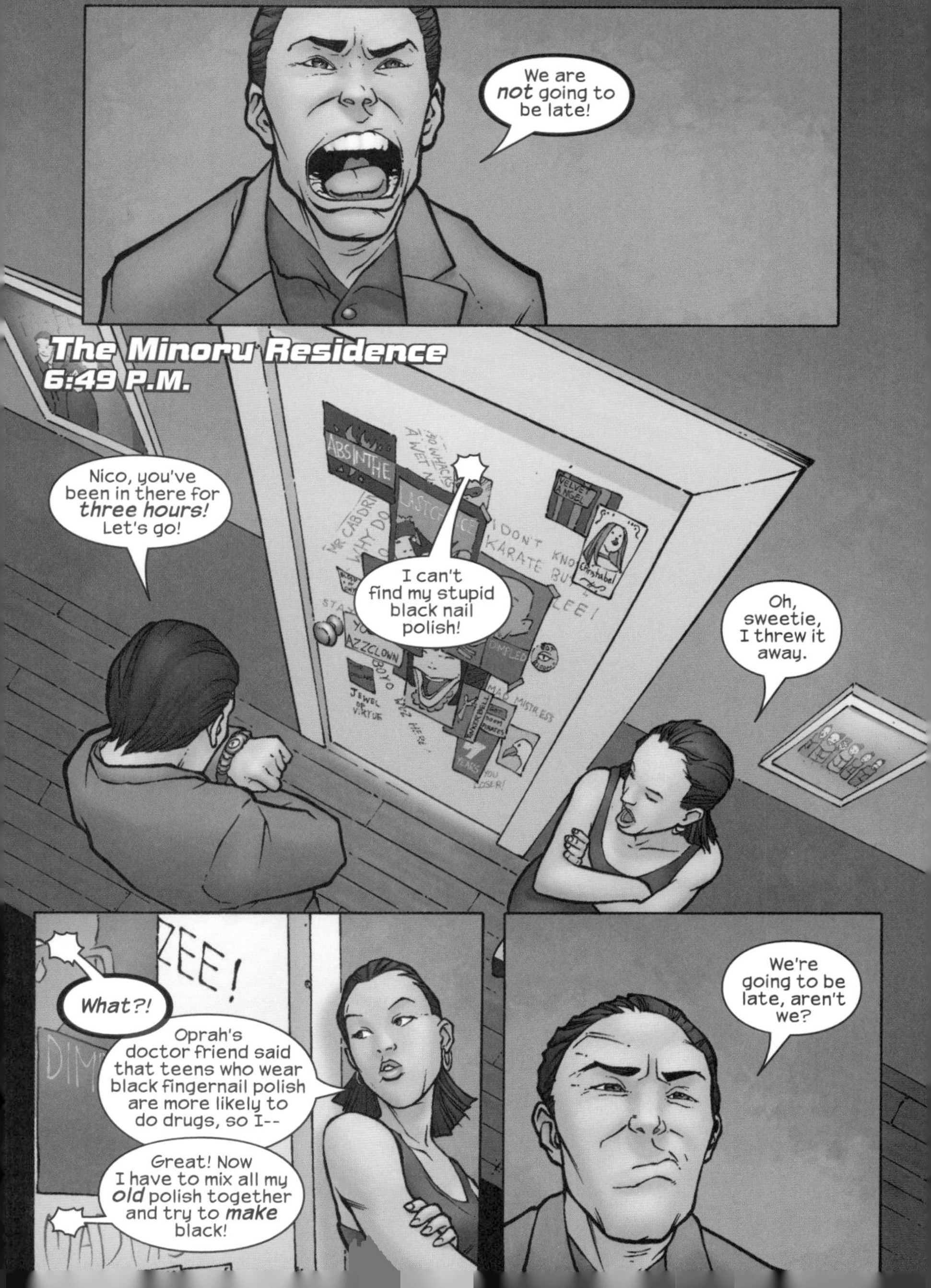
We are not going to be late!
The Minoru Residence 6:49 P.M.
Nico, you've been in there for three hours! Let's go!
I can't find my stupid black nail polish!
Oh, sweetie, I threw it away.
What?!
Oprah's doctor friend said that teens who wear black fingernail polish are more likely to do drugs, so I--
Great! Now I have to mix all my old polish together and try to make black!
We're going to be late, aren't we?

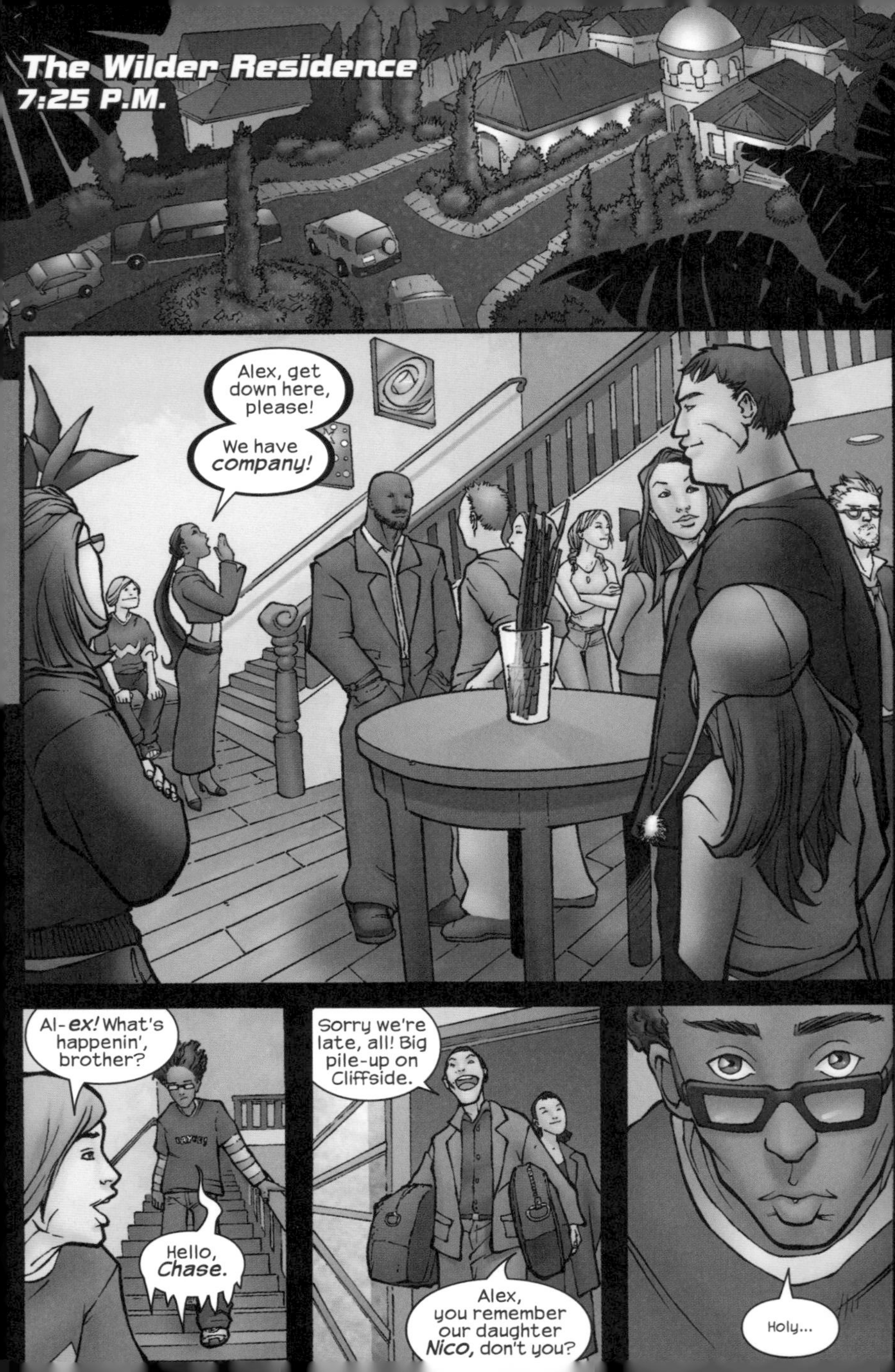
The Wilder Residence
7:25 P.M.
Alex, get down here, please!
We have company!
Al-ex! What's happenin', brother?
Hello, Chase.
Sorry we're late, all! Big pile-up on Cliffside.
Alex, you remember our daughter Nico, don't you?
Holy...

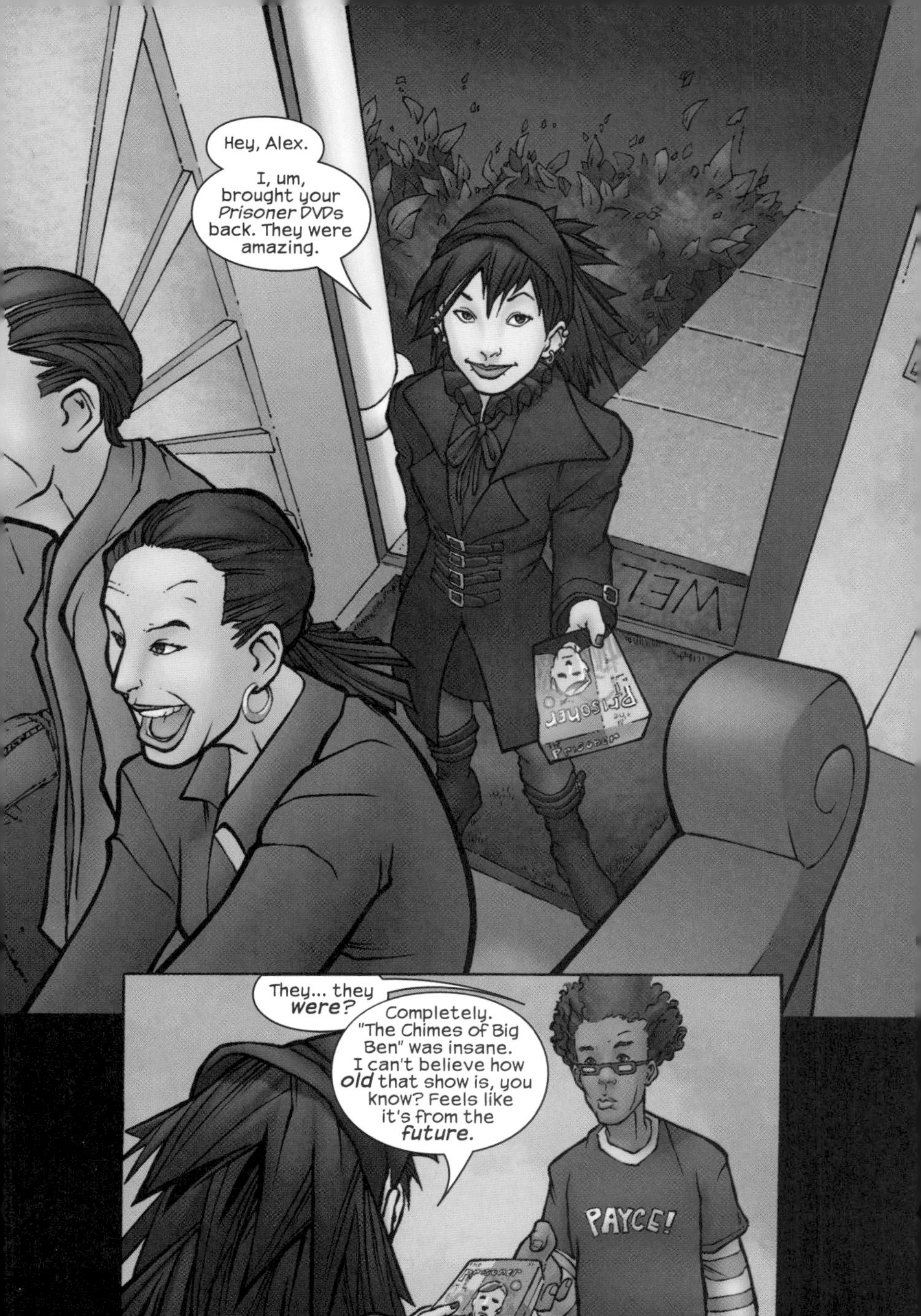
Hey, Alex.
I, um, brought your *Prisoner* DVDs back. They were amazing.
They... they *were*?
Completely. "The Chimes of Big Ben" was insane. I can't believe how *old* that show is, you know? Feels like it's from the *future.*
PAYCE!

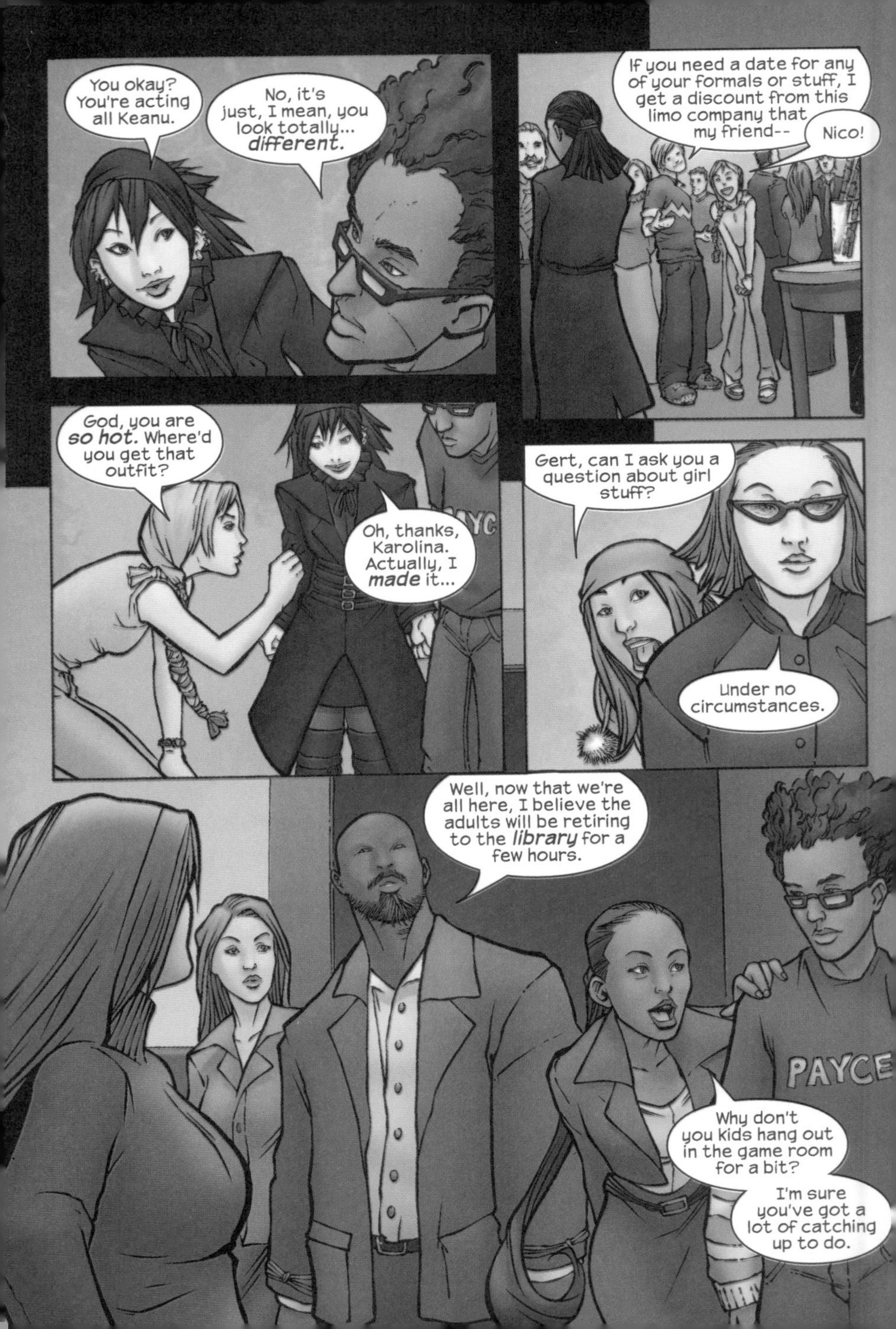
You okay? You're acting all Keanu.
No, it's just, I mean, you look totally... *different.*
If you need a date for any of your formals or stuff, I get a discount from this limo company that my friend--
Nico!
God, you are **so hot.** Where'd you get that outfit?
Oh, thanks, Karolina. Actually, I *made* it...
PAYC
Gert, can I ask you a question about girl stuff?
Under no circumstances.
Well, now that we're all here, I believe the adults will be retiring to the *library* for a few hours.
PAYCE
Why don't you kids hang out in the game room for a bit?
I'm sure you've got a lot of catching up to do.

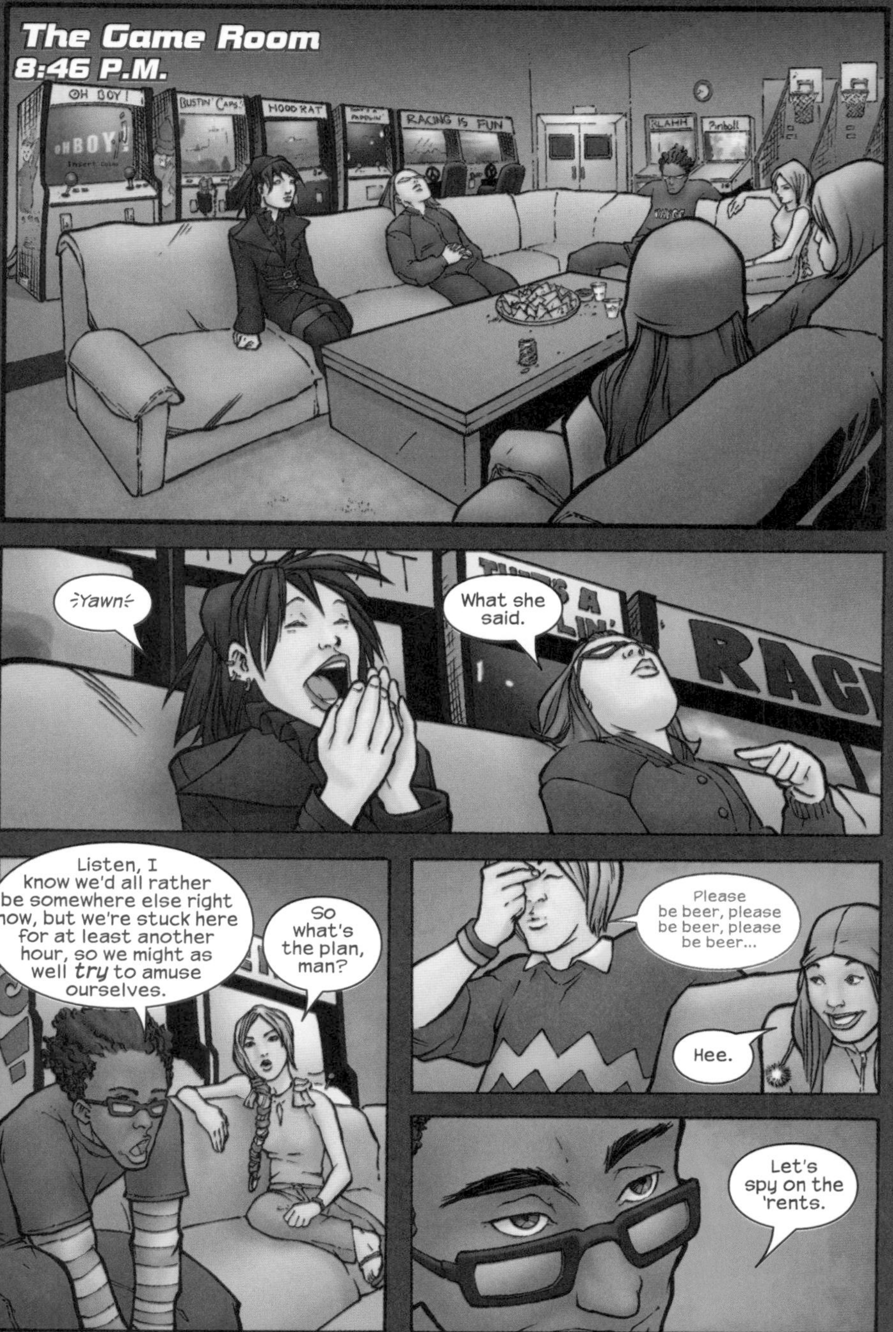
The Game Room
8:46 P.M.
OH BOY!
BUSTIN' CAPS!
HOOD RAT
RACING IS FUN
Pinball
≈Yawn≈
What she said.
Listen, I know we'd all rather be somewhere else right now, but we're stuck here for at least another hour, so we might as well *try* to amuse ourselves.
So what's the plan, man?
Please be beer, please be beer, please be beer...
Hee.
Let's spy on the 'rents.

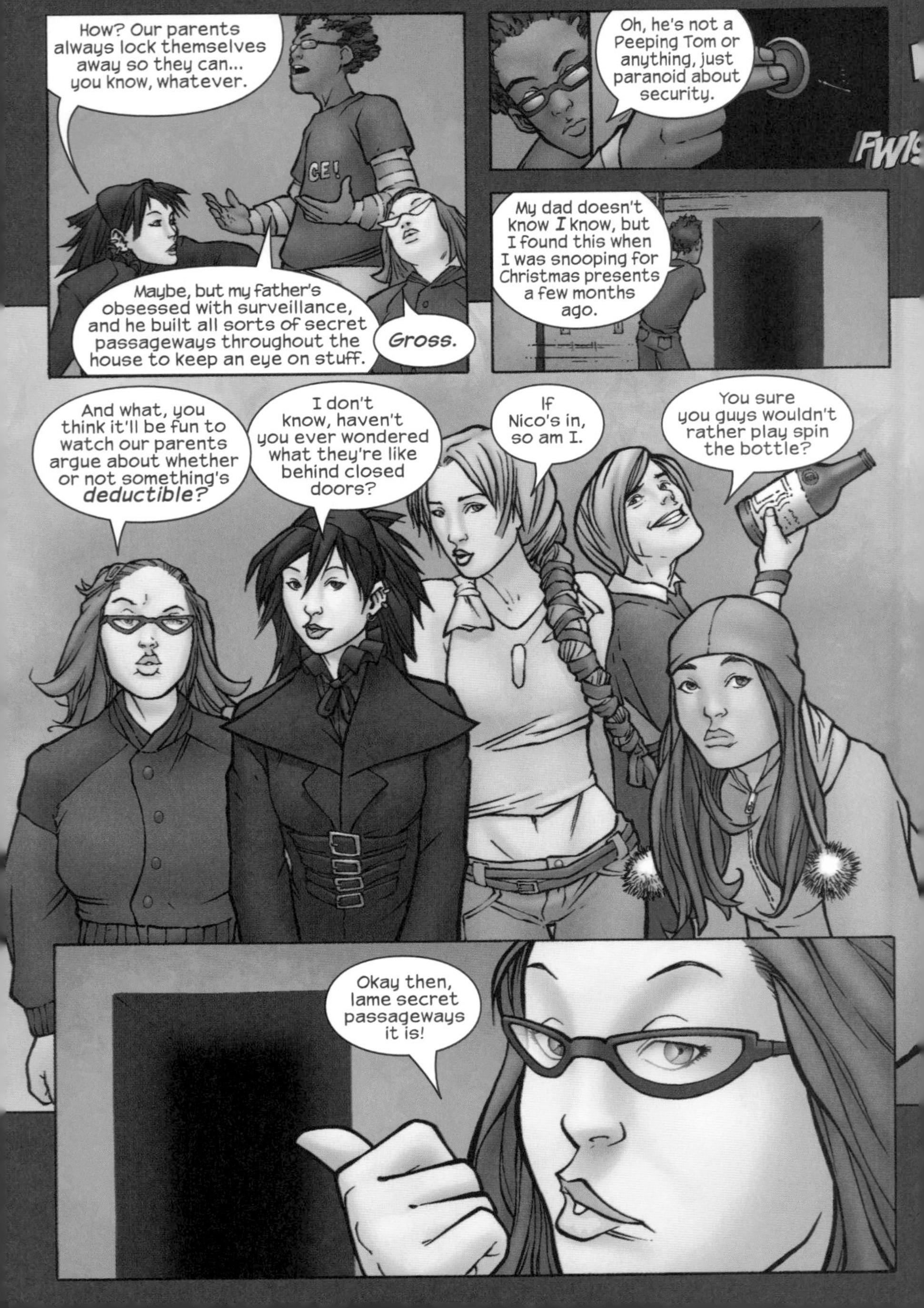
How? Our parents always lock themselves away so they can... you know, whatever.
Maybe, but my father's obsessed with surveillance, and he built all sorts of secret passageways throughout the house to keep an eye on stuff.
Gross.
Oh, he's not a Peeping Tom or anything, just paranoid about security.
FWIS
My dad doesn't know *I* know, but I found this when I was snooping for Christmas presents a few months ago.
And what, you think it'll be fun to watch our parents argue about whether or not something's *deductible?*
I don't know, haven't you ever wondered what they're like behind closed doors?
If Nico's in, so am I.
You sure you guys wouldn't rather play spin the bottle?
Okay then, lame secret passageways it is!

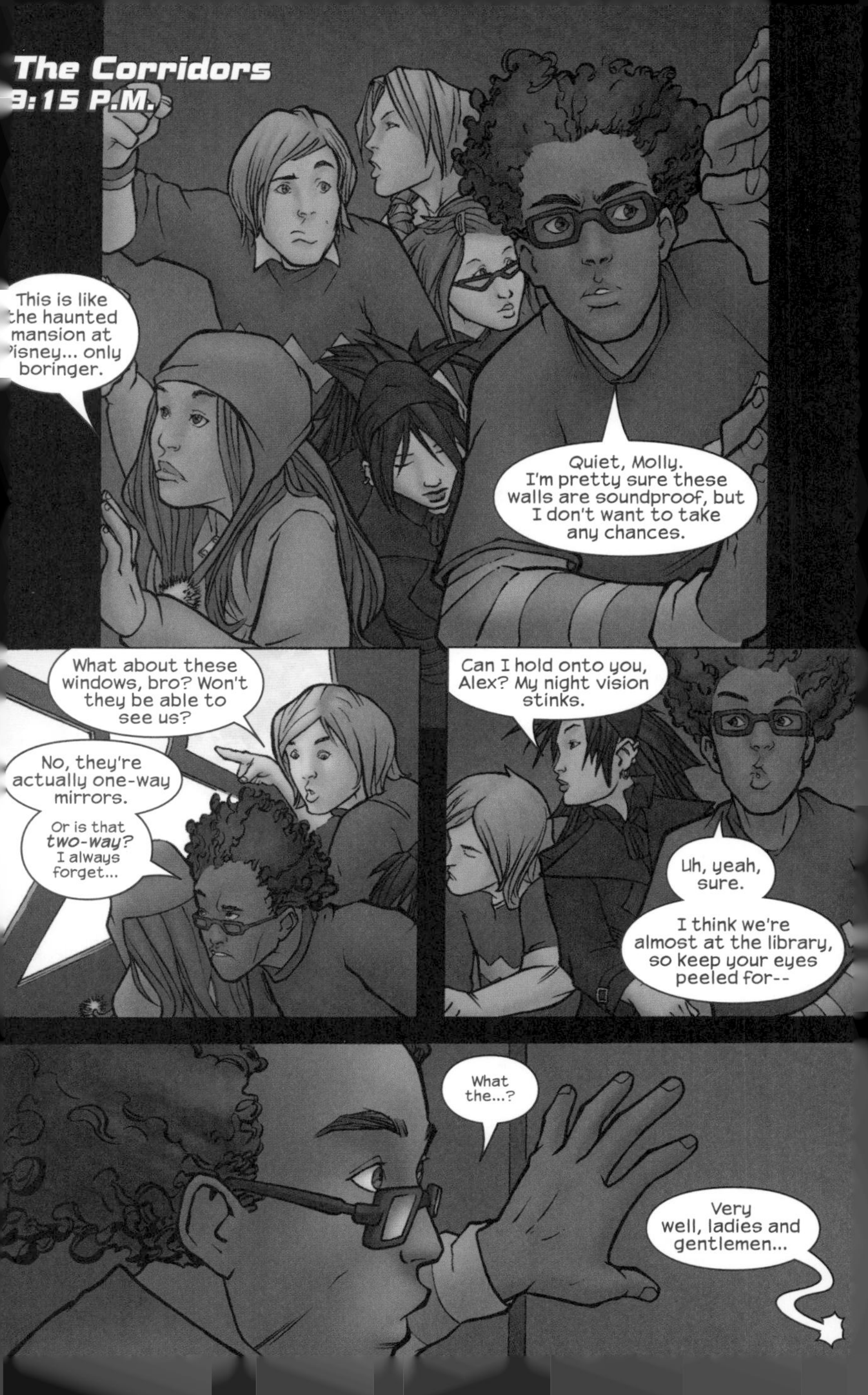
The Corridors
9:15 P.M.
This is like the haunted mansion at Disney... only boringer.
Quiet, Molly. I'm pretty sure these walls are soundproof, but I don't want to take any chances.
What about these windows, bro? Won't they be able to see us?
No, they're actually one-way mirrors.
Or is that *two-way*? I always forget...
Can I hold onto you, Alex? My night vision stinks.
Uh, yeah, sure.
I think we're almost at the library, so keep your eyes peeled for--
What the...?
Very well, ladies and gentlemen...

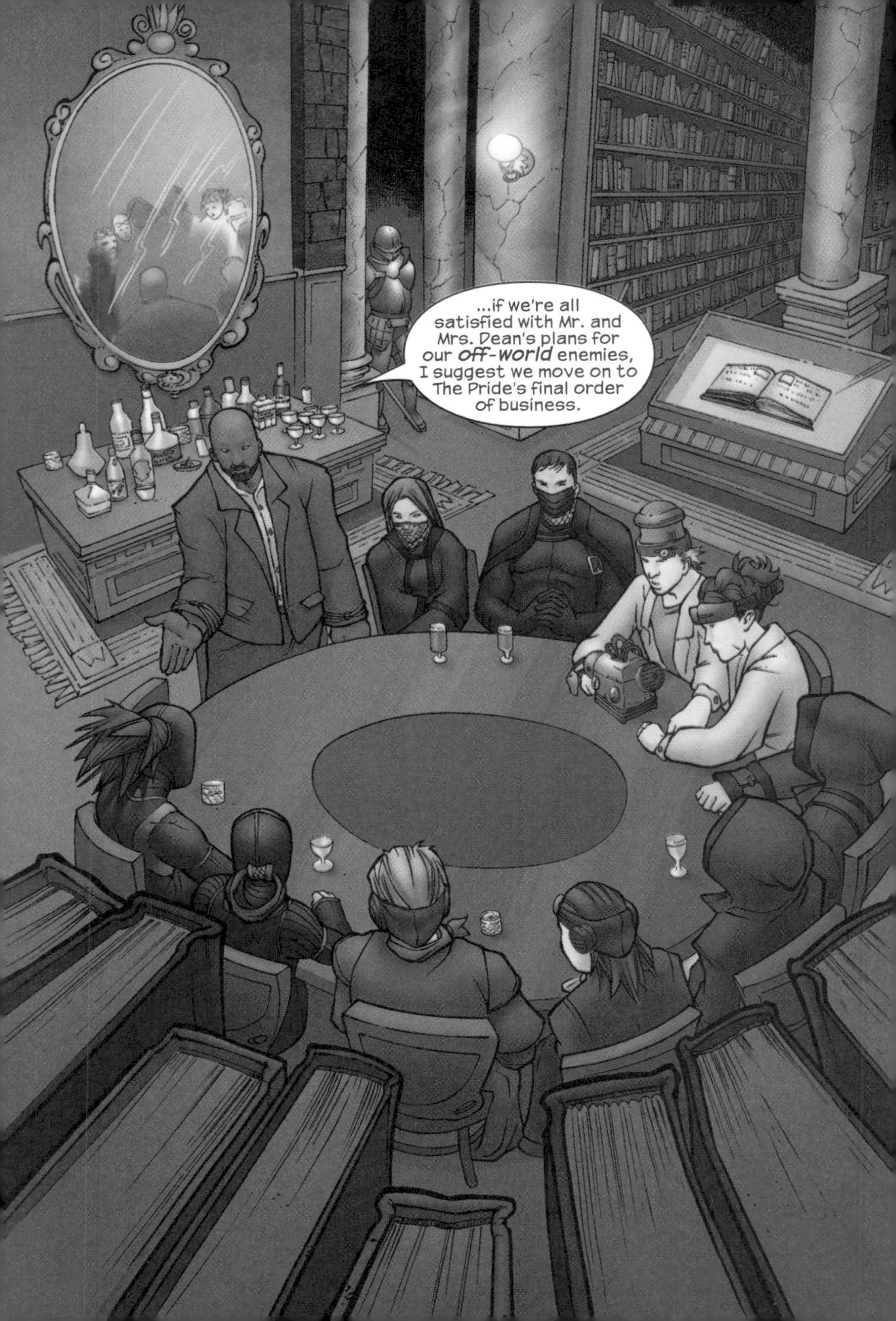
...if we're all satisfied with Mr. and Mrs. Dean's plans for our *off-world* enemies, I suggest we move on to The Pride's final order of business.

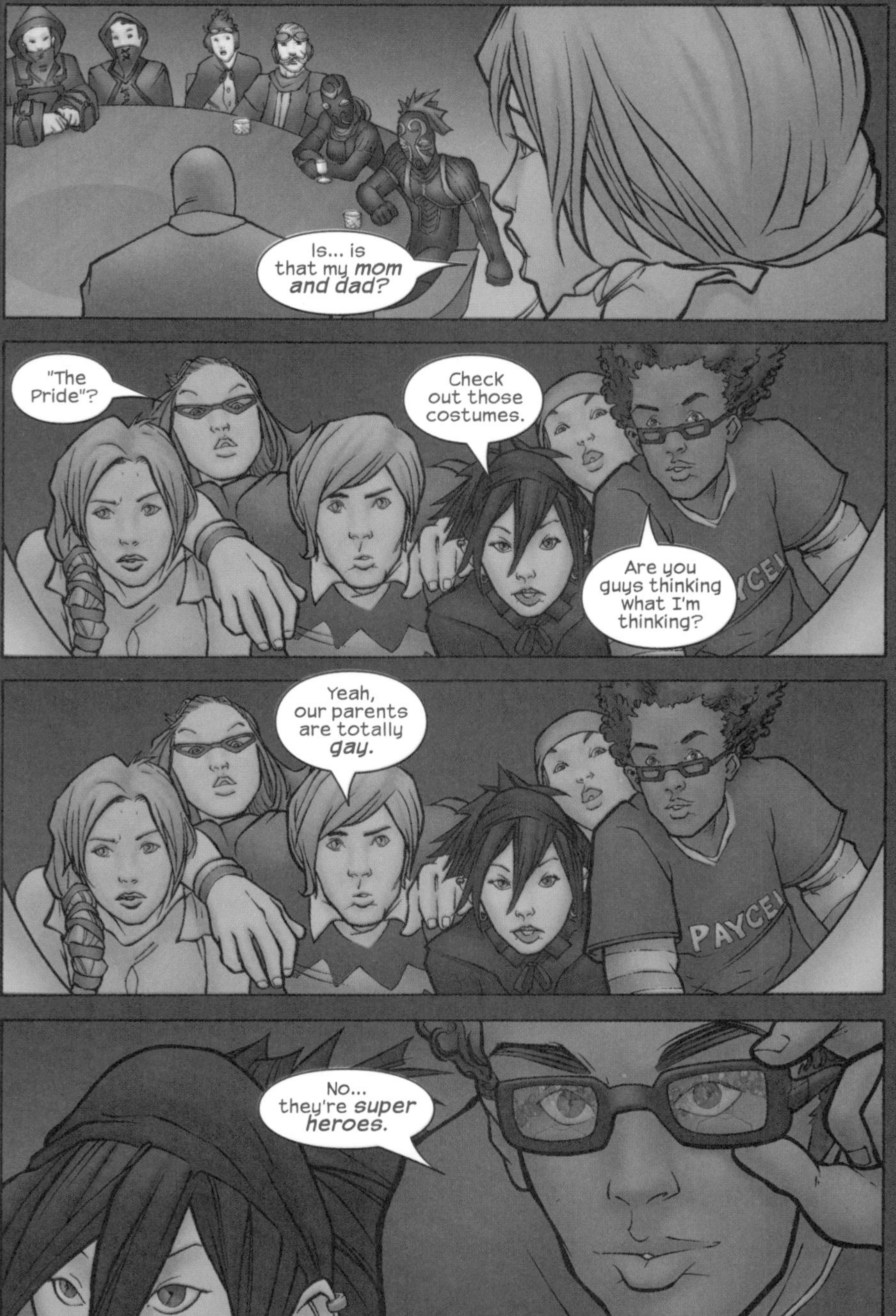
Is... is that my *mom and dad?*
"The Pride"?
Check out those costumes.
Are you guys thinking what I'm thinking?
Yeah, our parents are totally *gay.*
No... they're *super heroes.*

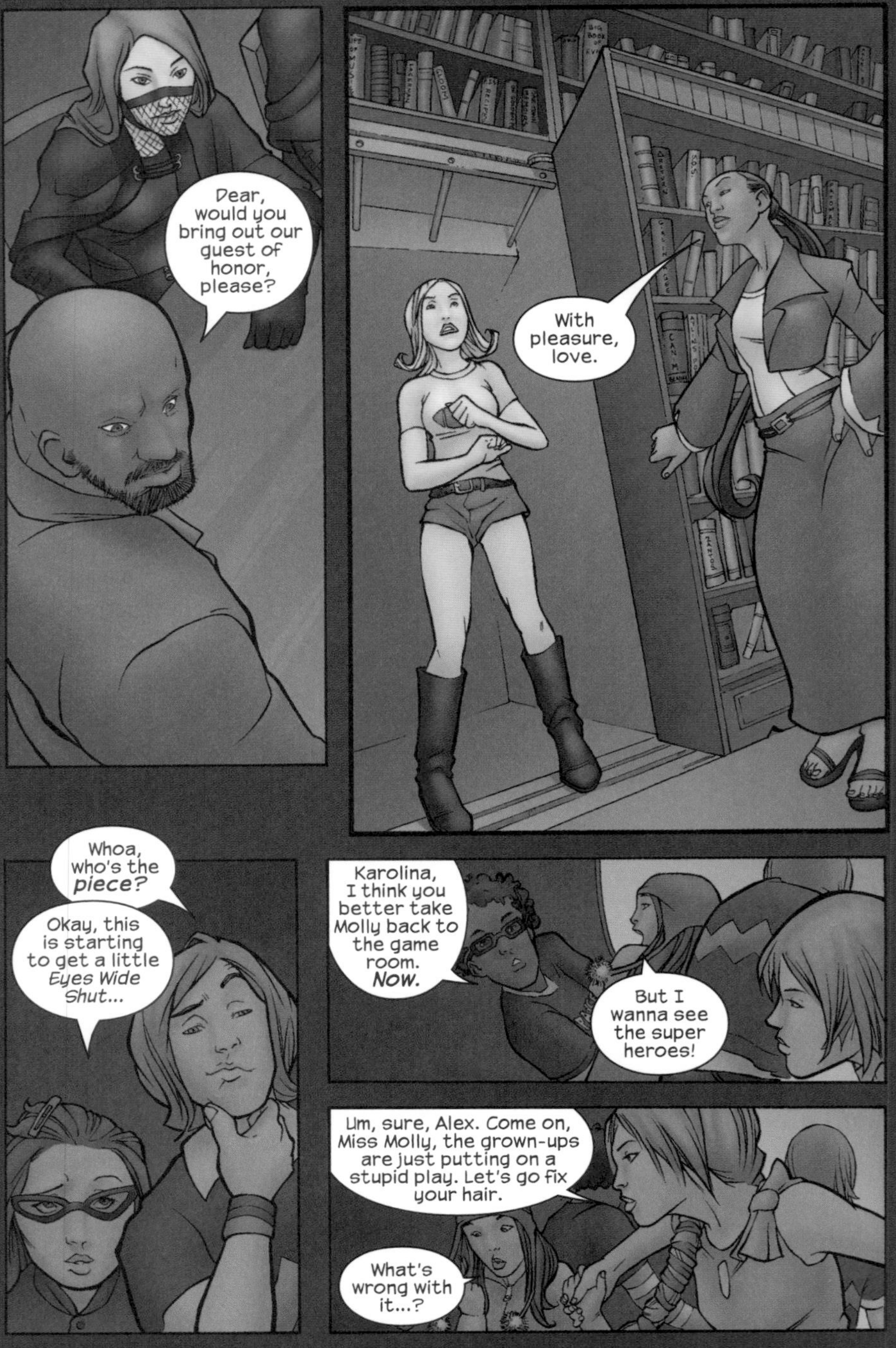
Dear, would you bring out our guest of honor, please?
With pleasure, love.
Whoa, who's the *piece*?
Okay, this is starting to get a little *Eyes Wide Shut*...
Karolina, I think you better take Molly back to the game room. **NOW.**
But I wanna see the super heroes!
Um, sure, Alex. Come on, Miss Molly, the grown-ups are just putting on a stupid play. Let's go fix your hair.
What's wrong with it...?

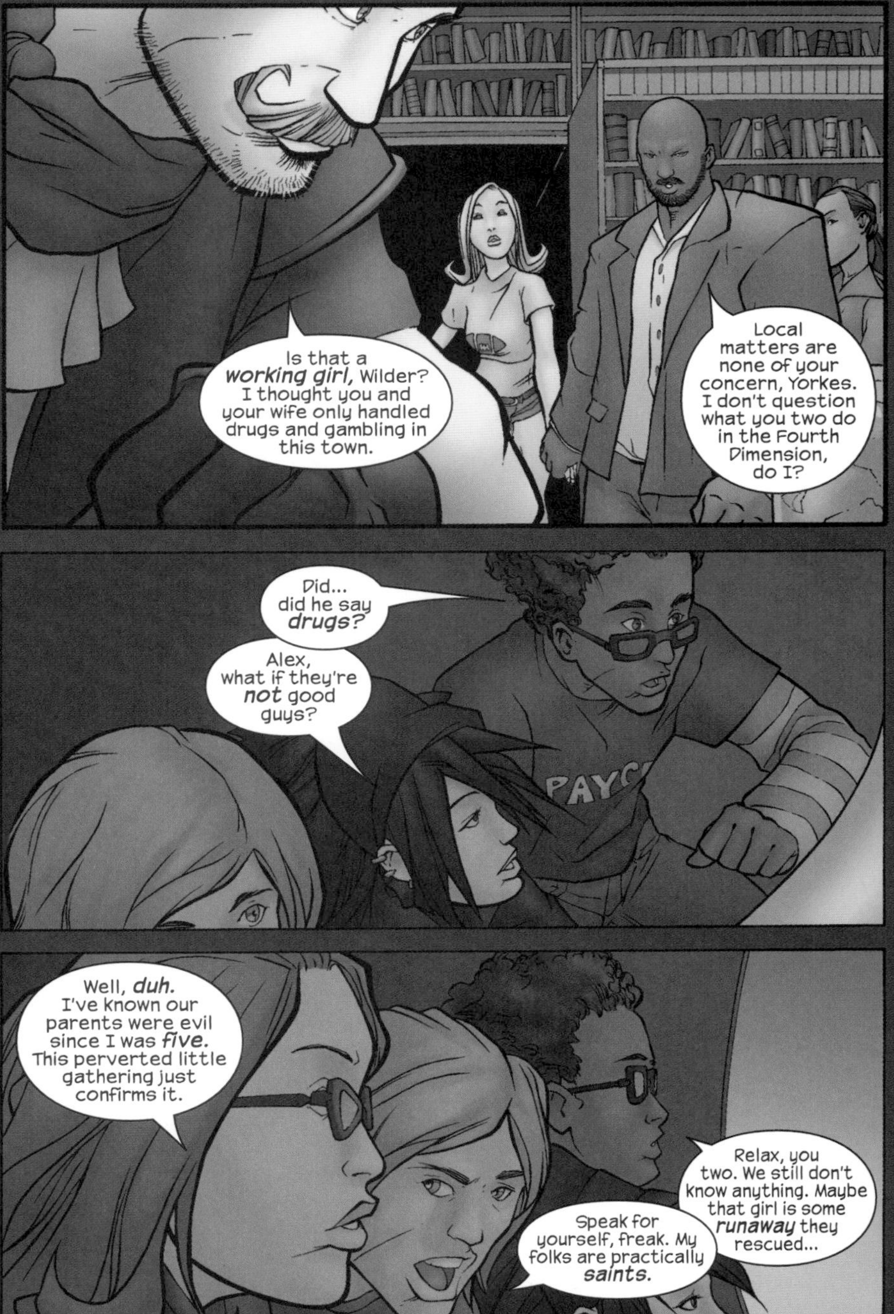

Is that a *working girl,* Wilder? I thought you and your wife only handled drugs and gambling in this town.
Local matters are none of your concern, Yorkes. I don't question what you two do in the Fourth Dimension, do I?
Did... did he say *drugs?*
Alex, what if they're *not* good guys?
PAYC
Well, *duh.* I've known our parents were evil since I was *five.* This perverted little gathering just confirms it.
Relax, you two. We still don't know anything. Maybe that girl is some *runaway* they rescued...
Speak for yourself, freak. My folks are practically *saints.*

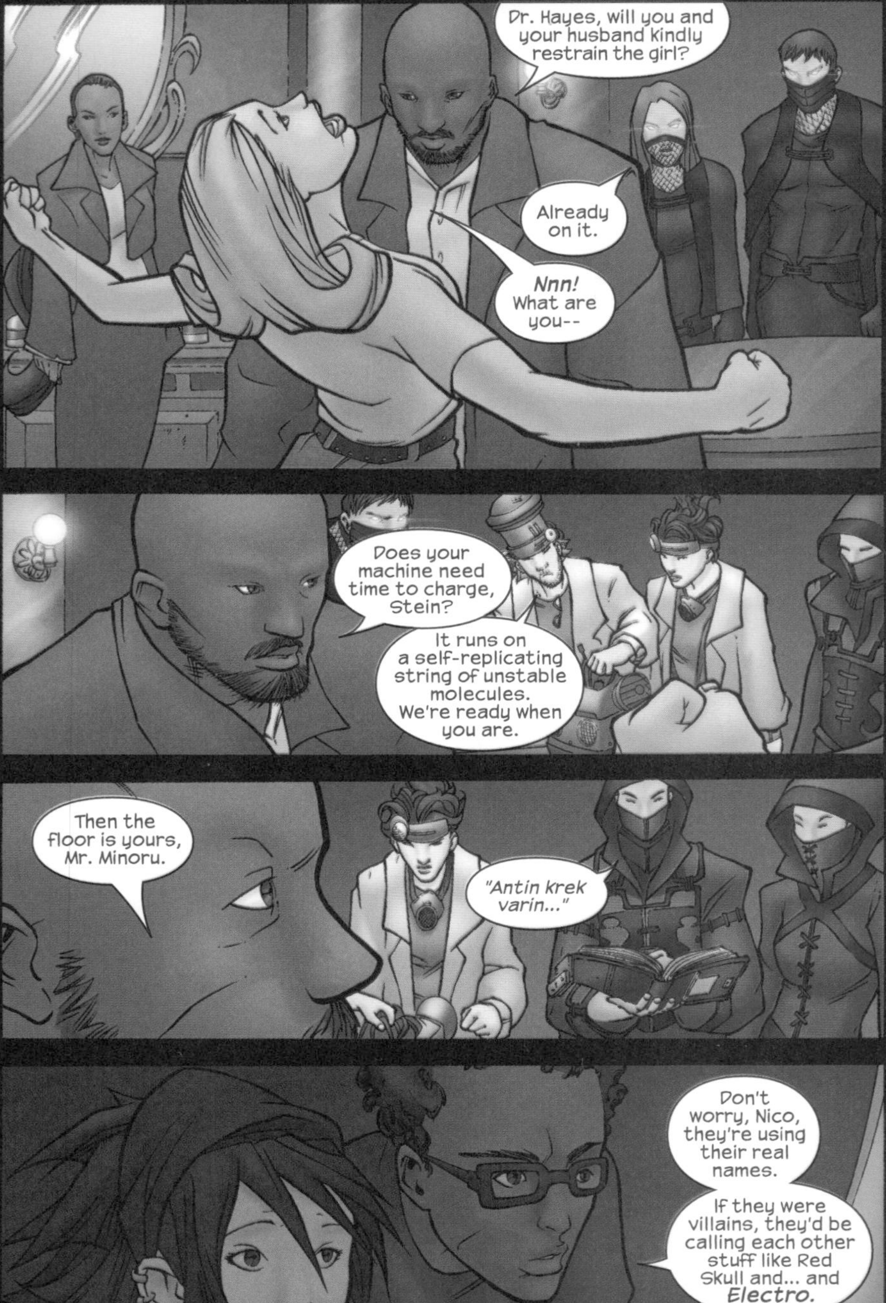
Dr. Hayes, will you and your husband kindly restrain the girl?
Already on it.
Nnn! What are you--
Does your machine need time to charge, Stein?
It runs on a self-replicating string of unstable molecules. We're ready when you are.
Then the floor is yours, Mr. Minoru.
"Antin krek varin..."
Don't worry, Nico, they're using their real names.
If they were villains, they'd be calling each other stuff like Red Skull and... and Electro.

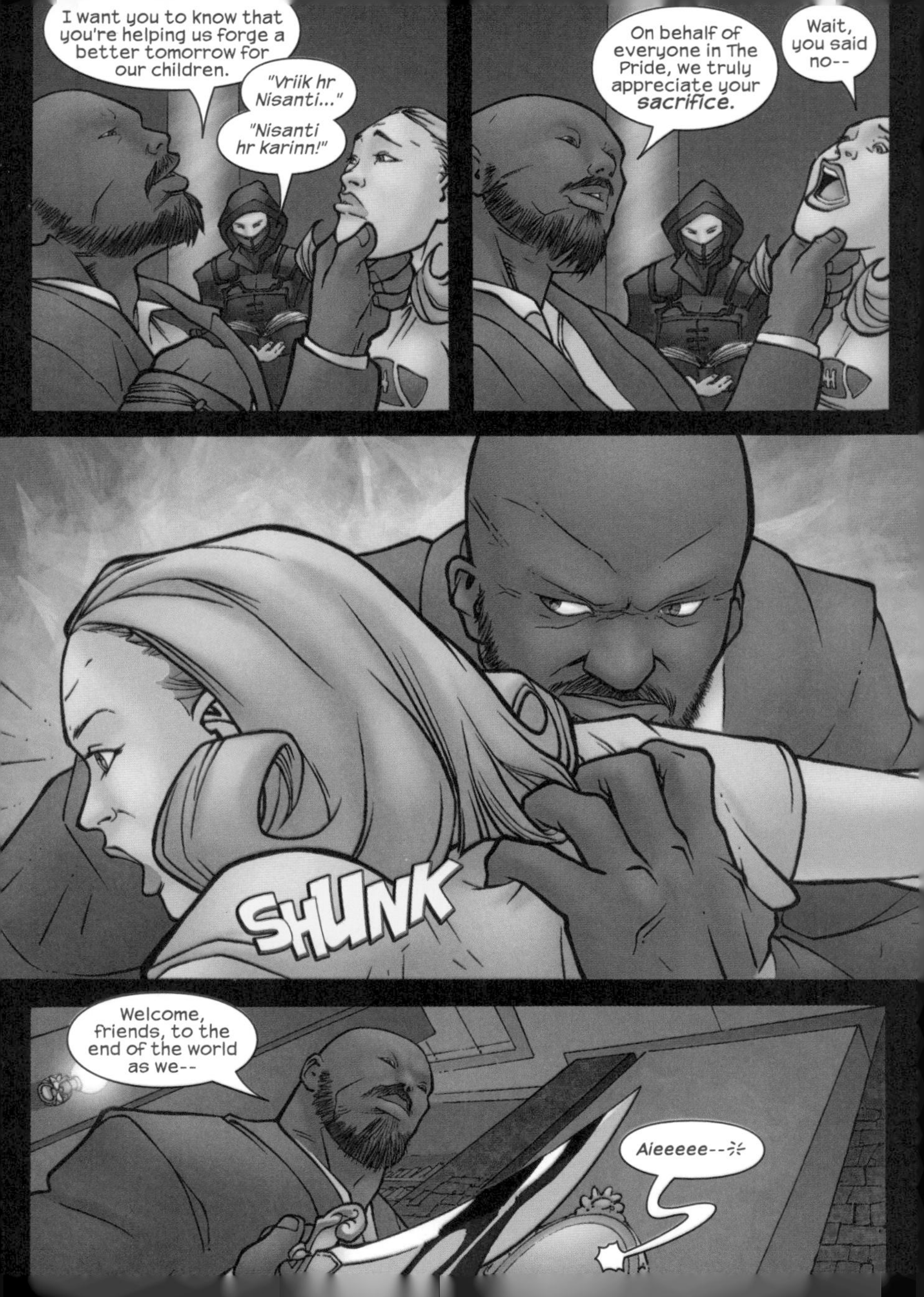

I want you to know that you're helping us forge a better tomorrow for our children.
"Vriik hr Nisanti..."
"Nisanti hr karinn!"
On behalf of everyone in The Pride, we truly appreciate your sacrifice.
Wait, you said no--
SHUNK
Welcome, friends, to the end of the world as we--
Aieeeee--

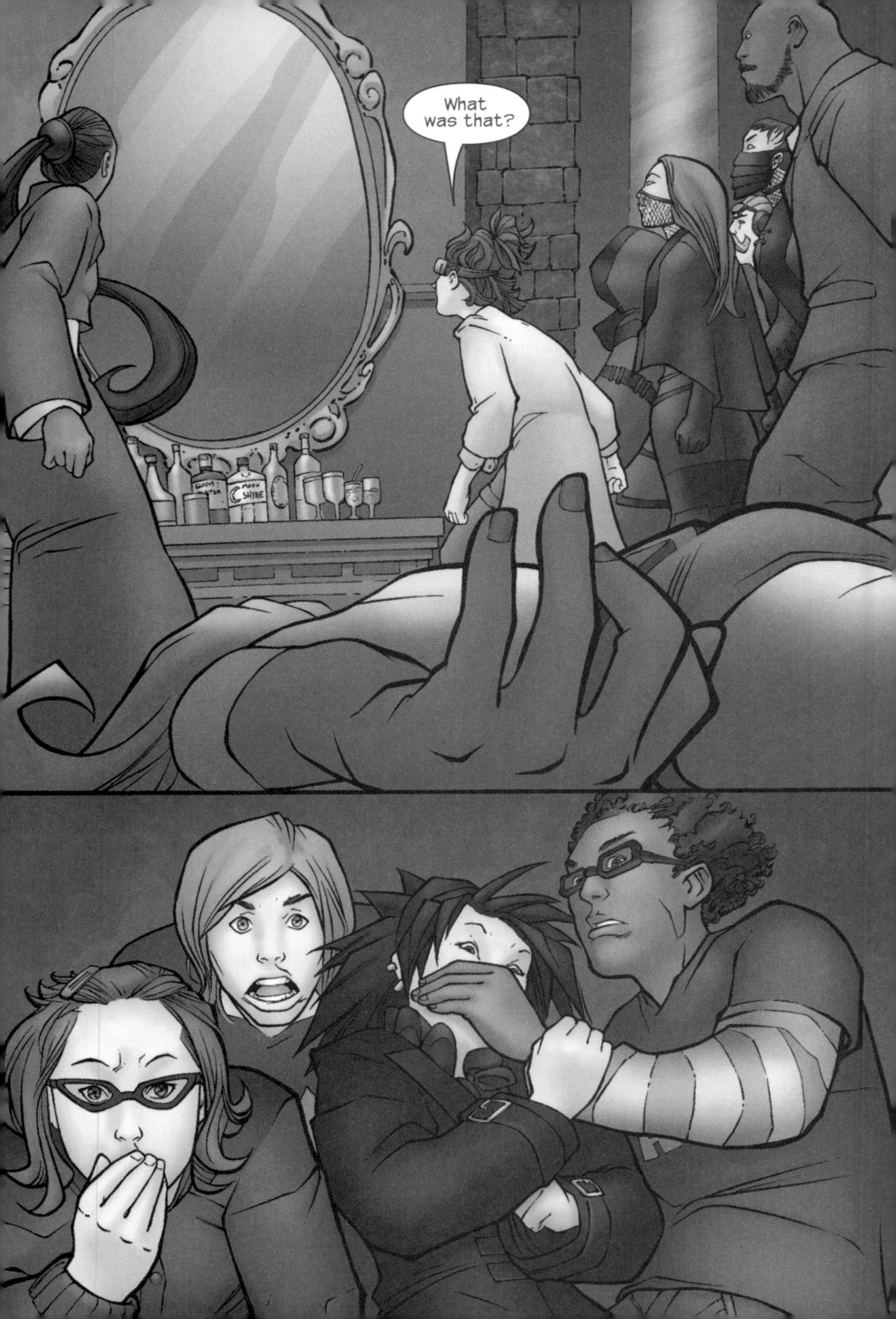
What was that?
GLOOM WATER
MOON SHYNE

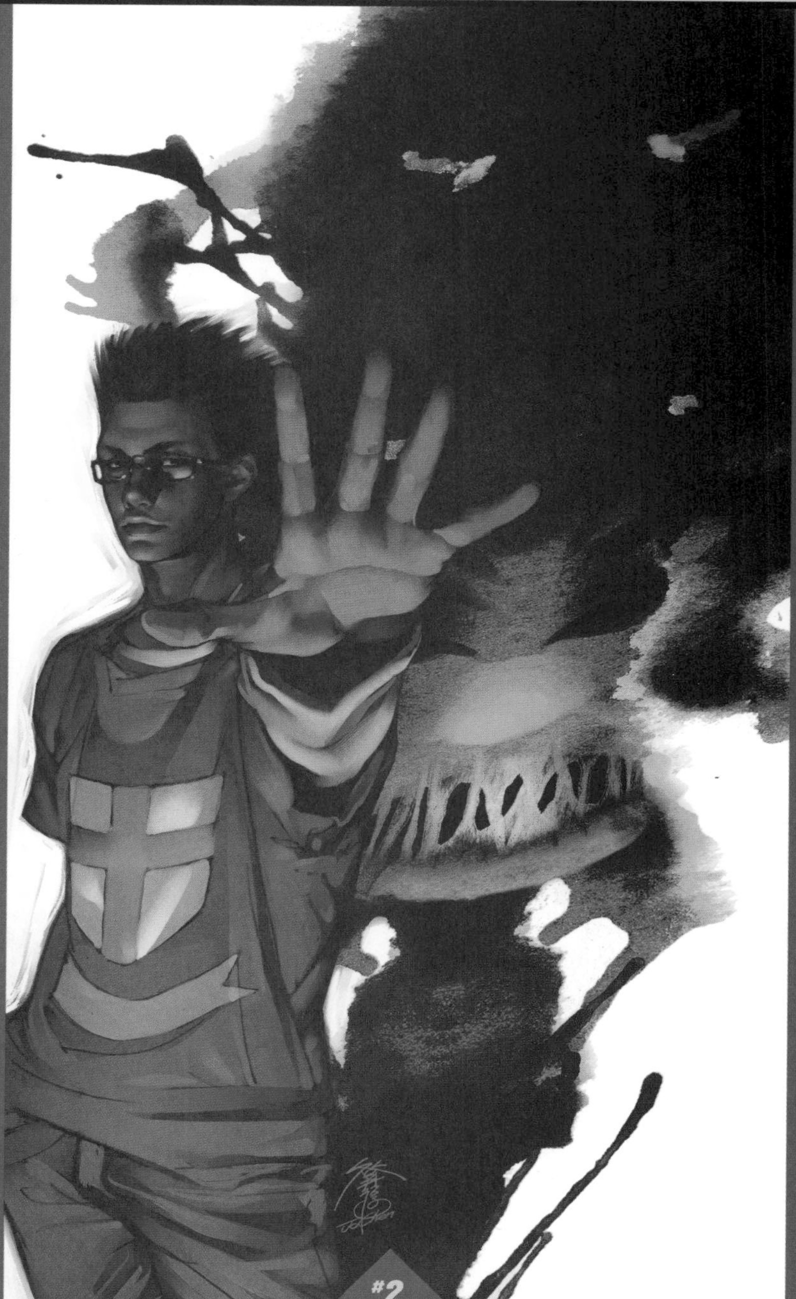
#2

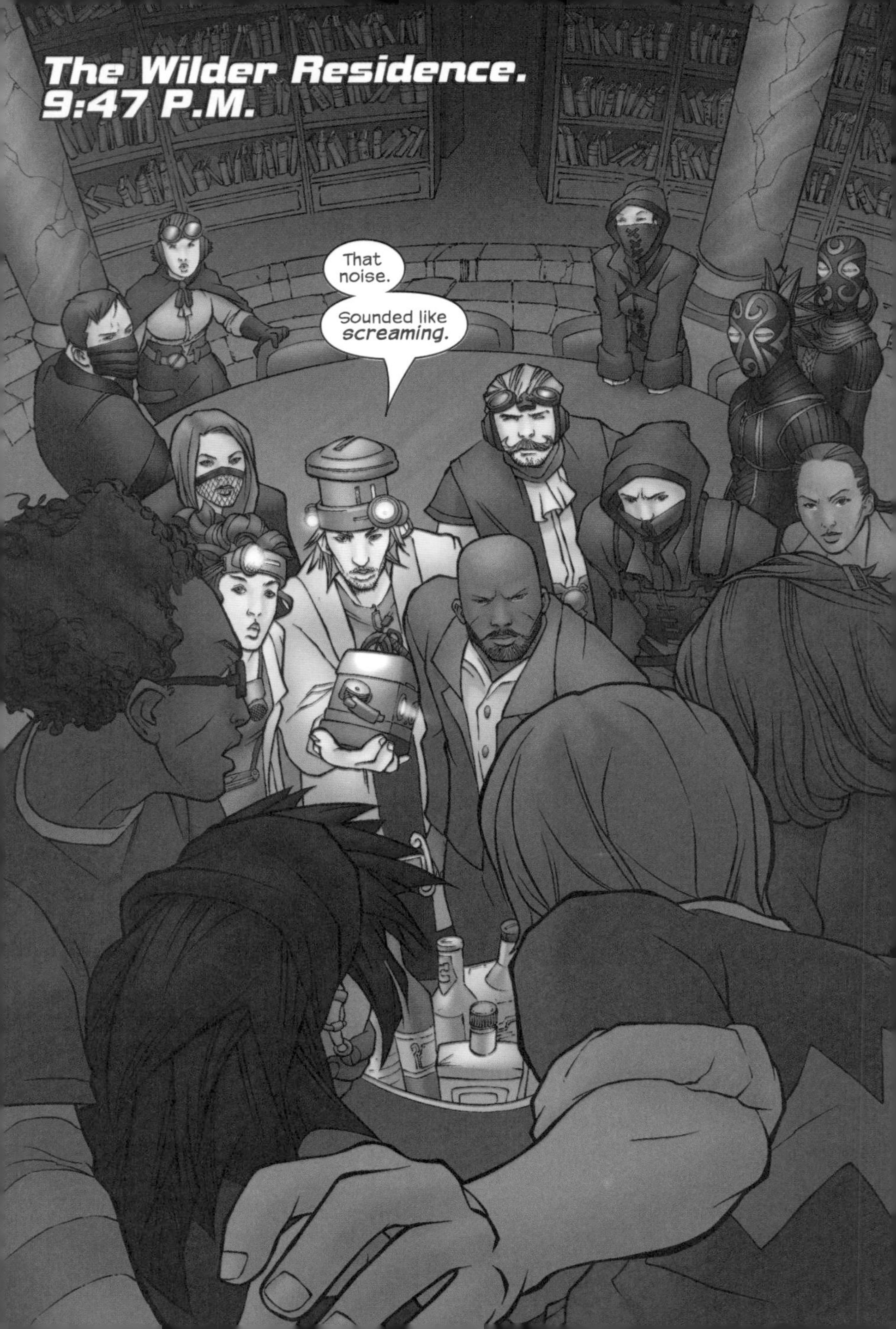
The Wilder Residence.
9:47 P.M.
That noise.
Sounded like *screaming.*

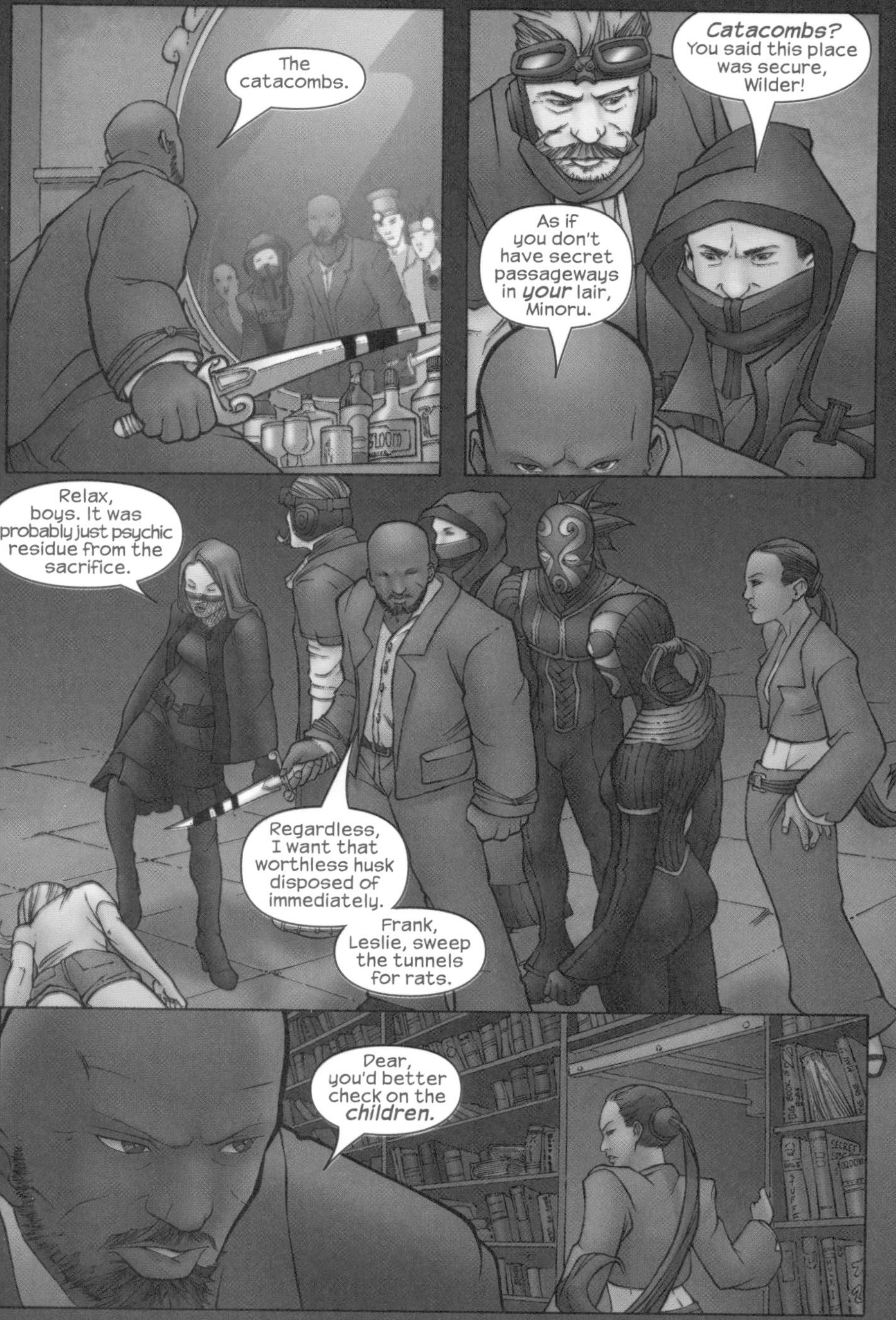
The catacombs.
Catacombs? You said this place was secure, Wilder!
As if you don't have secret passageways in your lair, Minoru.
Relax, boys. It was probably just psychic residue from the sacrifice.
Regardless, I want that worthless husk disposed of immediately.
Frank, Leslie, sweep the tunnels for rats.
Dear, you'd better check on the children.

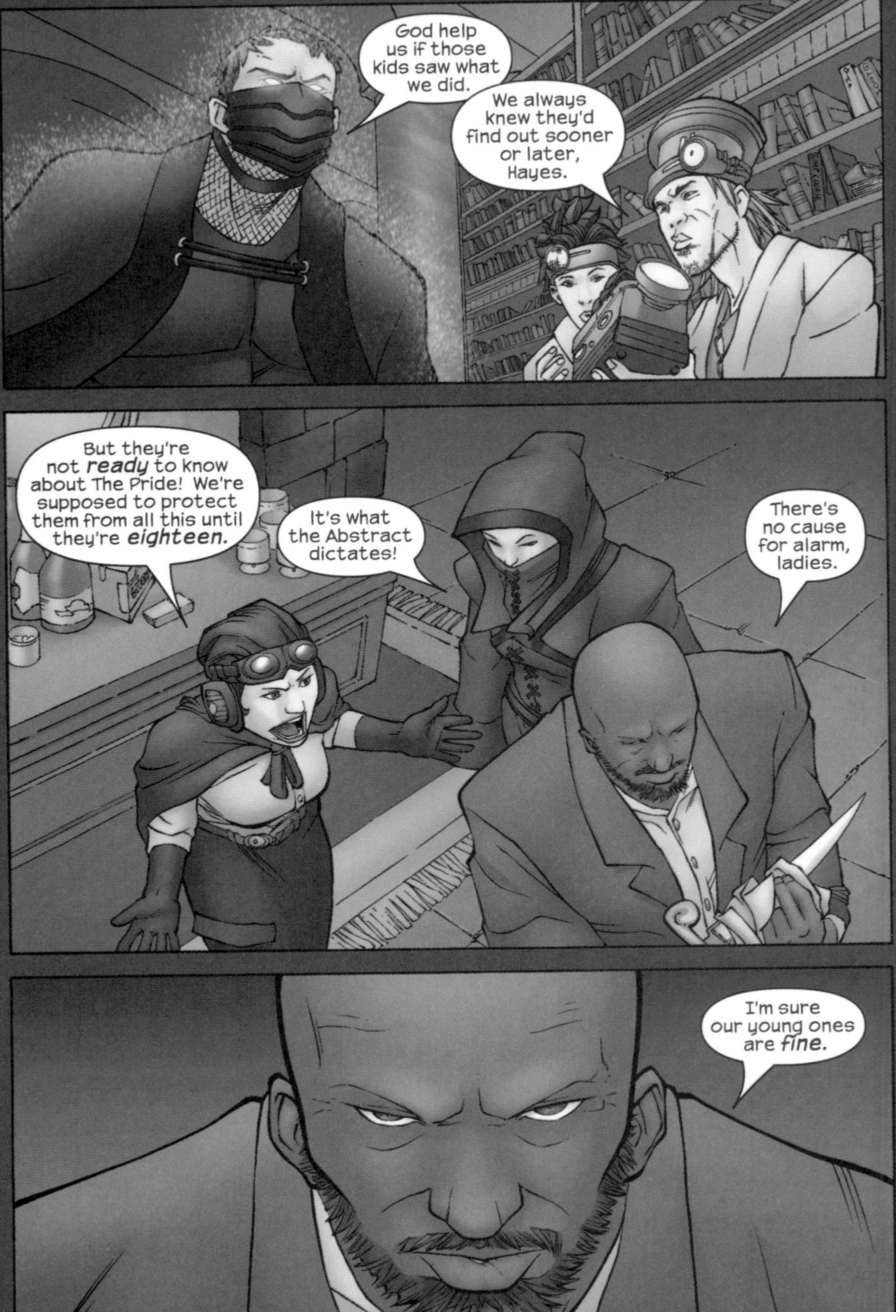
God help us if those kids saw what we did.
We always knew they'd find out sooner or later, Hayes.
But they're not **ready** to know about The Pride! We're supposed to protect them from all this until they're **eighteen.**
It's what the Abstract dictates!
There's no cause for alarm, ladies.
I'm sure our young ones are **fine.**

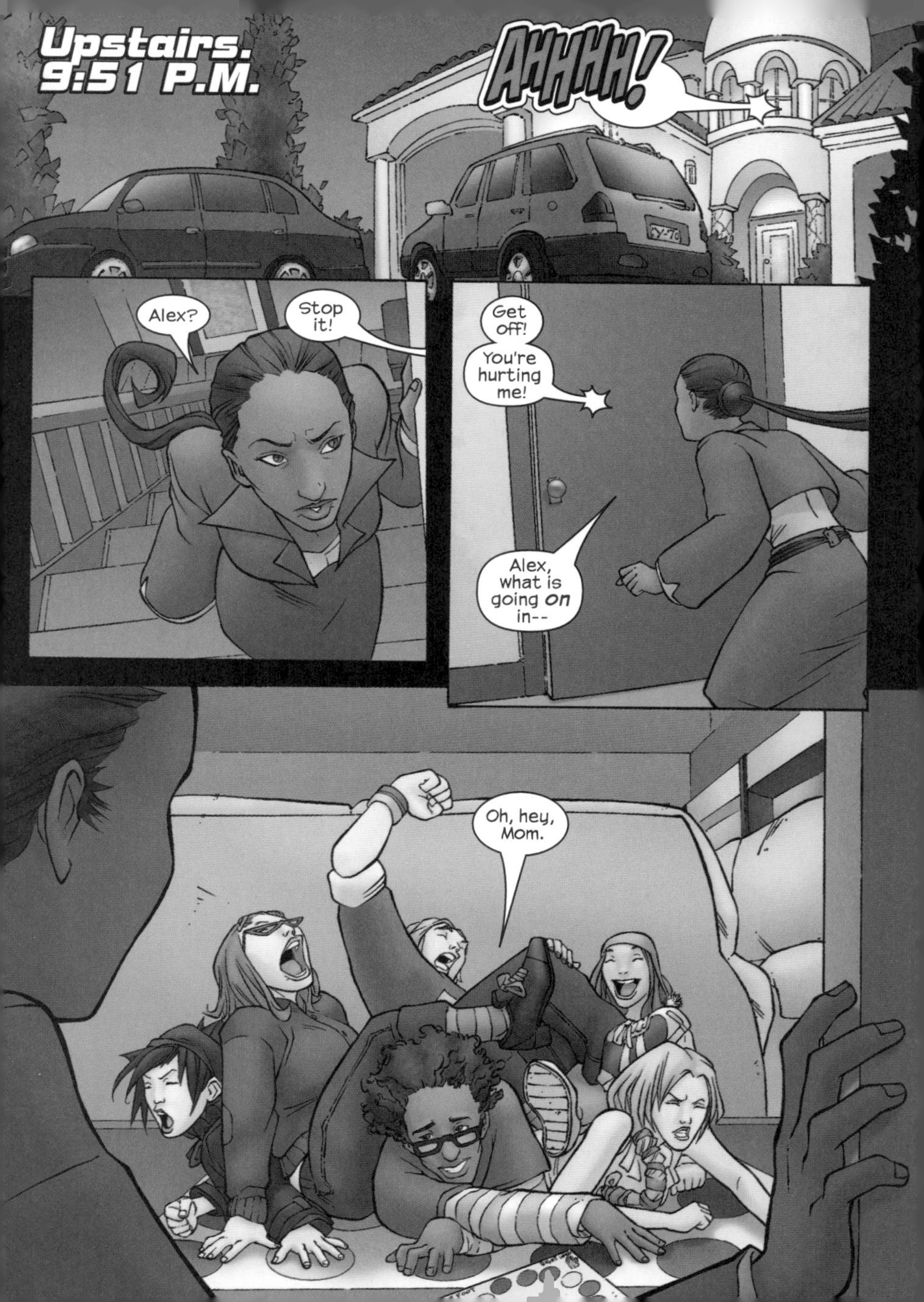
Upstairs. 9:51 P.M.
AHHHH!
Alex?
Stop it!
Get off!
You're hurting me!
Alex, what is going *on* in--
Oh, hey, Mom.

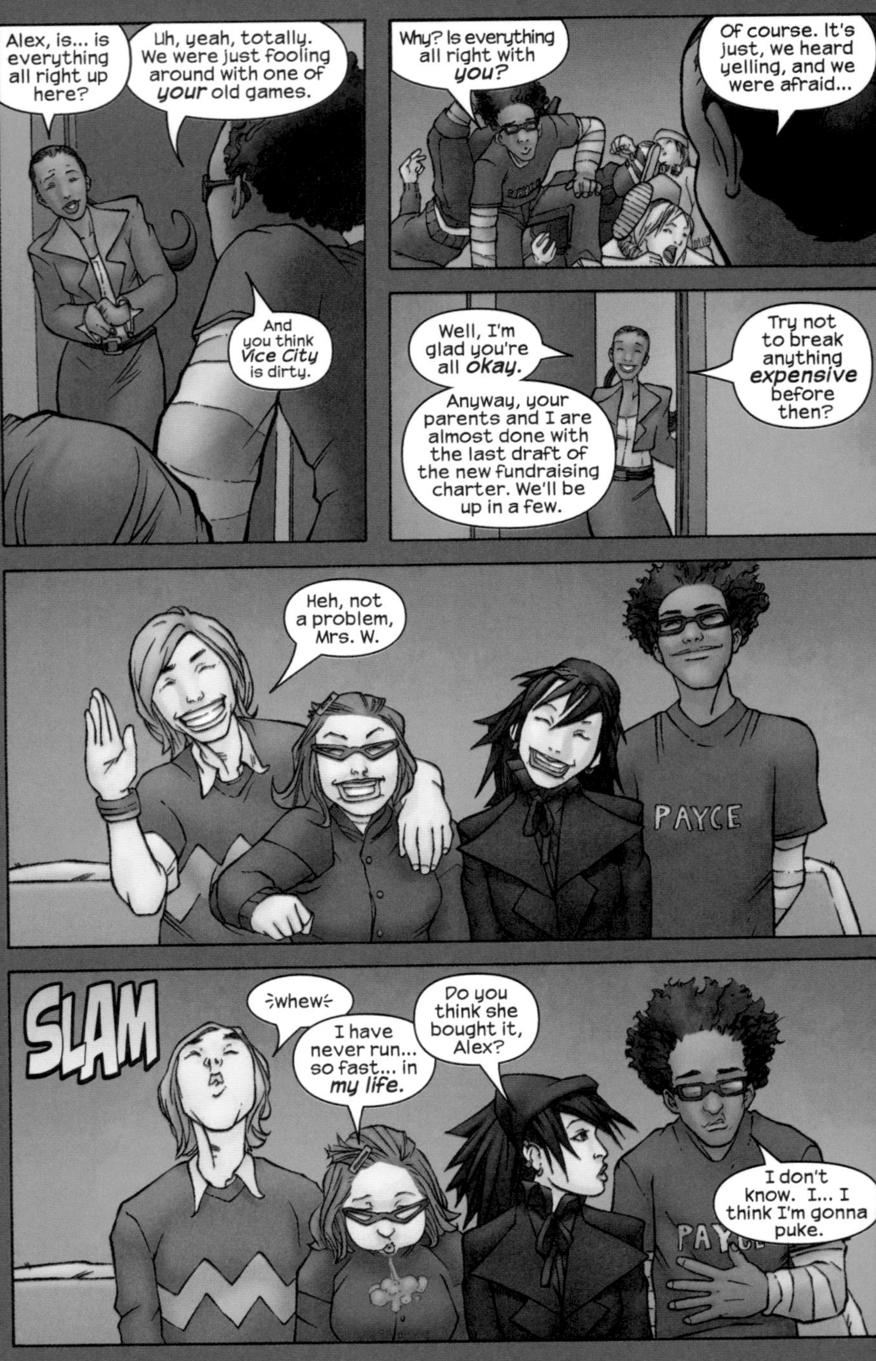

Alex, is... is everything all right up here?
Uh, yeah, totally. We were just fooling around with one of *your* old games.
And you think *Vice City* is dirty.
Why? Is everything all right with *you?*
Of course. It's just, we heard yelling, and we were afraid...
Well, I'm glad you're all *okay.*
Anyway, your parents and I are almost done with the last draft of the new fundraising charter. We'll be up in a few.
Try not to break anything *expensive* before then?
Heh, not a problem, Mrs. W.
PAYCE
SLAM
whew
I have never run... so fast... in *my life.*
Do you think she bought it, Alex?
I don't know. I... I think I'm gonna puke.

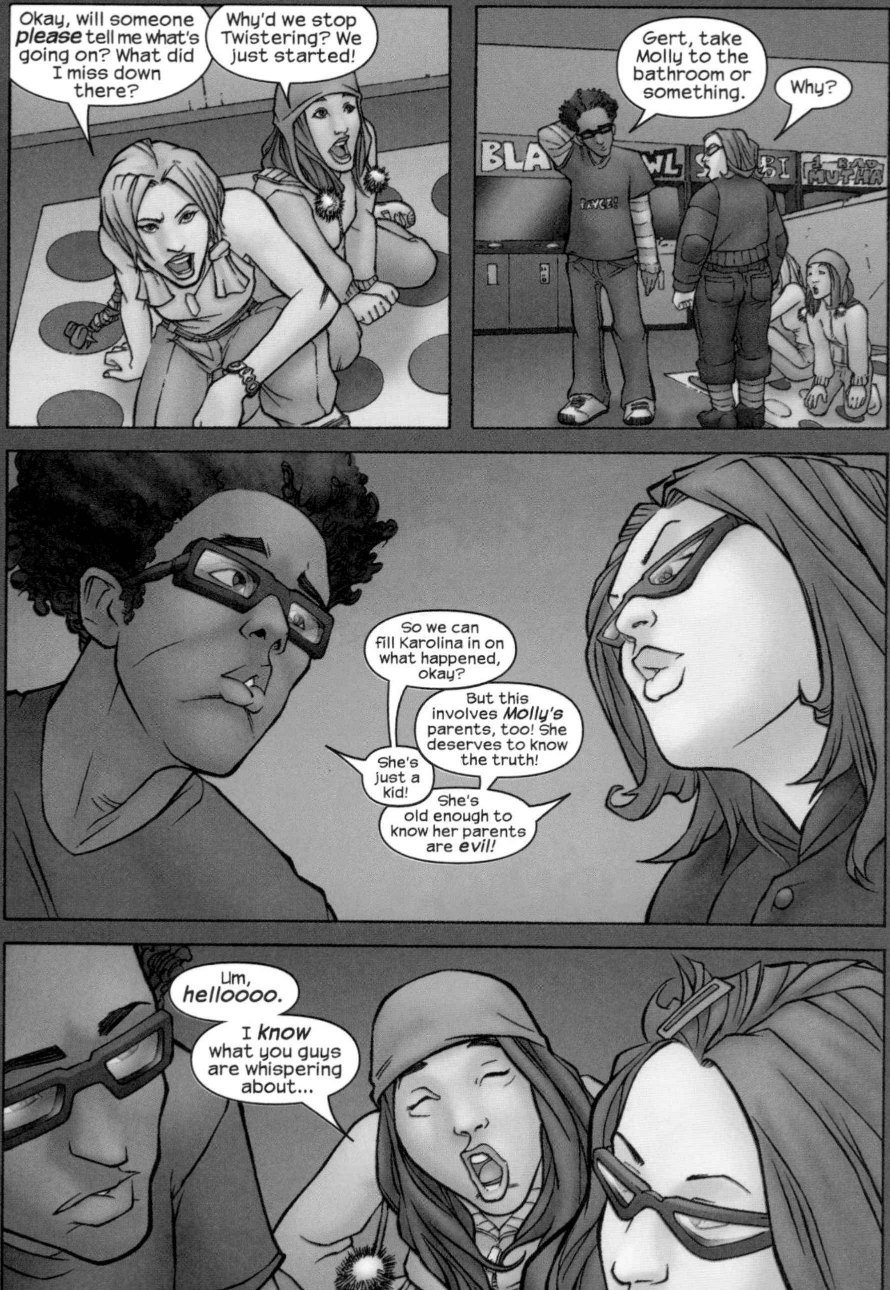
Okay, will someone *please* tell me what's going on? What did I miss down there?
Why'd we stop Twistering? We just started!
Gert, take Molly to the bathroom or something.
Why?
So we can fill Karolina in on what happened, okay?
But this involves *Molly's* parents, too! She deserves to know the truth!
She's just a kid!
She's old enough to know her parents are *evil!*
Um, *helloooo.*
I *know* what you guys are whispering about...

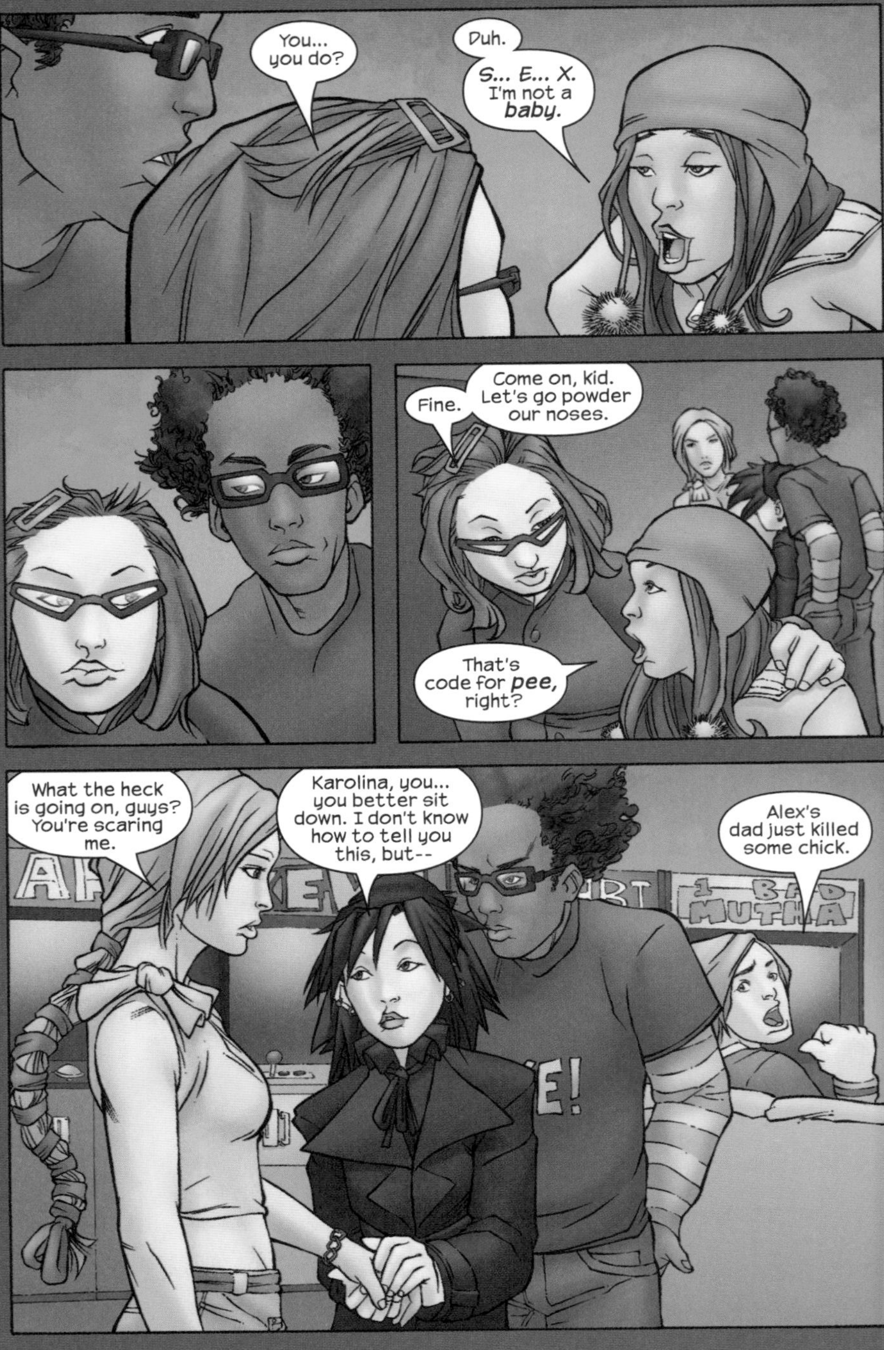
You... you do?
Duh.
S... E... X. I'm not a *baby.*
Fine.
Come on, kid. Let's go powder our noses.
That's code for *pee,* right?
What the heck is going on, guys? You're scaring me.
Karolina, you... you better sit down. I don't know how to tell you this, but--
Alex's dad just killed some chick.
1 BAD MUTHA
E!

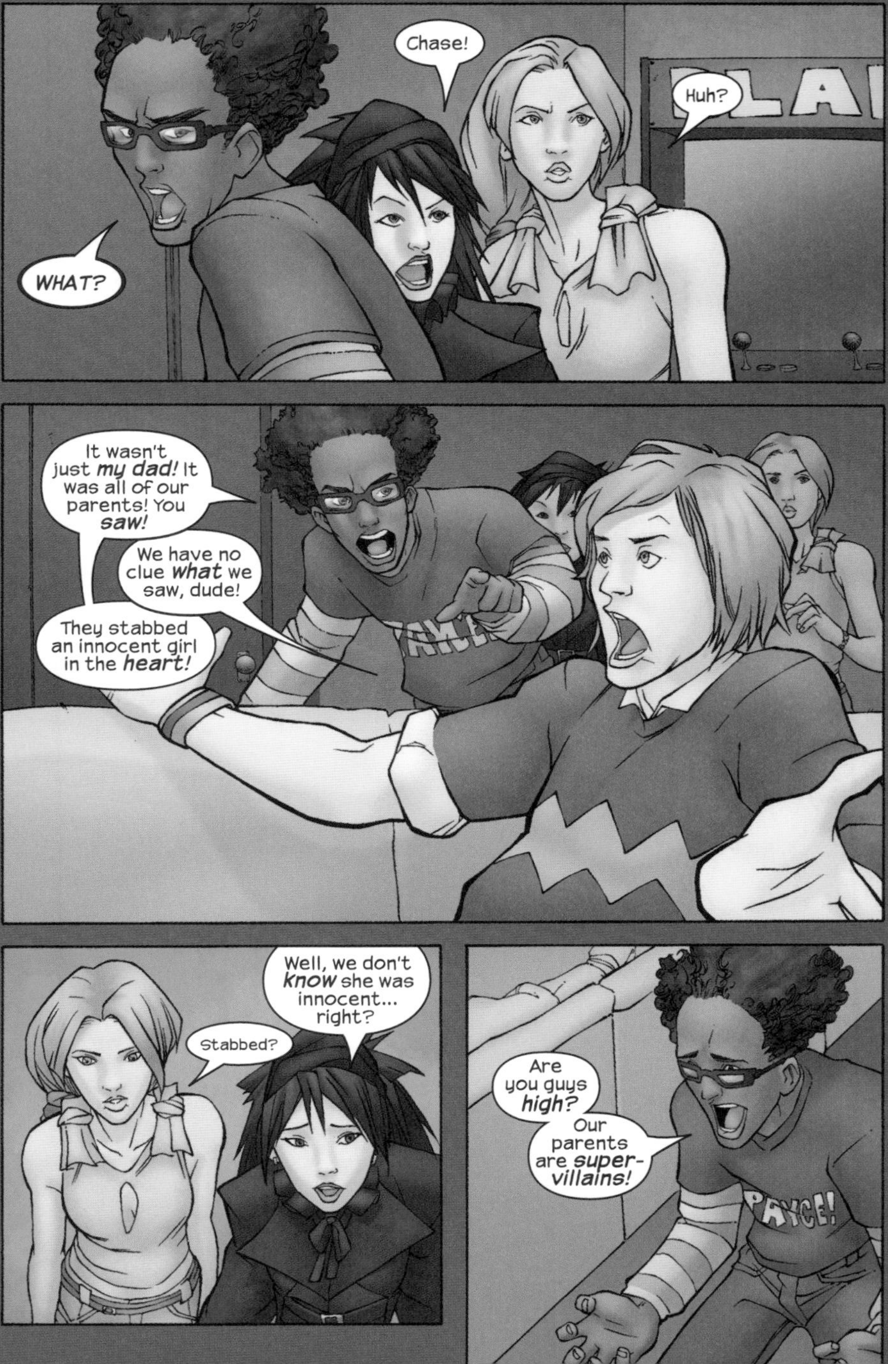
Chase!
Huh?
WHAT?
It wasn't just my dad! It was all of our parents! You saw!
We have no clue what we saw, dude!
They stabbed an innocent girl in the heart!
Well, we don't know she was innocent... right?
Stabbed?
Are you guys high?
Our parents are super-villains!

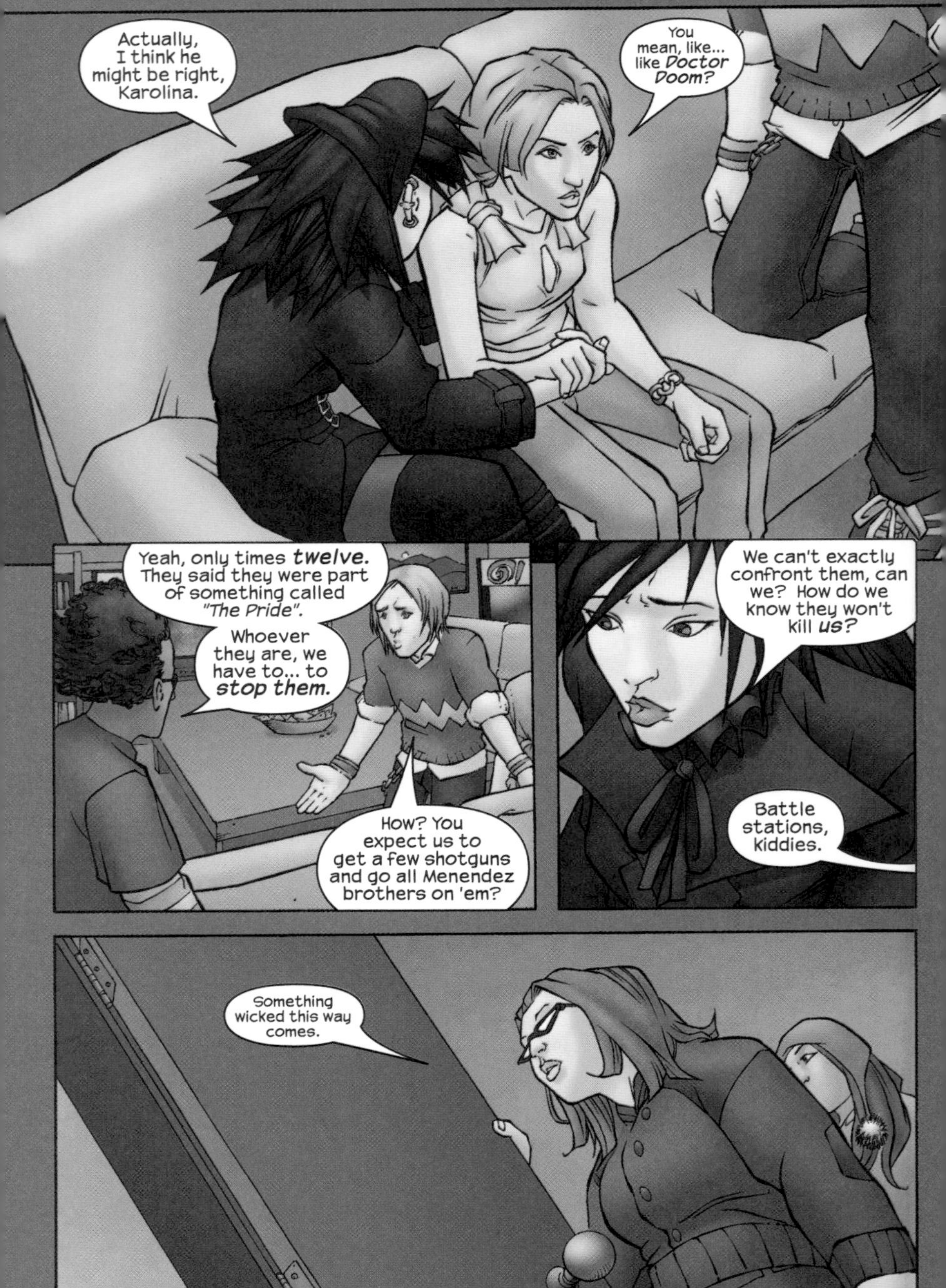

Actually, I think he might be right, Karolina.
You mean, like... like Doctor Doom?
Yeah, only times twelve. They said they were part of something called "The Pride".
Whoever they are, we have to... to stop them.
How? You expect us to get a few shotguns and go all Menendez brothers on 'em?
We can't exactly confront them, can we? How do we know they won't kill us?
Battle stations, kiddies.
Something wicked this way comes.

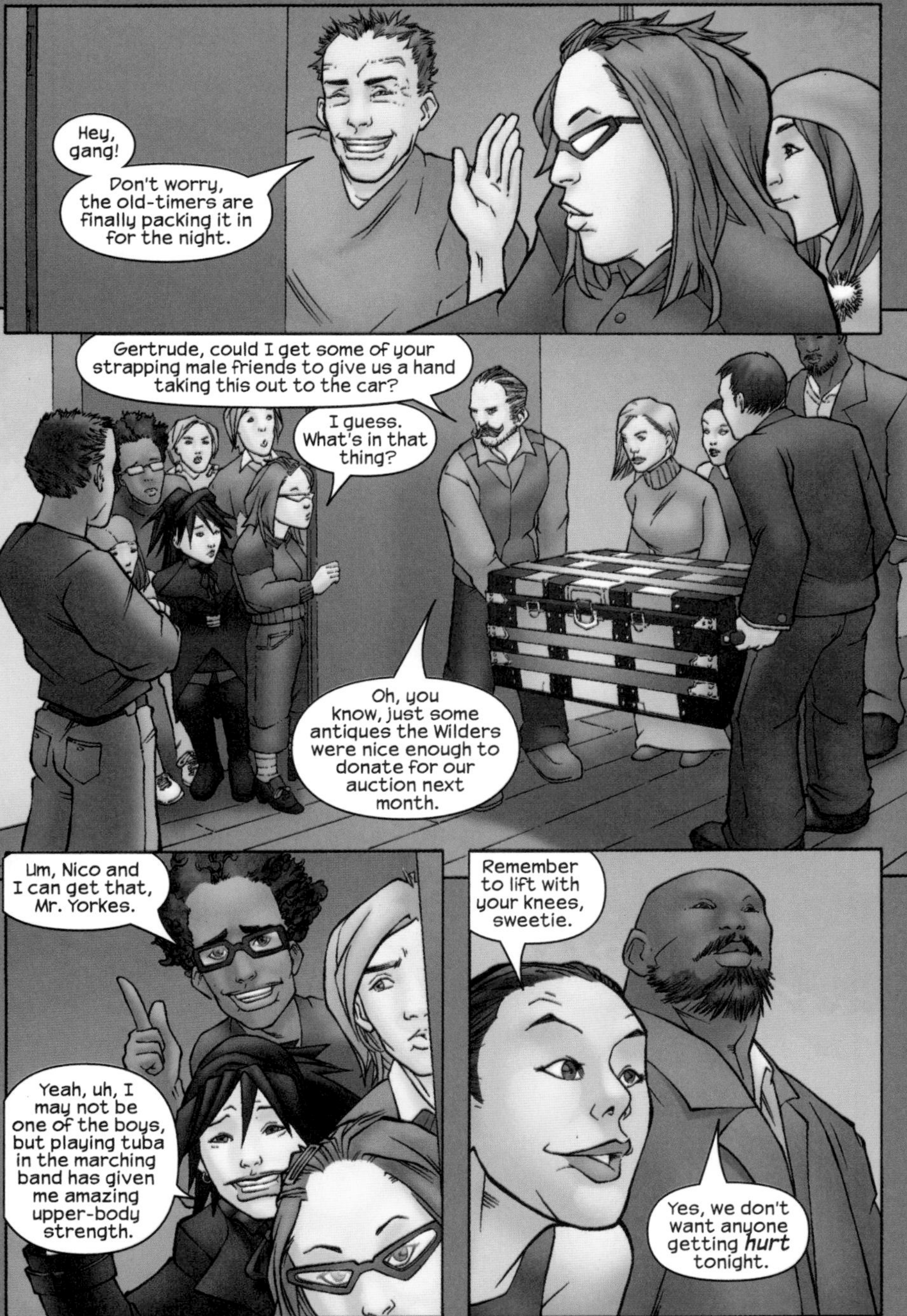
Hey, gang!
Don't worry, the old-timers are finally packing it in for the night.
Gertrude, could I get some of your strapping male friends to give us a hand taking this out to the car?
I guess. What's in that thing?
Oh, you know, just some antiques the Wilders were nice enough to donate for our auction next month.
Um, Nico and I can get that, Mr. Yorkes.
Yeah, uh, I may not be one of the boys, but playing tuba in the marching band has given me amazing upper-body strength.
Remember to lift with your knees, sweetie.
Yes, we don't want anyone getting *hurt* tonight.

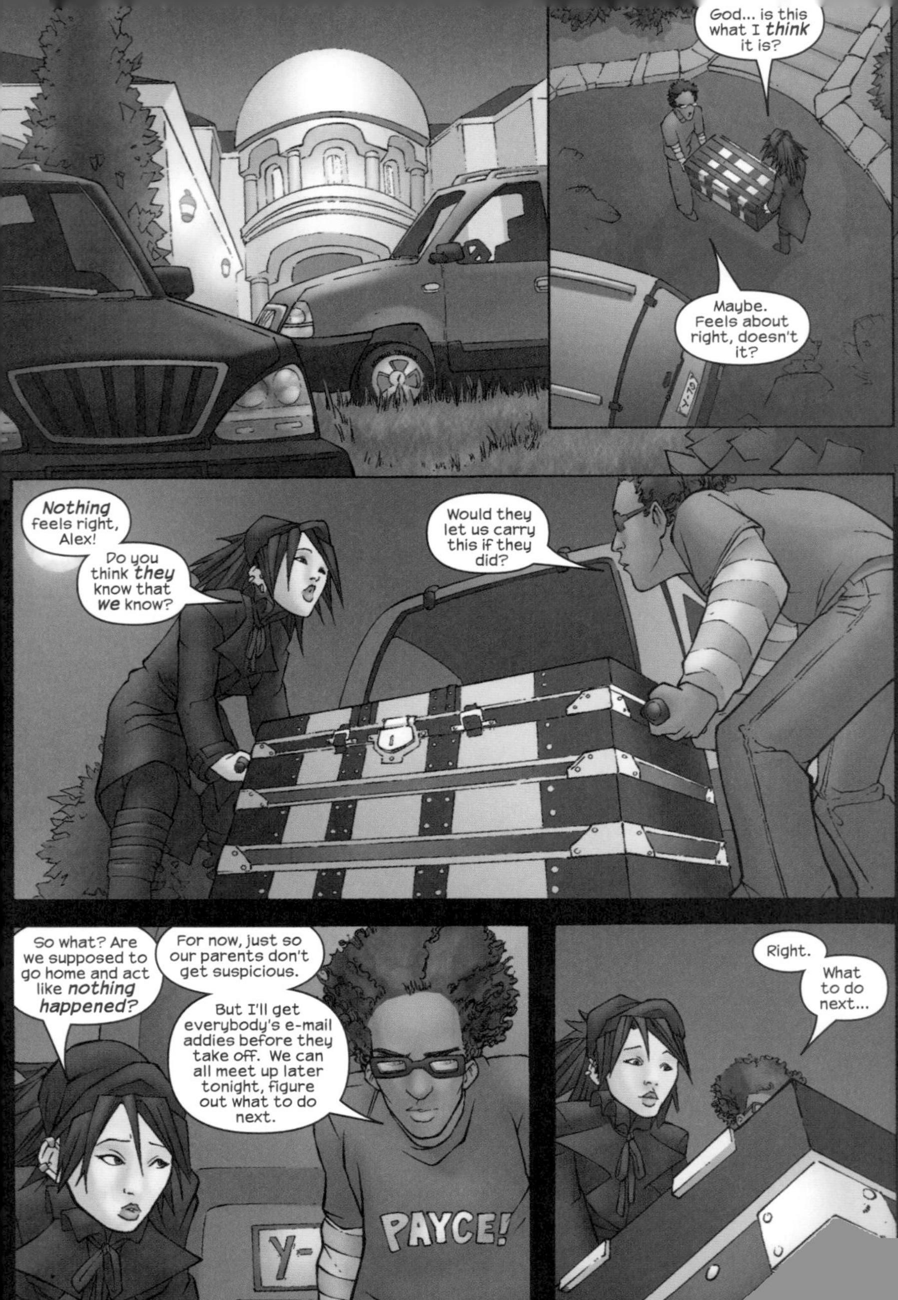
God... is this what I *think* it is?
Maybe. Feels about right, doesn't it?
Nothing feels right, Alex!
Do you think *they* know that *we* know?
Would they let us carry this if they did?
So what? Are we supposed to go home and act like *nothing happened?*
For now, just so our parents don't get suspicious.
But I'll get everybody's e-mail addies before they take off. We can all meet up later tonight, figure out what to do next.
Right.
What to do next...
PAYCE!

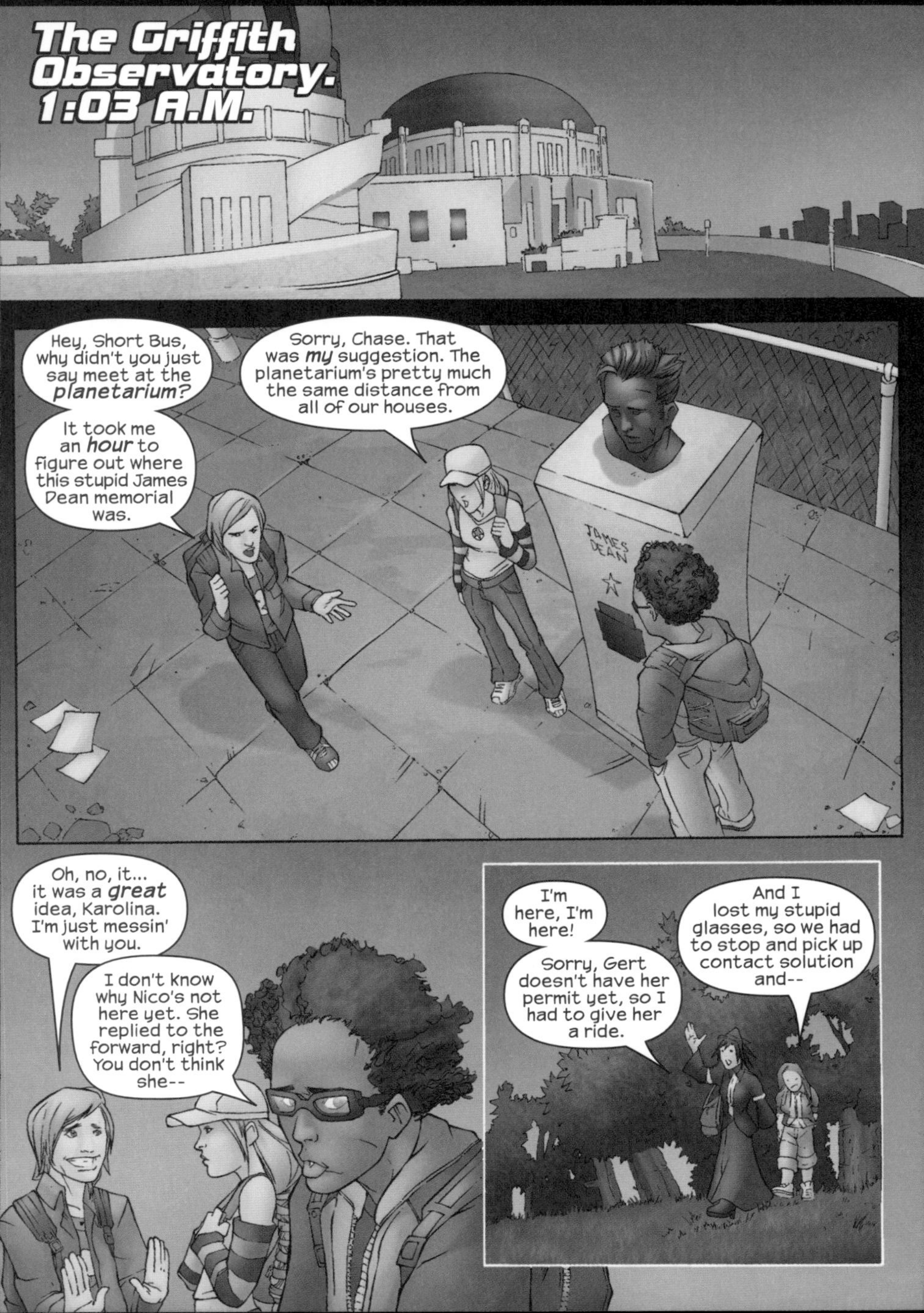
The Griffith Observatory. 1:03 A.M.
Hey, Short Bus, why didn't you just say meet at the *planetarium*?
It took me an *hour* to figure out where this stupid James Dean memorial was.
Sorry, Chase. That was *my* suggestion. The planetarium's pretty much the same distance from all of our houses.
JAMES DEAN
Oh, no, it... it was a *great* idea, Karolina. I'm just messin' with you.
I don't know why Nico's not here yet. She replied to the forward, right? You don't think she--
I'm here, I'm here!
Sorry, Gert doesn't have her permit yet, so I had to give her a ride.
And I lost my stupid glasses, so we had to stop and pick up contact solution and--

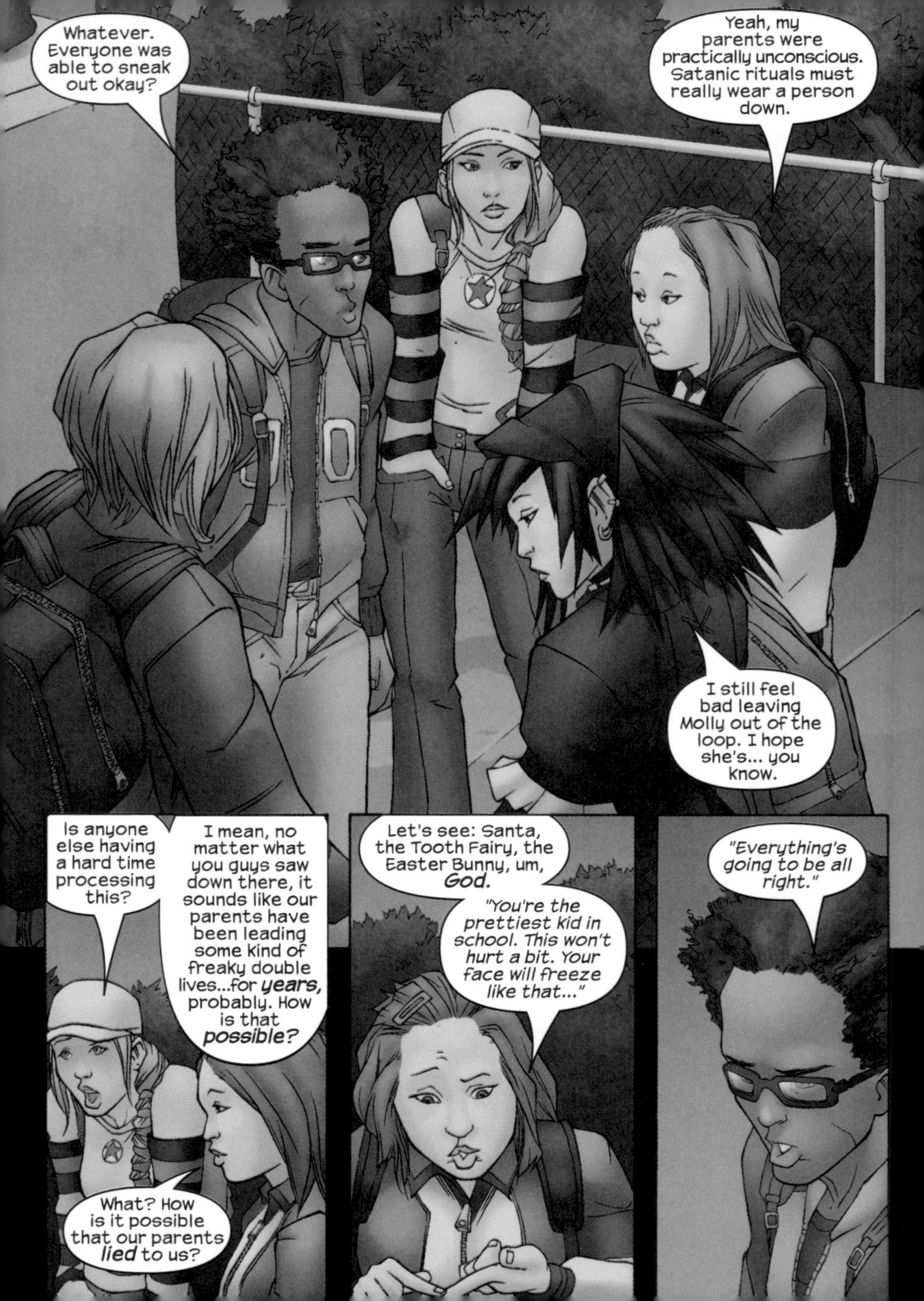
Whatever. Everyone was able to sneak out okay?
Yeah, my parents were practically unconscious. Satanic rituals must really wear a person down.
I still feel bad leaving Molly out of the loop. I hope she's... you know.
Is anyone else having a hard time processing this?
I mean, no matter what you guys saw down there, it sounds like our parents have been leading some kind of freaky double lives...for *years,* probably. How is that ***possible?***
What? How is it possible that our parents ***lied*** to us?
Let's see: Santa, the Tooth Fairy, the Easter Bunny, um, ***God.***
"You're the prettiest kid in school. This won't hurt a bit. Your face will freeze like that..."
"Everything's going to be all right."

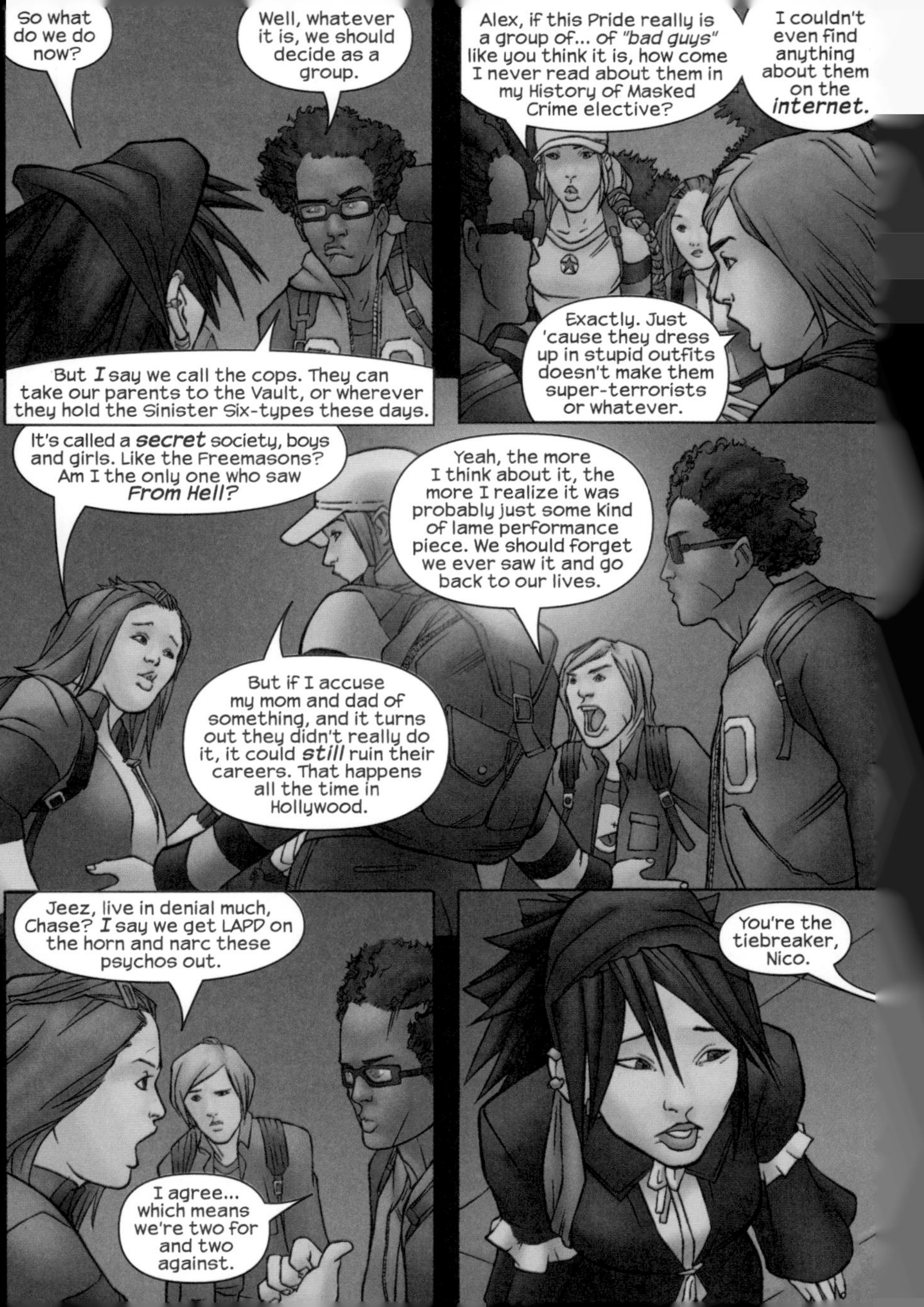
So what do we do now?
Well, whatever it is, we should decide as a group.
But *I* say we call the cops. They can take our parents to the Vault, or wherever they hold the Sinister Six-types these days.
Alex, if this Pride really is a group of... of *"bad guys"* like you think it is, how come I never read about them in my History of Masked Crime elective?
I couldn't even find anything about them on the *internet.*
Exactly. Just 'cause they dress up in stupid outfits doesn't make them super-terrorists or whatever.
It's called a *secret* society, boys and girls. Like the Freemasons? Am I the only one who saw *From Hell?*
Yeah, the more I think about it, the more I realize it was probably just some kind of lame performance piece. We should forget we ever saw it and go back to our lives.
But if I accuse my mom and dad of something, and it turns out they didn't really do it, it could *still* ruin their careers. That happens all the time in Hollywood.
Jeez, live in denial much, Chase? *I* say we get LAPD on the horn and narc these psychos out.
I agree... which means we're two for and two against.
You're the tiebreaker, Nico.

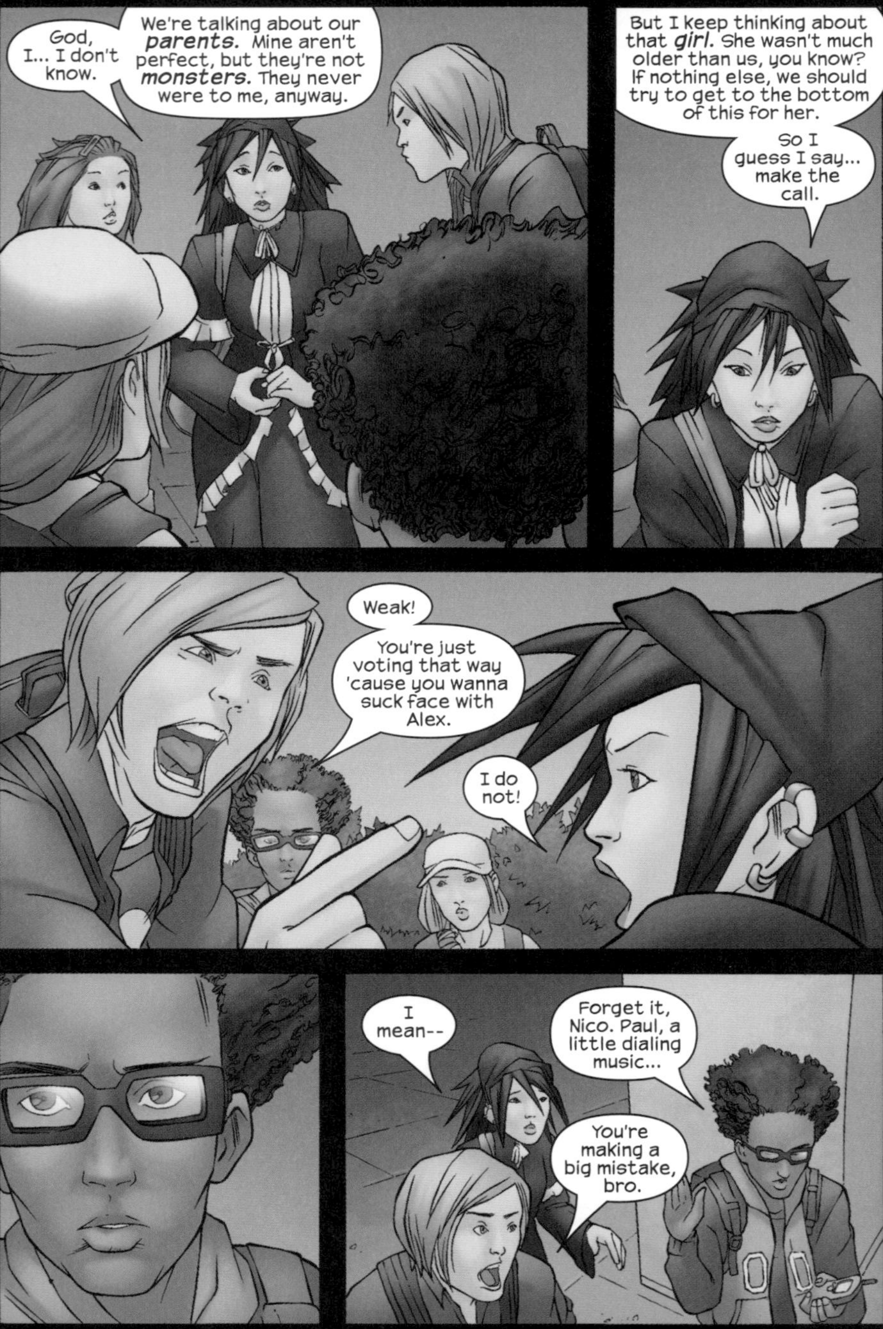
God, I... I don't know.
We're talking about our *parents.* Mine aren't perfect, but they're not *monsters.* They never were to me, anyway.
But I keep thinking about that *girl.* She wasn't much older than us, you know? If nothing else, we should try to get to the bottom of this for her.
So I guess I say... make the call.
Weak!
You're just voting that way 'cause you wanna suck face with Alex.
I do not!
I mean--
Forget it, Nico. Paul, a little dialing music...
You're making a big mistake, bro.

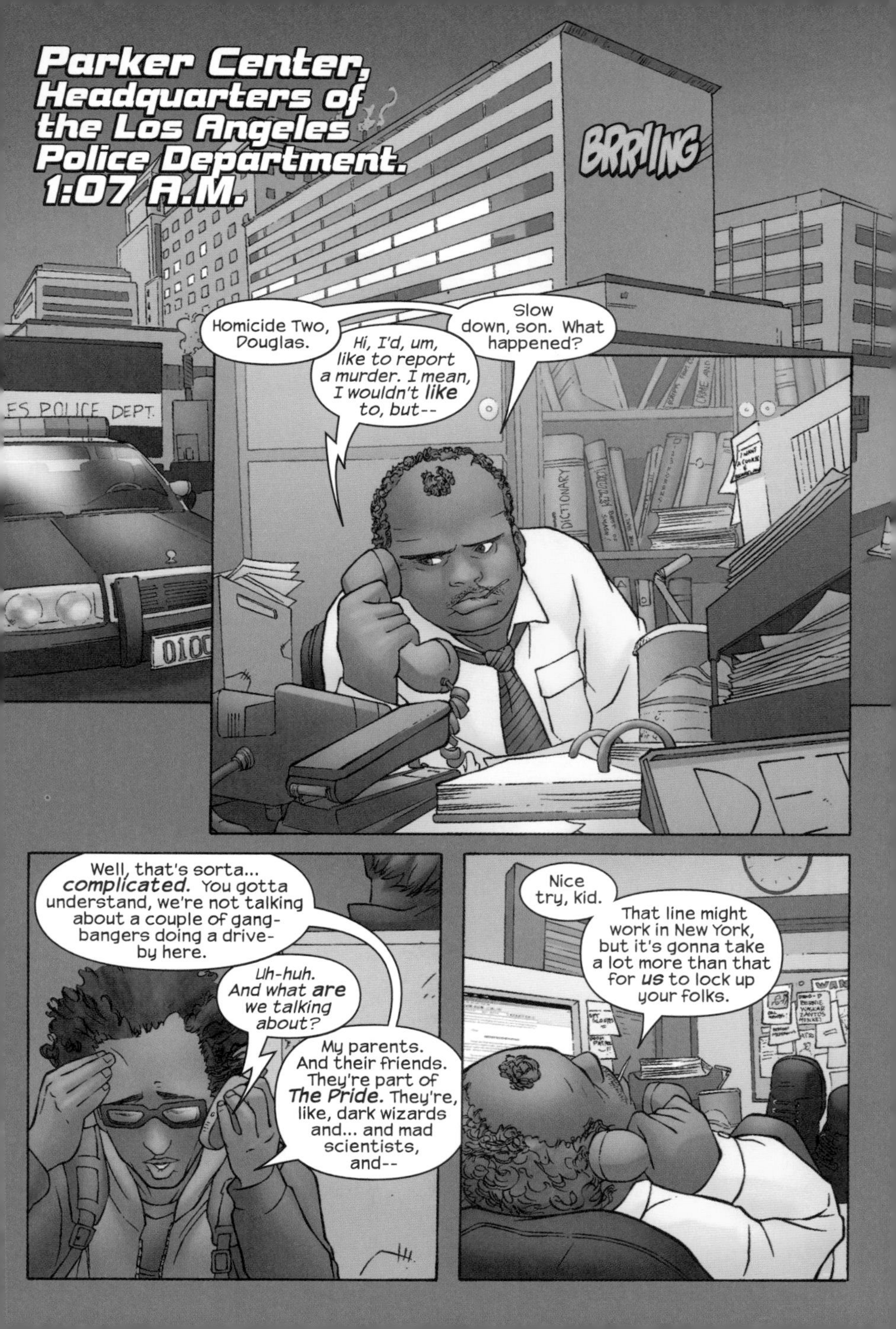
Parker Center, Headquarters of the Los Angeles Police Department. 1:07 A.M.
BRRIING
ES POLICE DEPT.
Homicide Two, Douglas.
Hi, I'd, um, like to report a murder. I mean, I wouldn't *like* to, but--
Slow down, son. What happened?
DICTIONARY
Well, that's sorta... *complicated.* You gotta understand, we're not talking about a couple of gang-bangers doing a drive-by here.
Uh-huh. And what *are* we talking about?
My parents. And their friends. They're part of *The Pride.* They're, like, dark wizards and... and mad scientists, and--
Nice try, kid.
That line might work in New York, but it's gonna take a lot more than that for *us* to lock up your folks.

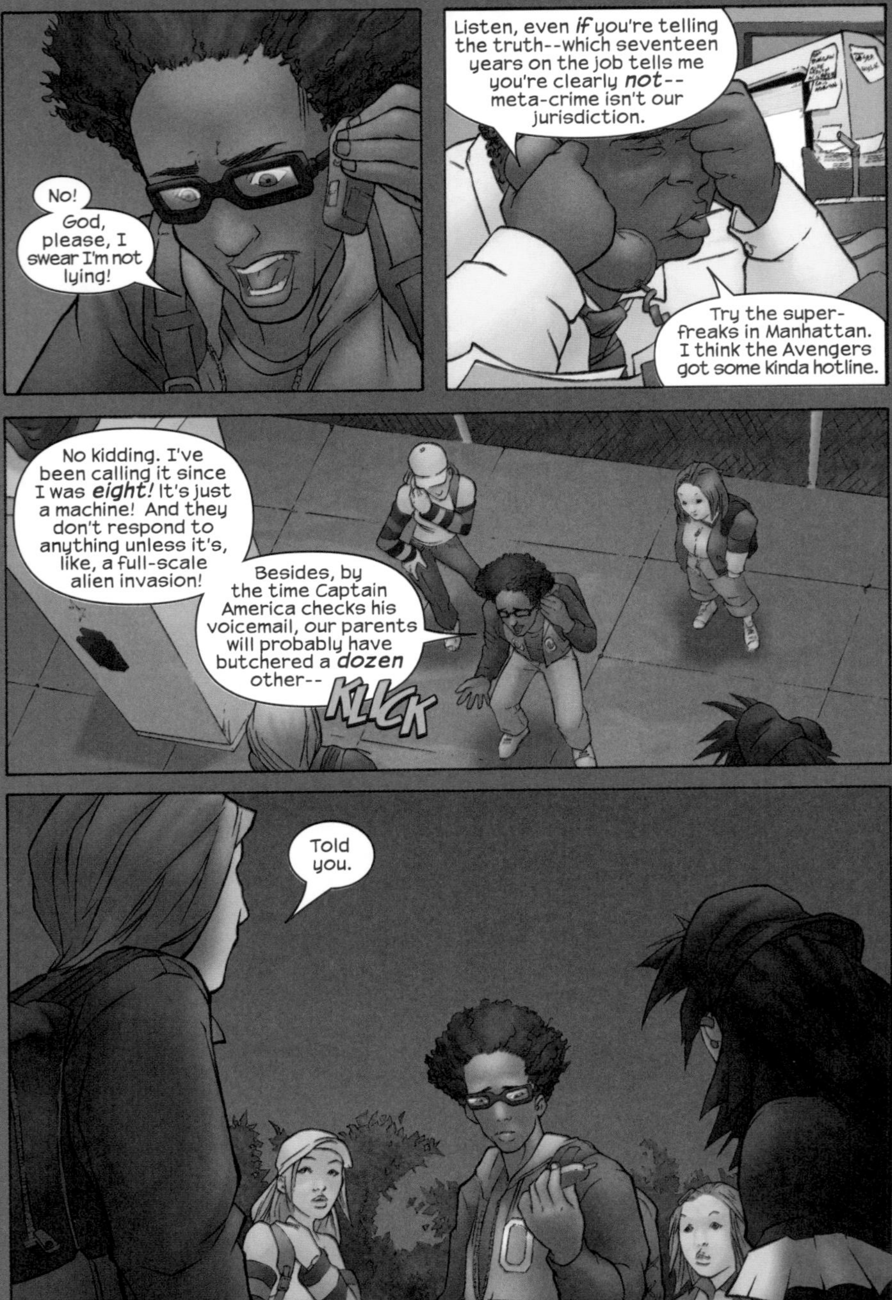
No!
God, please, I swear I'm not lying!
Listen, even *if* you're telling the truth--which seventeen years on the job tells me you're clearly *not*--meta-crime isn't our jurisdiction.
Try the super-freaks in Manhattan. I think the Avengers got some kinda hotline.
No kidding. I've been calling it since I was *eight!* It's just a machine! And they don't respond to anything unless it's, like, a full-scale alien invasion!
Besides, by the time Captain America checks his voicemail, our parents will probably have butchered a *dozen* other--
KLICK
Told you.

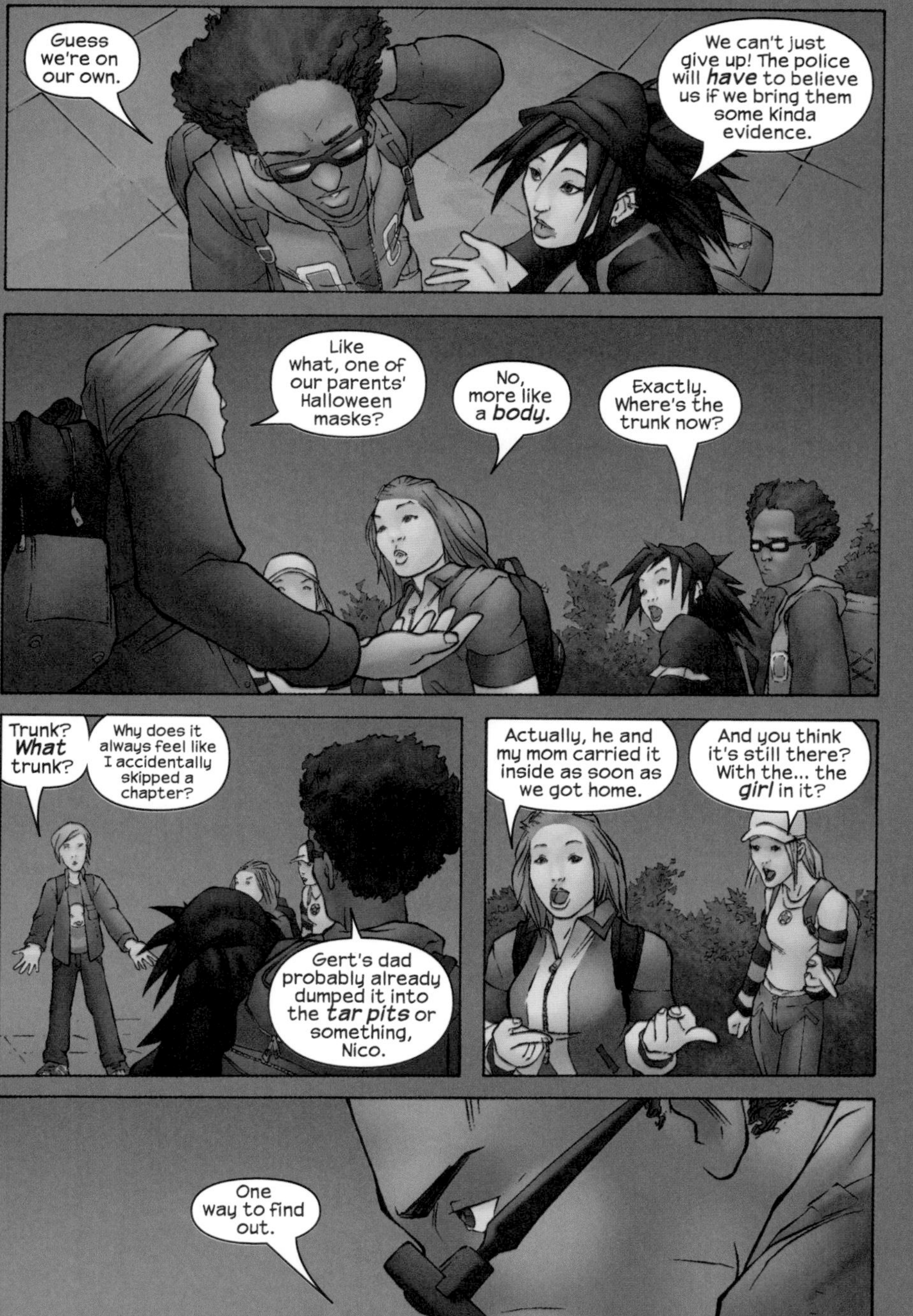
Guess we're on our own.
We can't just give up! The police will *have* to believe us if we bring them some kinda evidence.
Like what, one of our parents' Halloween masks?
No, more like a *body.*
Exactly. Where's the trunk now?
Trunk? *What* trunk?
Why does it always feel like I accidentally skipped a chapter?
Gert's dad probably already dumped it into the *tar pits* or something, Nico.
Actually, he and my mom carried it inside as soon as we got home.
And you think it's still there? With the... the *girl* in it?
One way to find out.

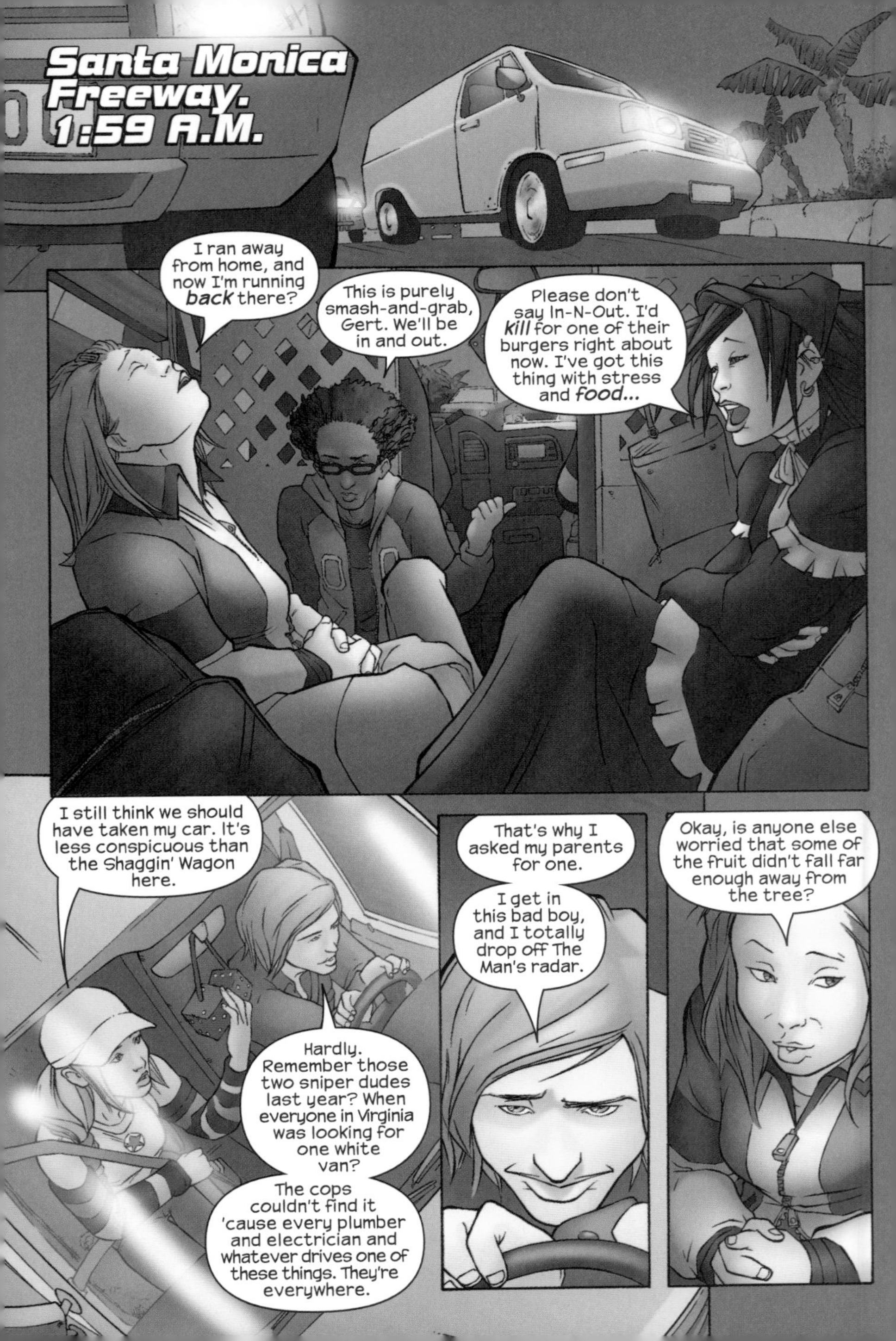
Santa Monica Freeway. 1:59 A.M.
I ran away from home, and now I'm running back there?
This is purely smash-and-grab, Gert. We'll be in and out.
Please don't say In-N-Out. I'd kill for one of their burgers right about now. I've got this thing with stress and food...
I still think we should have taken my car. It's less conspicuous than the Shaggin' Wagon here.
Hardly. Remember those two sniper dudes last year? When everyone in Virginia was looking for one white van?
The cops couldn't find it 'cause every plumber and electrician and whatever drives one of these things. They're everywhere.
That's why I asked my parents for one.
I get in this bad boy, and I totally drop off The Man's radar.
Okay, is anyone else worried that some of the fruit didn't fall far enough away from the tree?

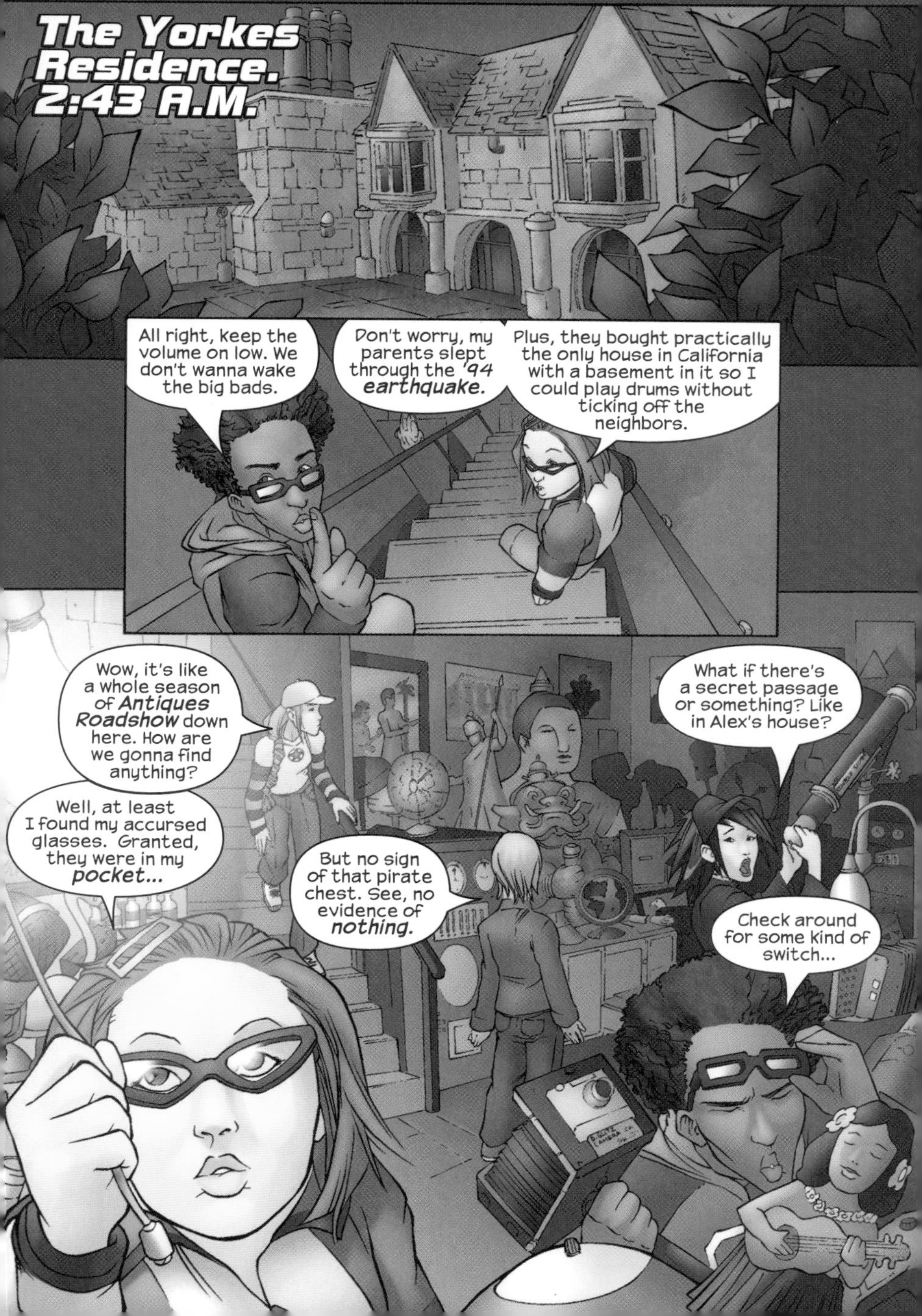

The Yorkes Residence. 2:43 A.M.
All right, keep the volume on low. We don't wanna wake the big bads.
Don't worry, my parents slept through the '94 earthquake.
Plus, they bought practically the only house in California with a basement in it so I could play drums without ticking off the neighbors.
Wow, it's like a whole season of Antiques Roadshow down here. How are we gonna find anything?
What if there's a secret passage or something? Like in Alex's house?
Well, at least I found my accursed glasses. Granted, they were in my pocket...
But no sign of that pirate chest. See, no evidence of nothing.
Check around for some kind of switch...

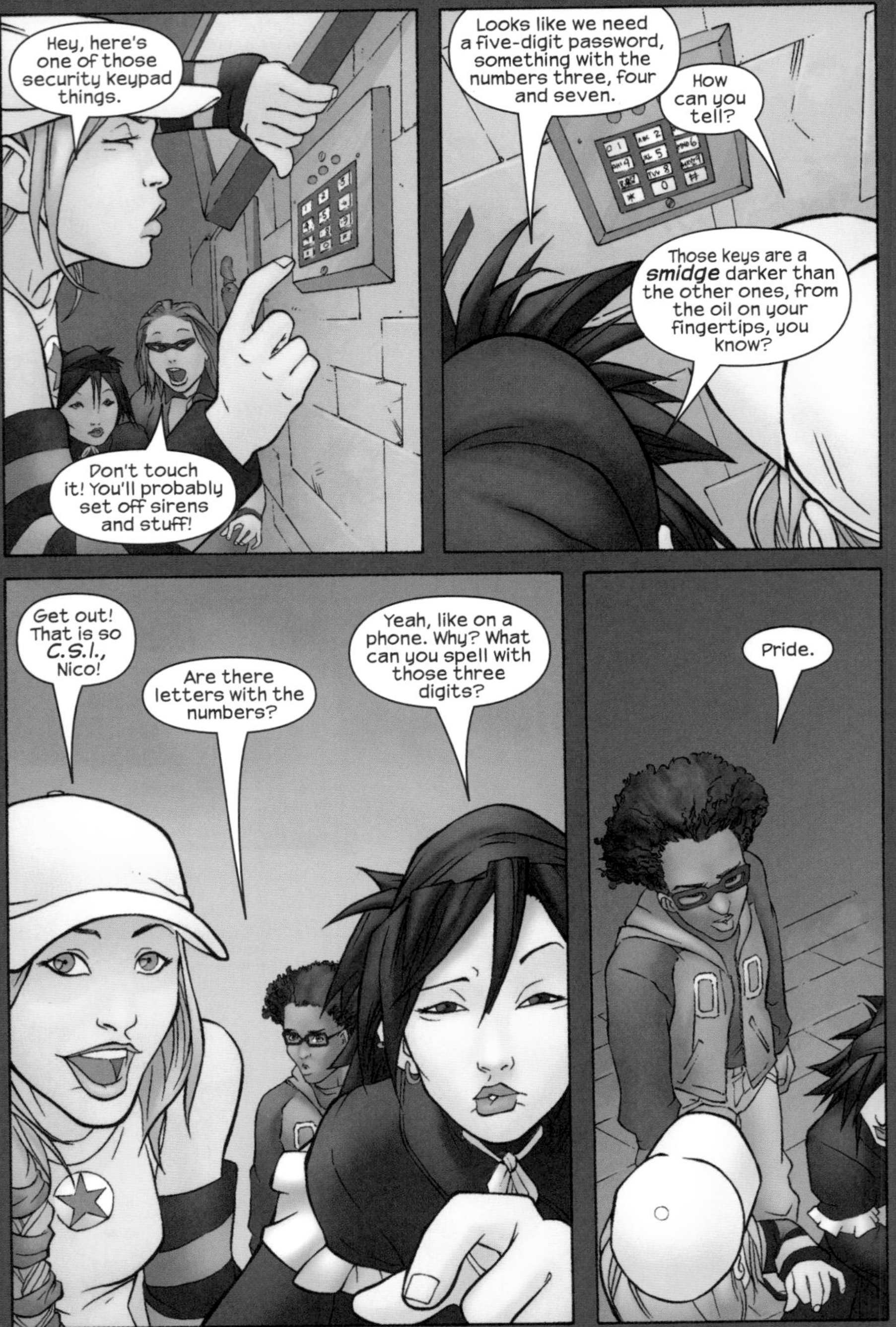
Hey, here's one of those security keypad things.
Don't touch it! You'll probably set off sirens and stuff!
Looks like we need a five-digit password, something with the numbers three, four and seven.
How can you tell?
Those keys are a smidge darker than the other ones, from the oil on your fingertips, you know?
Get out! That is so C.S.I., Nico!
Are there letters with the numbers?
Yeah, like on a phone. Why? What can you spell with those three digits?
Pride.

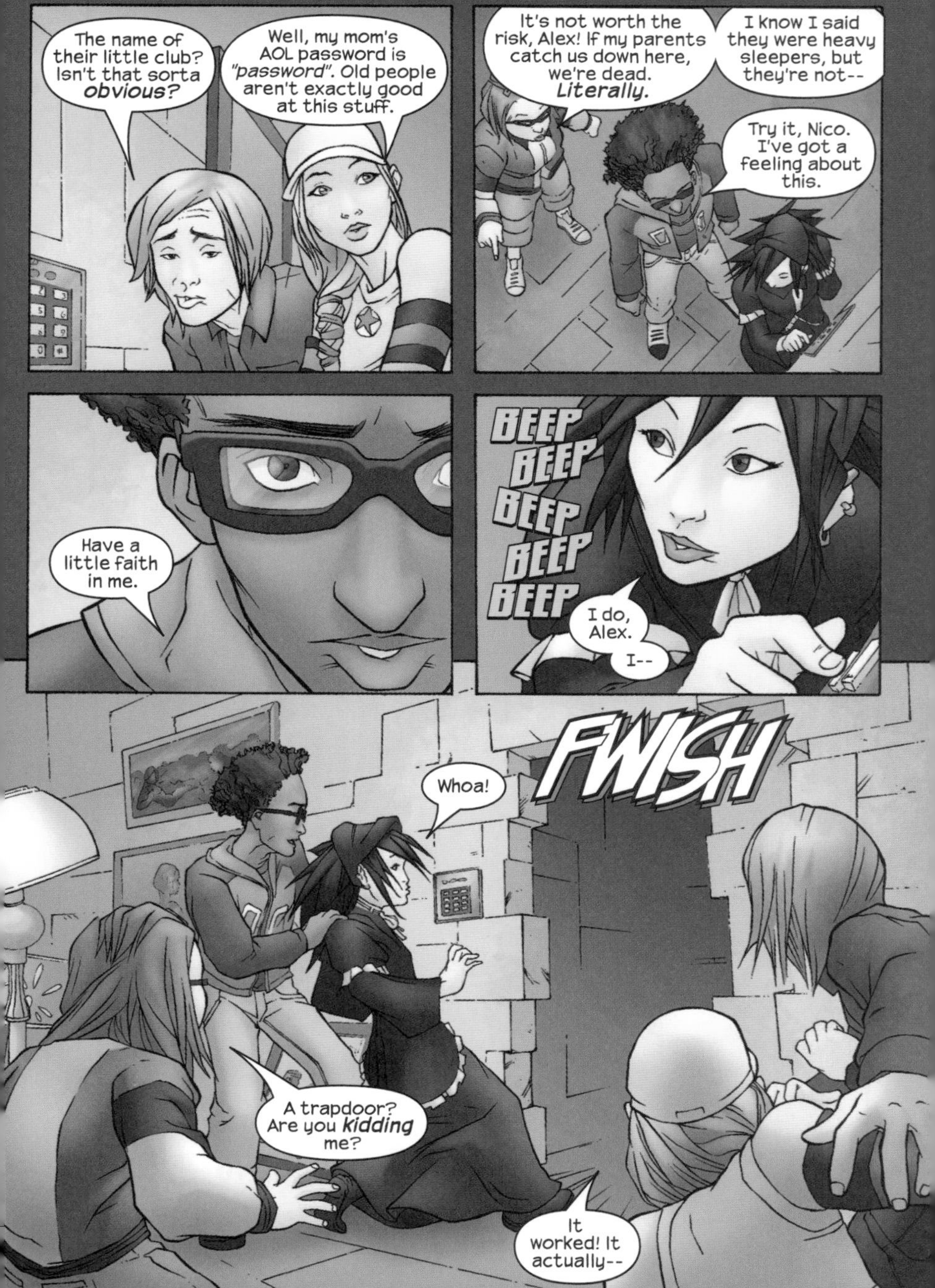
The name of their little club? Isn't that sorta obvious?
Well, my mom's AOL password is "password". Old people aren't exactly good at this stuff.
It's not worth the risk, Alex! If my parents catch us down here, we're dead. Literally.
I know I said they were heavy sleepers, but they're not--
Try it, Nico. I've got a feeling about this.
Have a little faith in me.
BEEP BEEP BEEP BEEP BEEP
I do, Alex.
I--
FWISH
Whoa!
A trapdoor? Are you kidding me?
It worked! It actually--

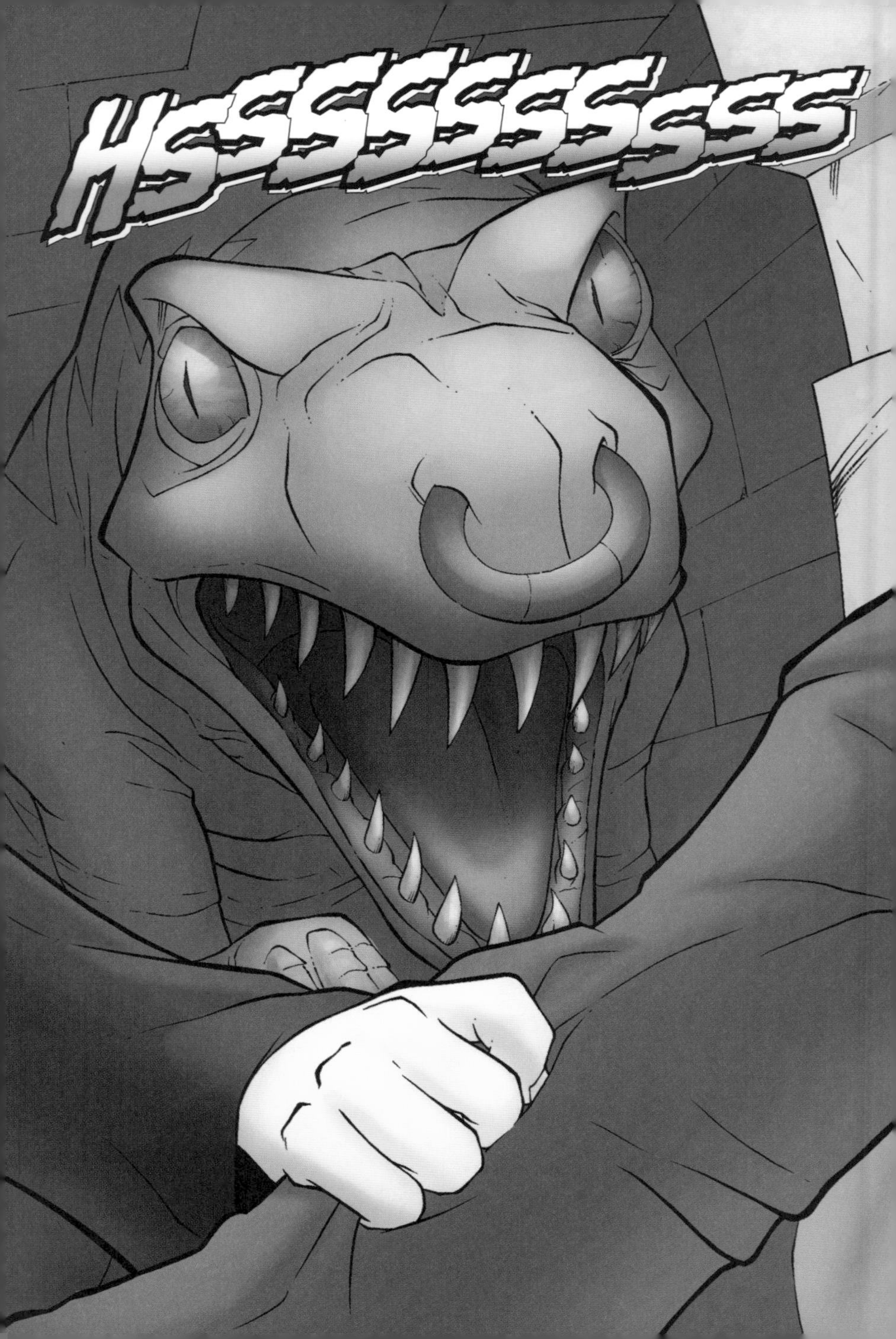
HSSSSSSSSS

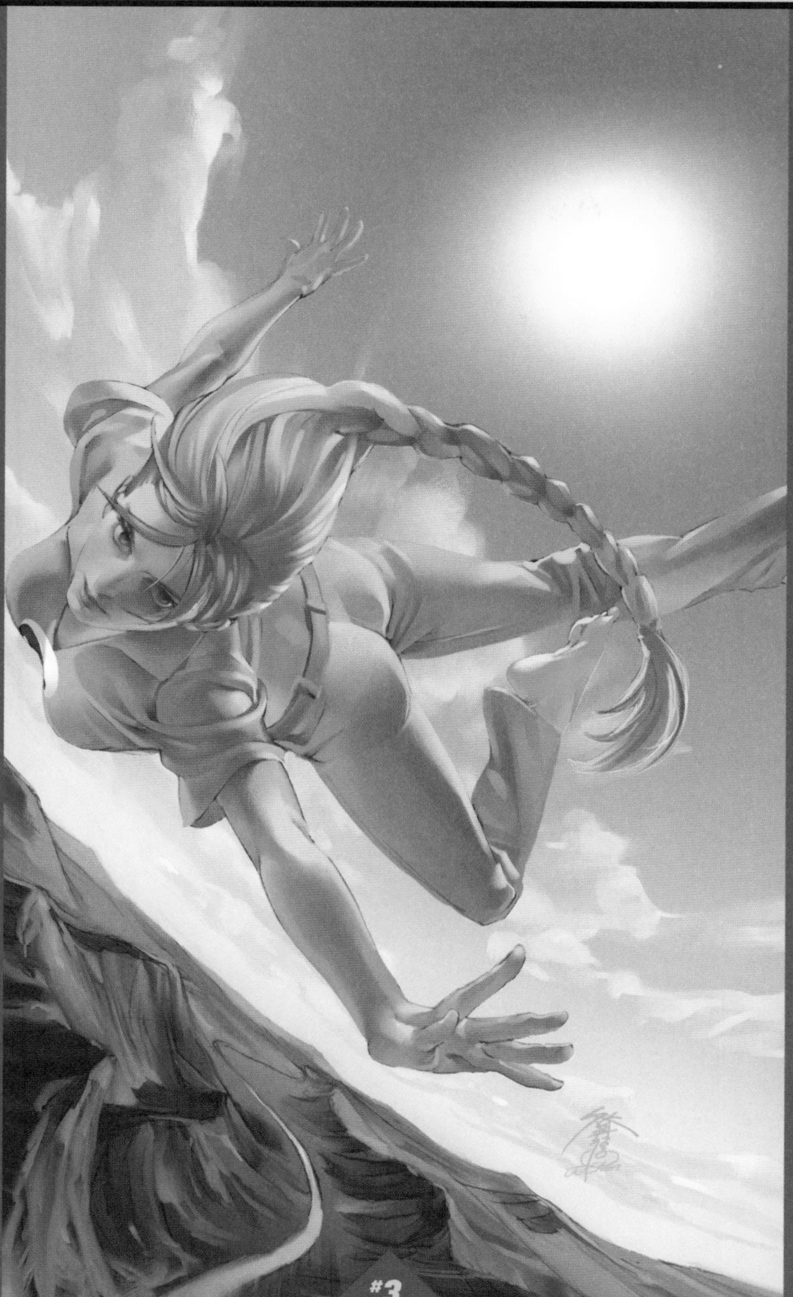

#3

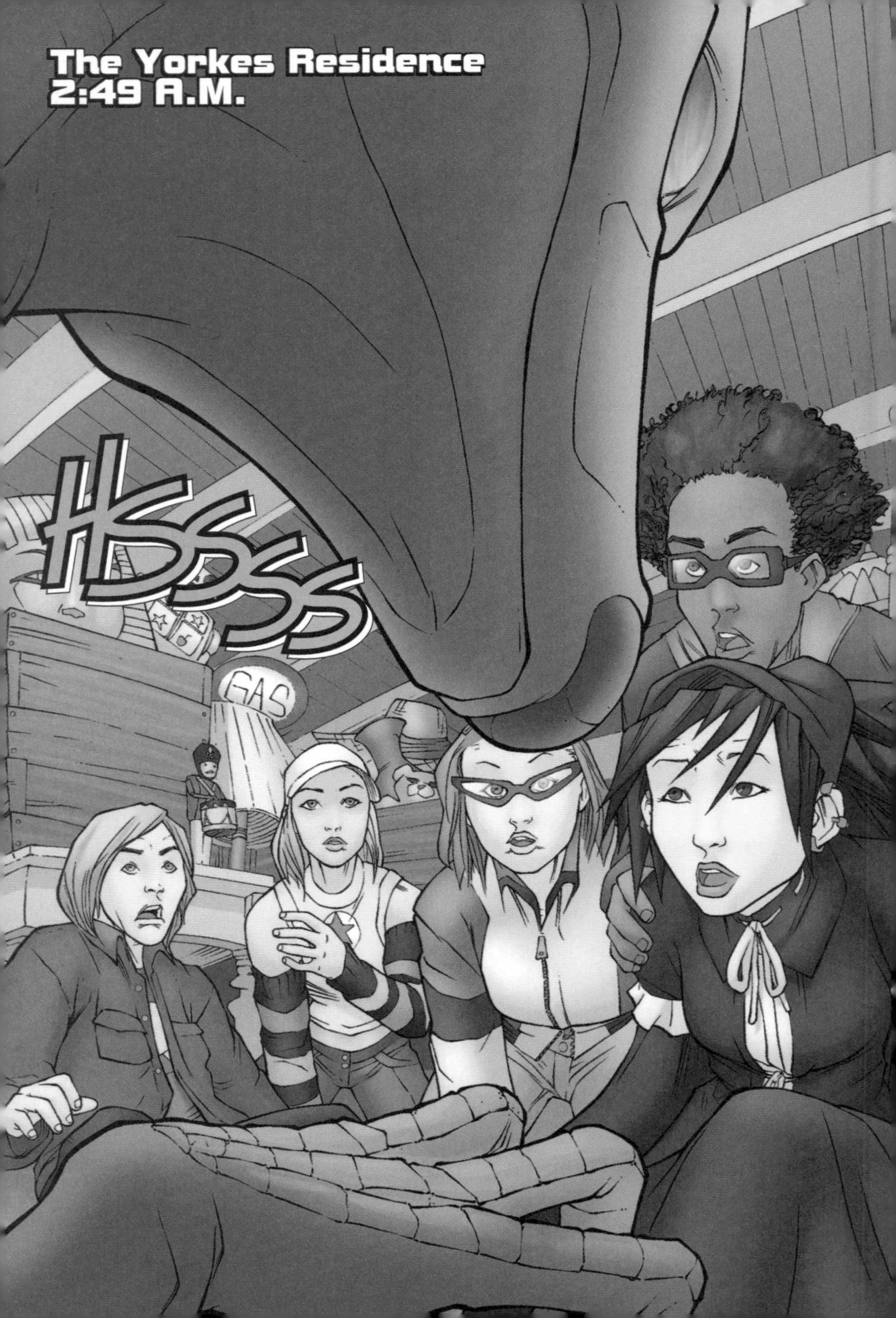

The Yorkes Residence
2:49 A.M.
HSSSS
GAS

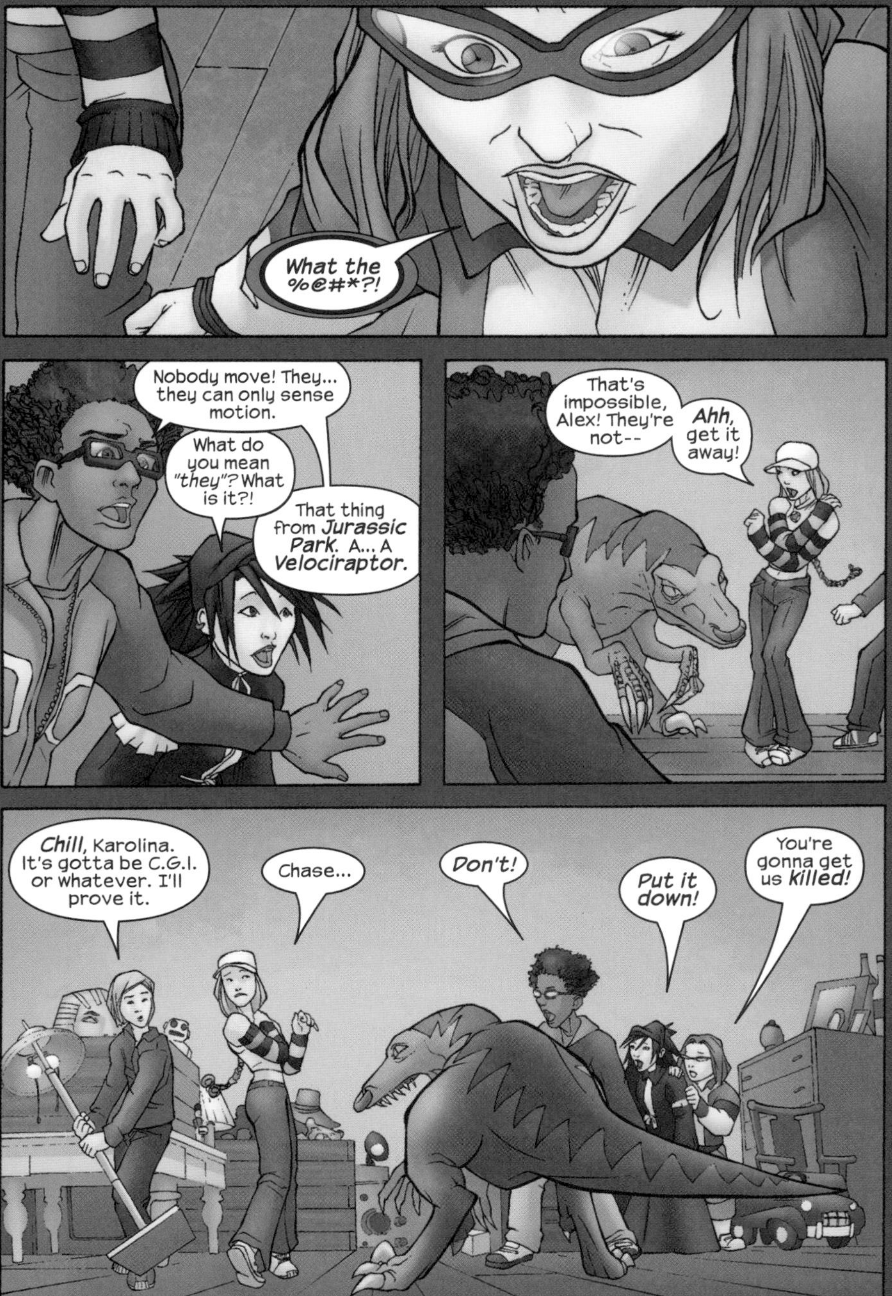
What the %@#*?!
Nobody move! They... they can only sense motion.
What do you mean "they"? What is it?!
That thing from Jurassic Park. A... A Velociraptor.
That's impossible, Alex! They're not--
Ahh, get it away!
Chill, Karolina. It's gotta be C.G.I. or whatever. I'll prove it.
Chase...
Don't!
Put it down!
You're gonna get us killed!

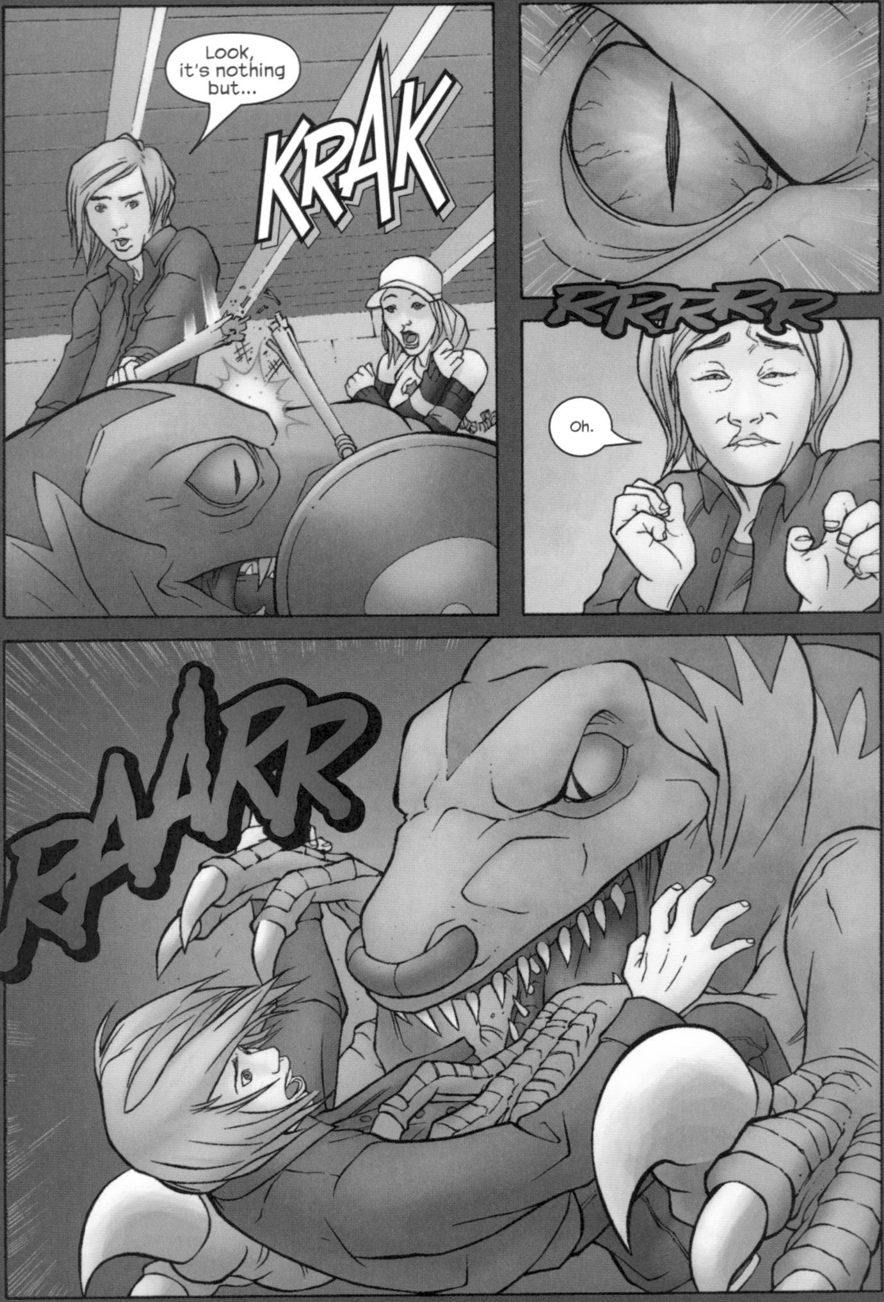
Look, it's nothing but...
KRAK
RRRRRR
Oh.
RAARR

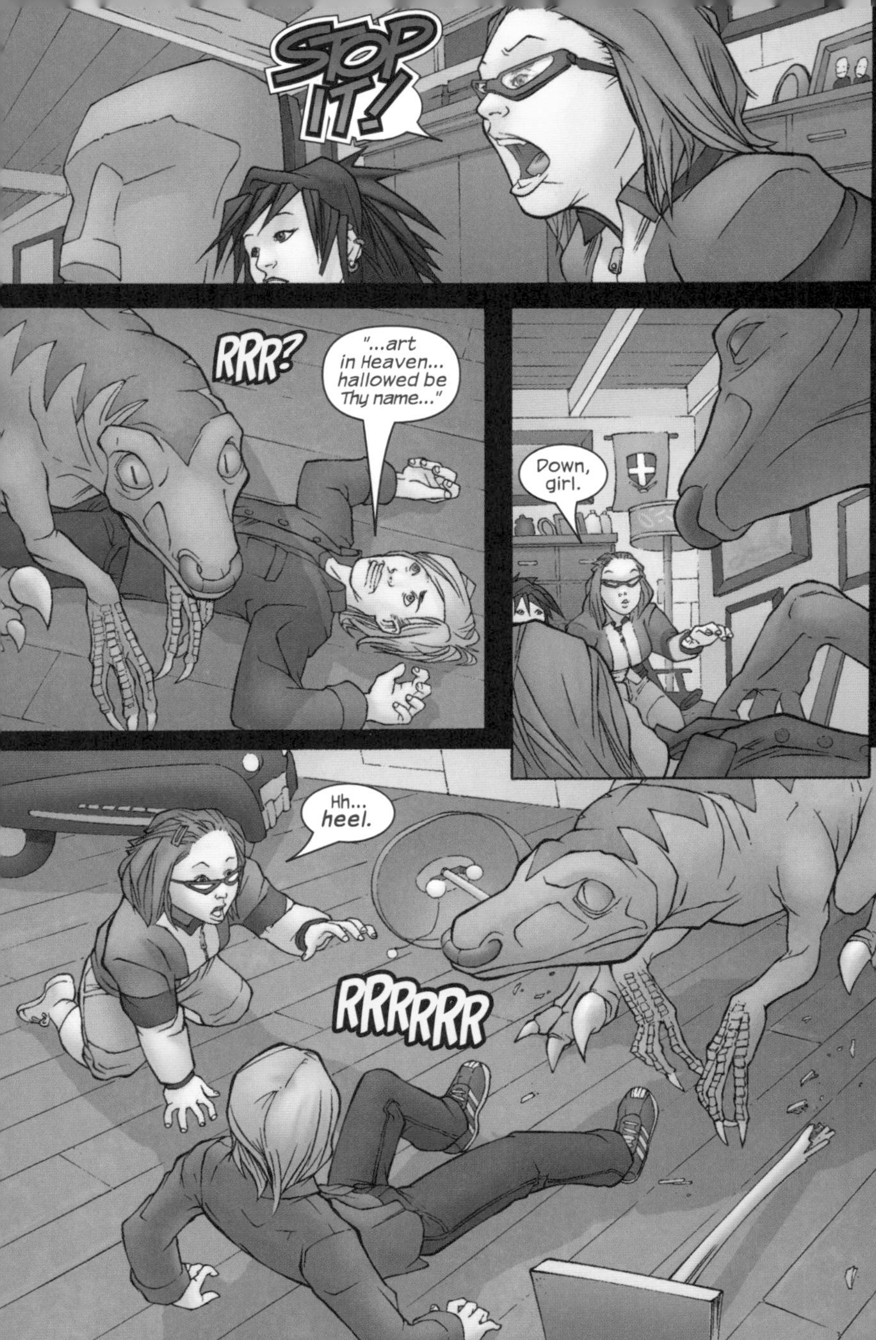
STOP IT!
RRR?
"...art in Heaven... hallowed be Thy name..."
Down, girl.
Hh... heel.
RRRRRR

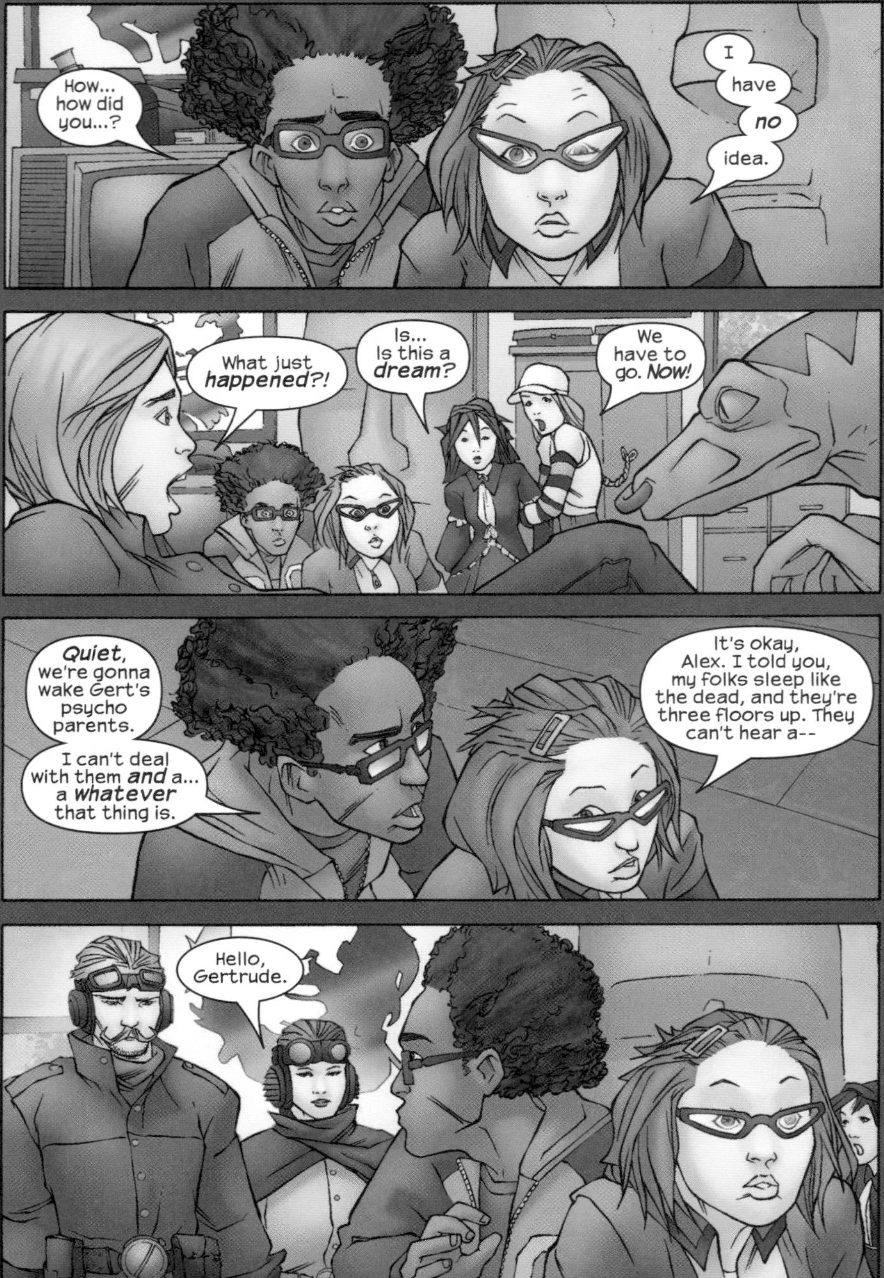

How... how did you...?
I have no idea.
What just happened?!
Is... Is this a dream?
We have to go. Now!
Quiet, we're gonna wake Gert's psycho parents.
I can't deal with them and a... a whatever that thing is.
It's okay, Alex. I told you, my folks sleep like the dead, and they're three floors up. They can't hear a--
Hello, Gertrude.

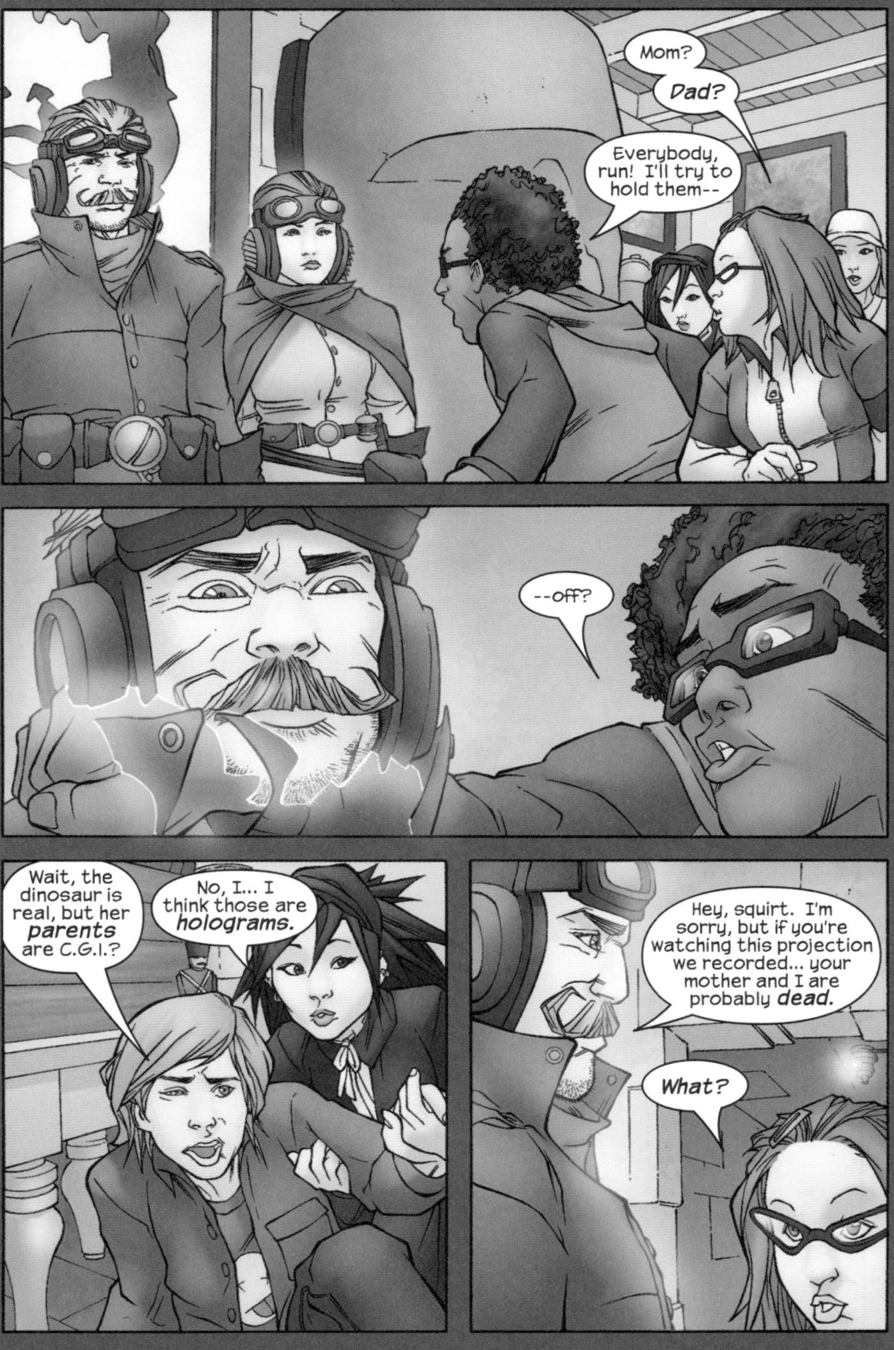
Mom?
Dad?
Everybody, run! I'll try to hold them--
--off?
Wait, the dinosaur is real, but her parents are C.G.I.?
No, I... I think those are holograms.
Hey, squirt. I'm sorry, but if you're watching this projection we recorded... your mother and I are probably dead.
What?

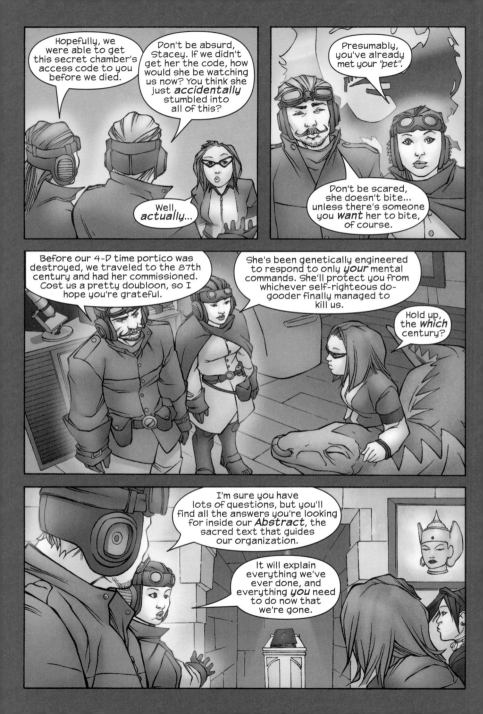

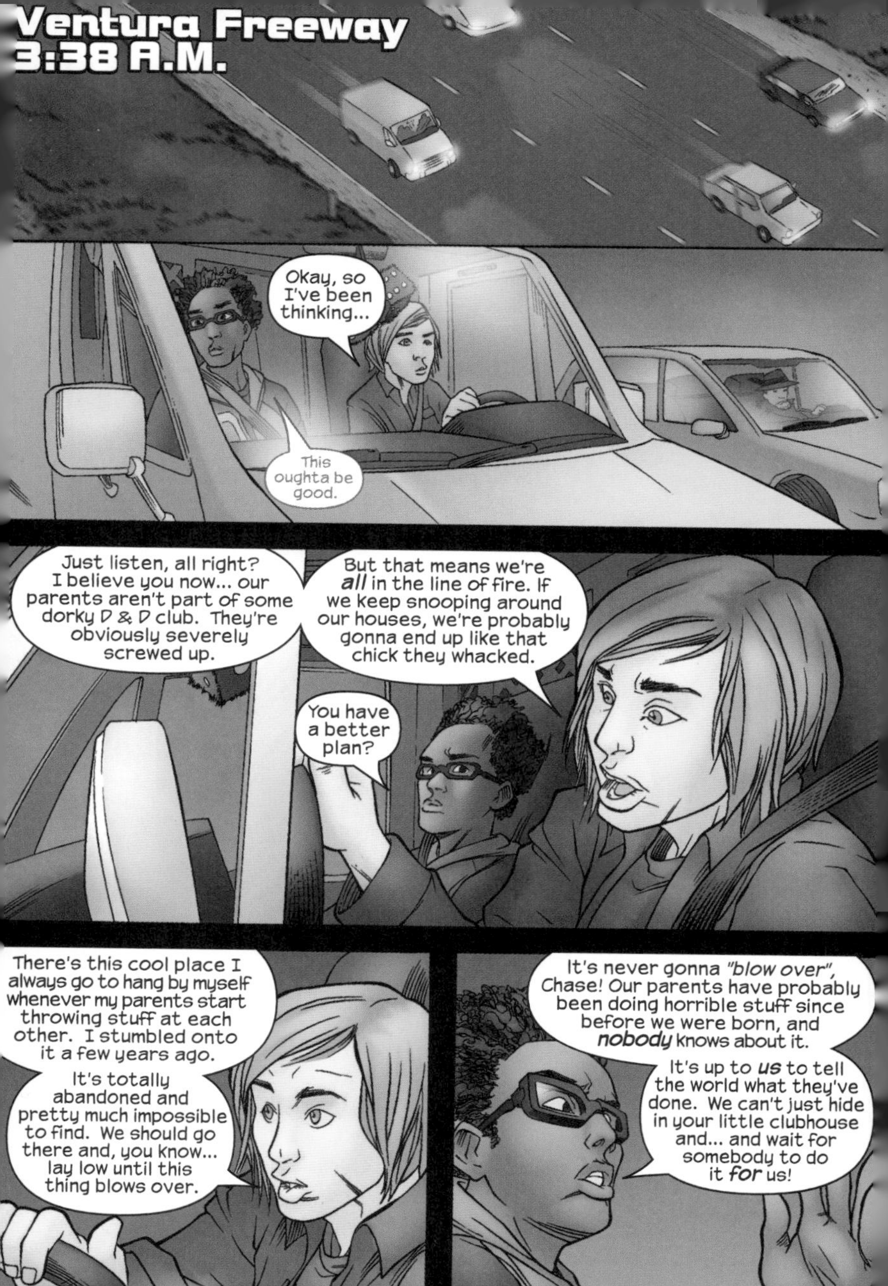

Ventura Freeway 3:38 A.M.
Okay, so I've been thinking...
This oughta be good.
Just listen, all right? I believe you now... our parents aren't part of some dorky D & D club. They're obviously severely screwed up.
But that means we're *all* in the line of fire. If we keep snooping around our houses, we're probably gonna end up like that chick they whacked.
You have a better plan?
There's this cool place I always go to hang by myself whenever my parents start throwing stuff at each other. I stumbled onto it a few years ago.
It's totally abandoned and pretty much impossible to find. We should go there and, you know... lay low until this thing blows over.
It's never gonna *"blow over"*, Chase! Our parents have probably been doing horrible stuff since before we were born, and *nobody* knows about it.
It's up to *us* to tell the world what they've done. We can't just hide in your little clubhouse and... and wait for somebody to do it *for* us!

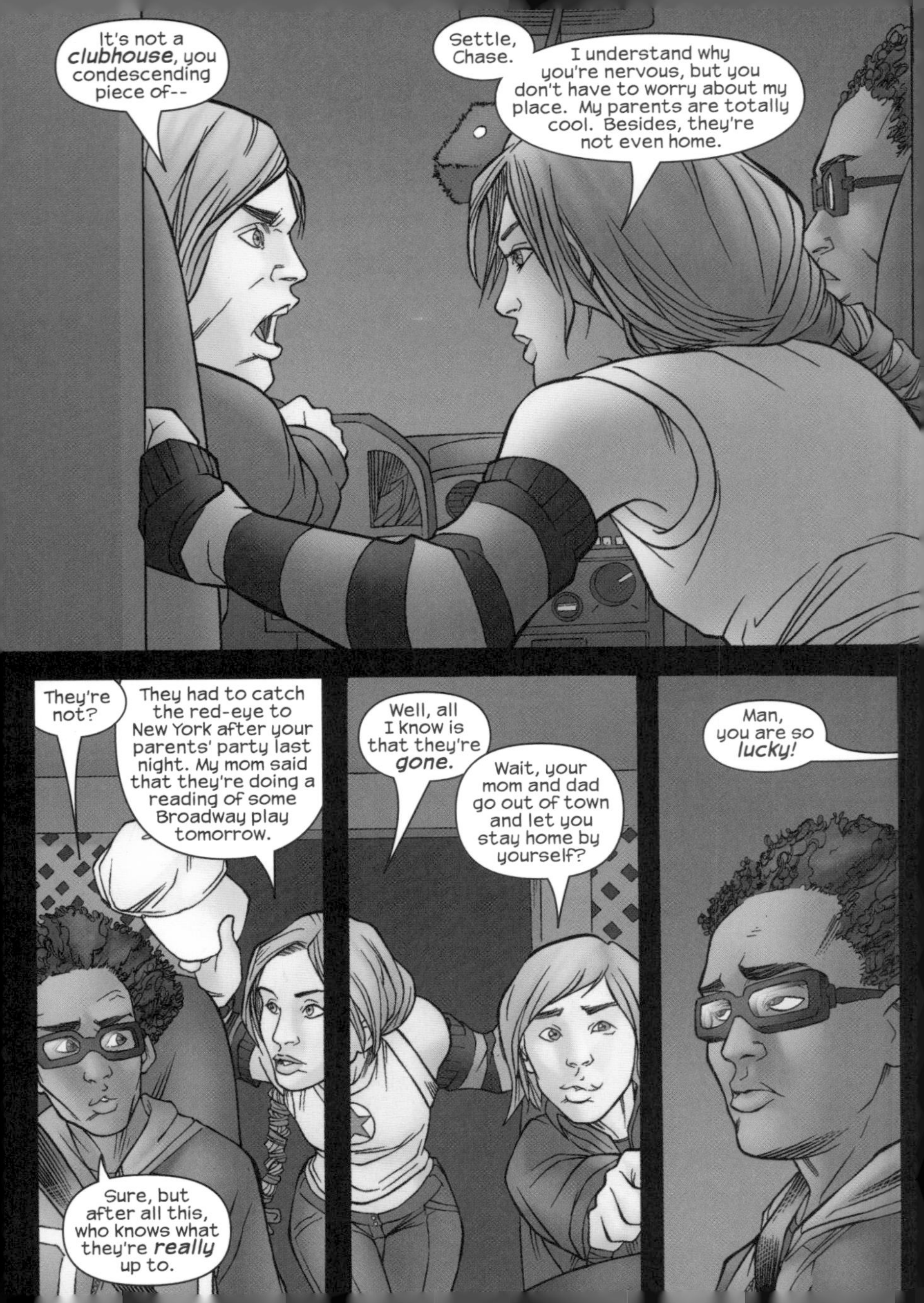
It's not a *clubhouse*, you condescending piece of--
Settle, Chase.
I understand why you're nervous, but you don't have to worry about my place. My parents are totally cool. Besides, they're not even home.
They're not?
They had to catch the red-eye to New York after your parents' party last night. My mom said that they're doing a reading of some Broadway play tomorrow.
Sure, but after all this, who knows what they're *really* up to.
Well, all I know is that they're *gone*.
Wait, your mom and dad go out of town and let you stay home by yourself?
Man, you are so *lucky*!

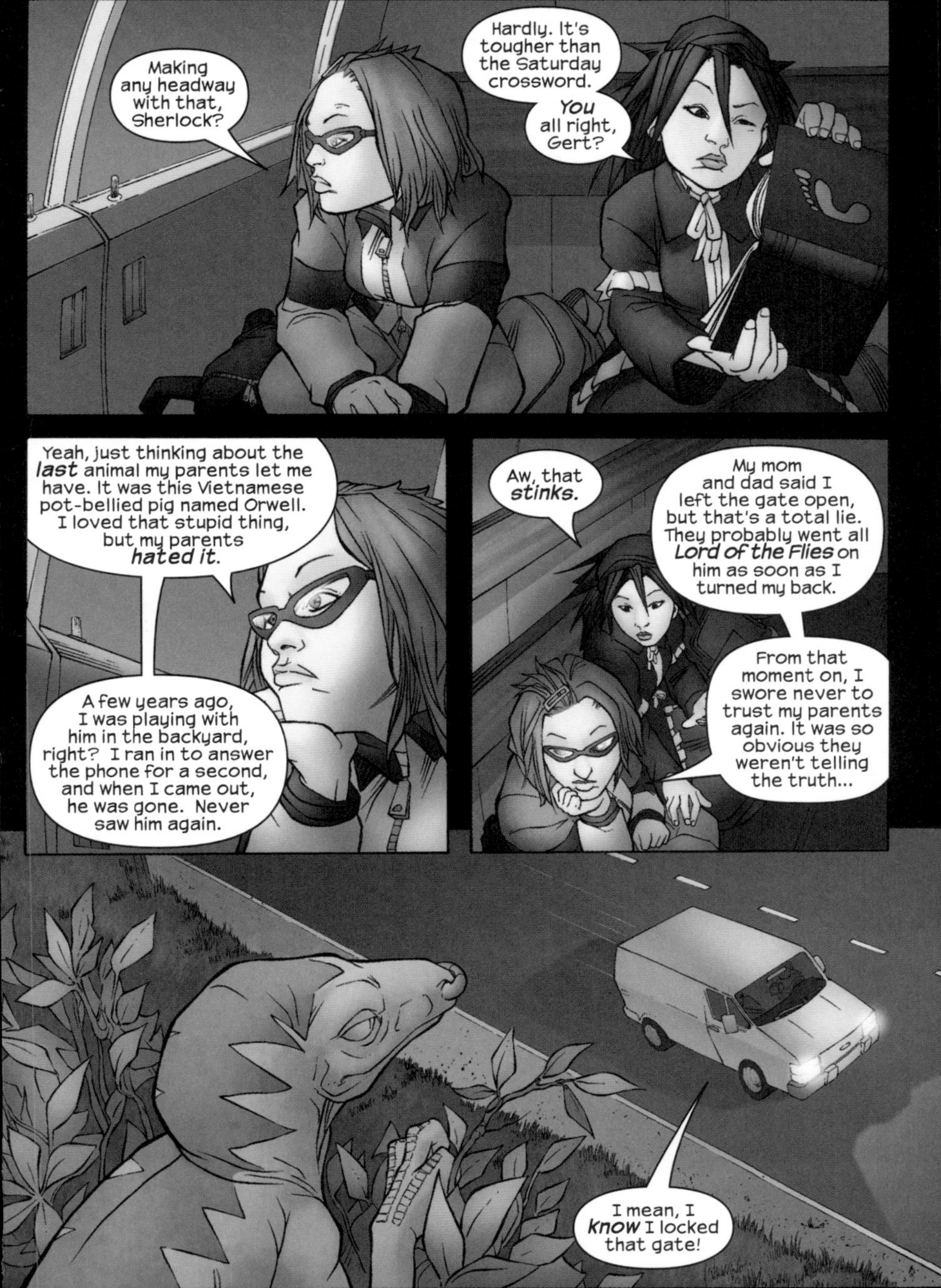
Making any headway with that, Sherlock?
Hardly. It's tougher than the Saturday crossword.
You all right, Gert?
Yeah, just thinking about the *last* animal my parents let me have. It was this Vietnamese pot-bellied pig named Orwell. I loved that stupid thing, but my parents *hated it*.
A few years ago, I was playing with him in the backyard, right? I ran in to answer the phone for a second, and when I came out, he was gone. Never saw him again.
Aw, that *stinks.*
My mom and dad said I left the gate open, but that's a total lie. They probably went all *Lord of the Flies* on him as soon as I turned my back.
From that moment on, I swore never to trust my parents again. It was so obvious they weren't telling the truth...
I mean, I *know* I locked that gate!

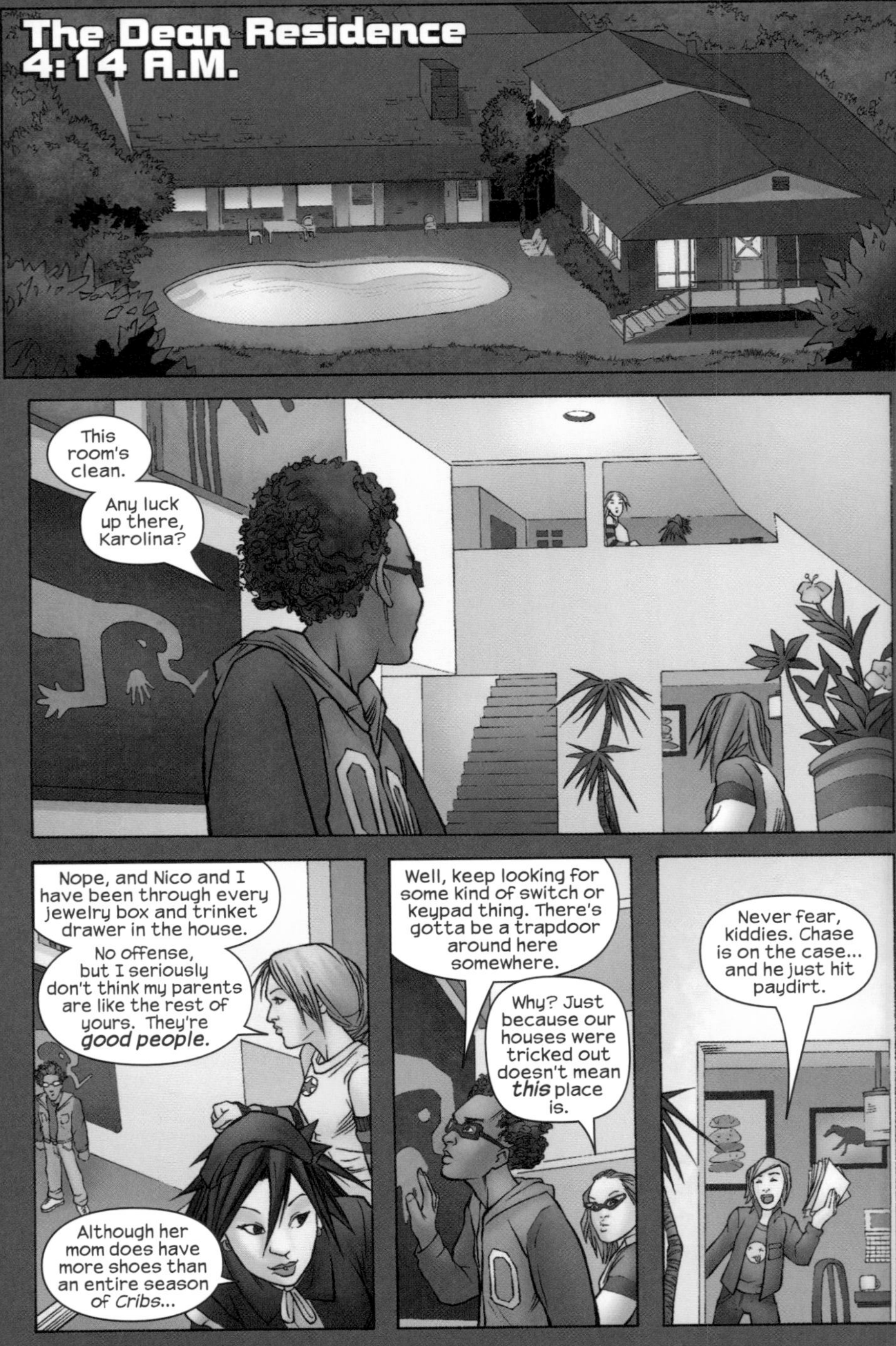
The Dean Residence
4:14 A.M.
This room's clean.
Any luck up there, Karolina?
Nope, and Nico and I have been through every jewelry box and trinket drawer in the house.
No offense, but I seriously don't think my parents are like the rest of yours. They're *good people.*
Although her mom does have more shoes than an entire season of *Cribs*...
Well, keep looking for some kind of switch or keypad thing. There's gotta be a trapdoor around here somewhere.
Why? Just because our houses were tricked out doesn't mean *this* place is.
Never fear, kiddies. Chase is on the case... and he just hit paydirt.

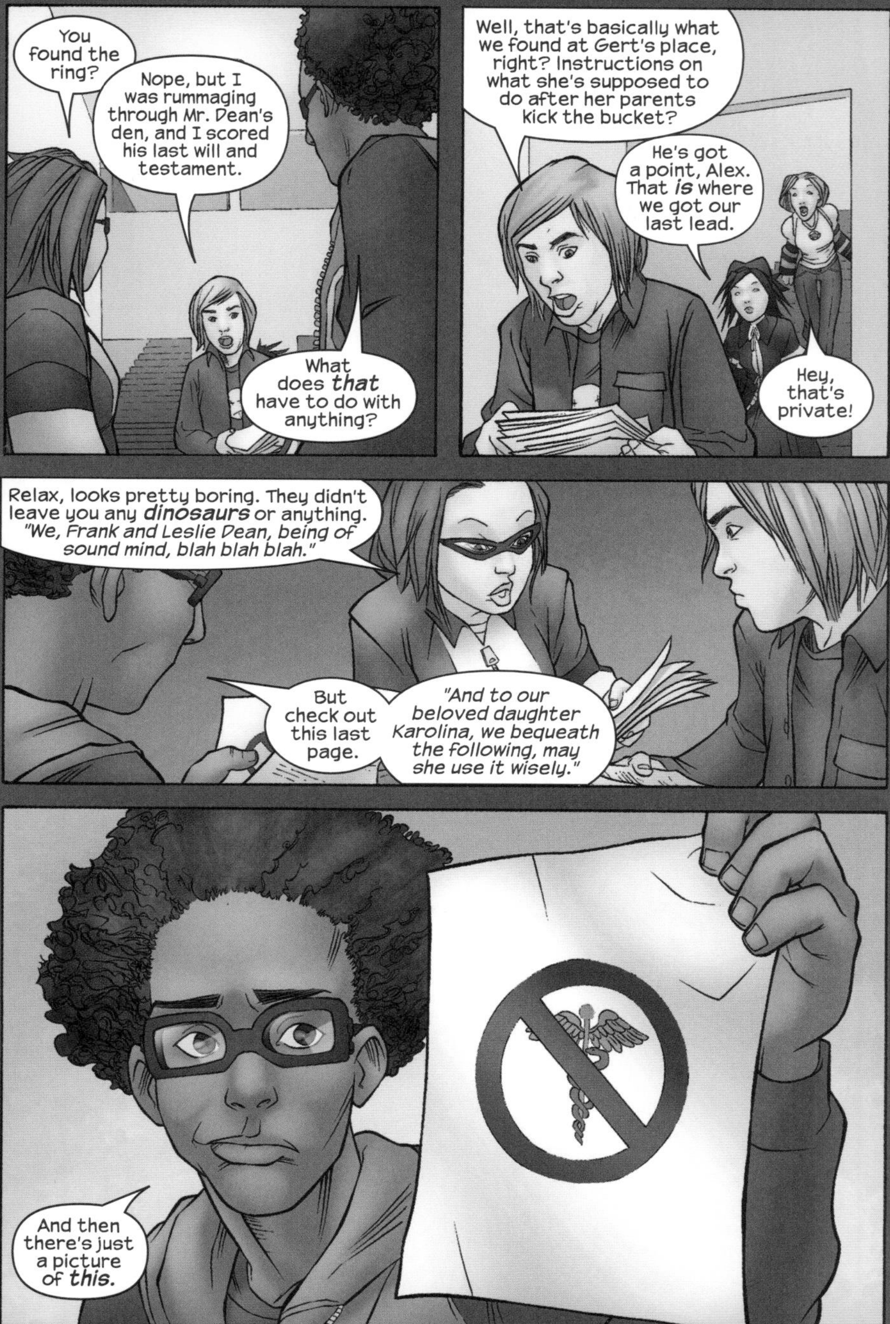
You found the ring?
Nope, but I was rummaging through Mr. Dean's den, and I scored his last will and testament.
What does *that* have to do with anything?
Well, that's basically what we found at Gert's place, right? Instructions on what she's supposed to do after her parents kick the bucket?
He's got a point, Alex. That *is* where we got our last lead.
Hey, that's private!
Relax, looks pretty boring. They didn't leave you any **dinosaurs** or anything. *"We, Frank and Leslie Dean, being of sound mind, blah blah blah."*
But check out this last page.
"And to our beloved daughter Karolina, we bequeath the following, may she use it wisely."
And then there's just a picture of **this.**

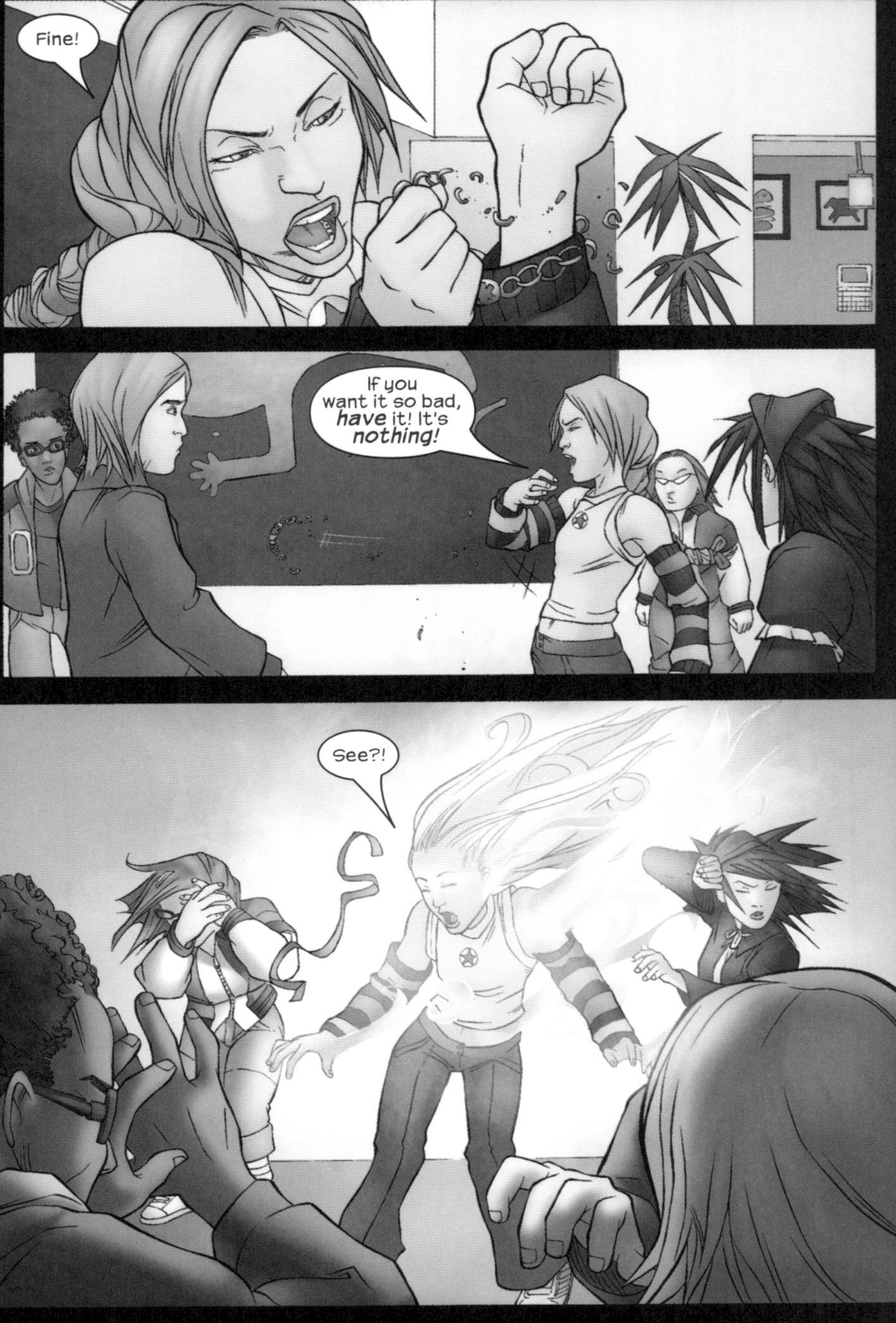
Fine!
If you want it so bad, **have** it! It's **nothing!**
See?!

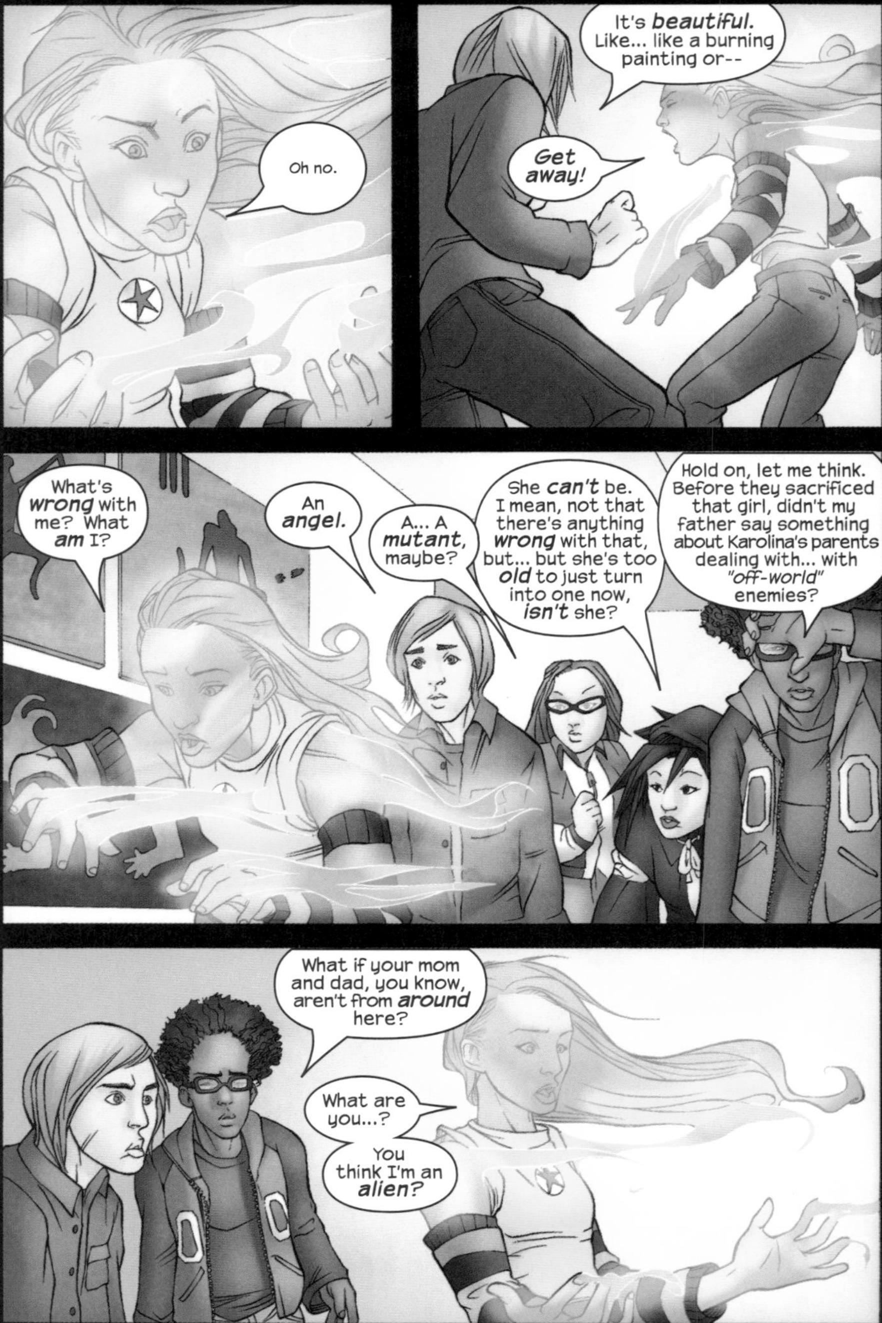
Oh no.
It's *beautiful.* Like... like a burning painting or--
Get away!
What's *wrong* with me? What *am* I?
An *angel.*
A... A *mutant,* maybe?
She *can't* be. I mean, not that there's anything *wrong* with that, but... but she's too *old* to just turn into one now, *isn't* she?
Hold on, let me think. Before they sacrificed that girl, didn't my father say something about Karolina's parents dealing with... with *"off-world"* enemies?
What if your mom and dad, you know, aren't from *around* here?
What are you...?
You think I'm an *alien?*

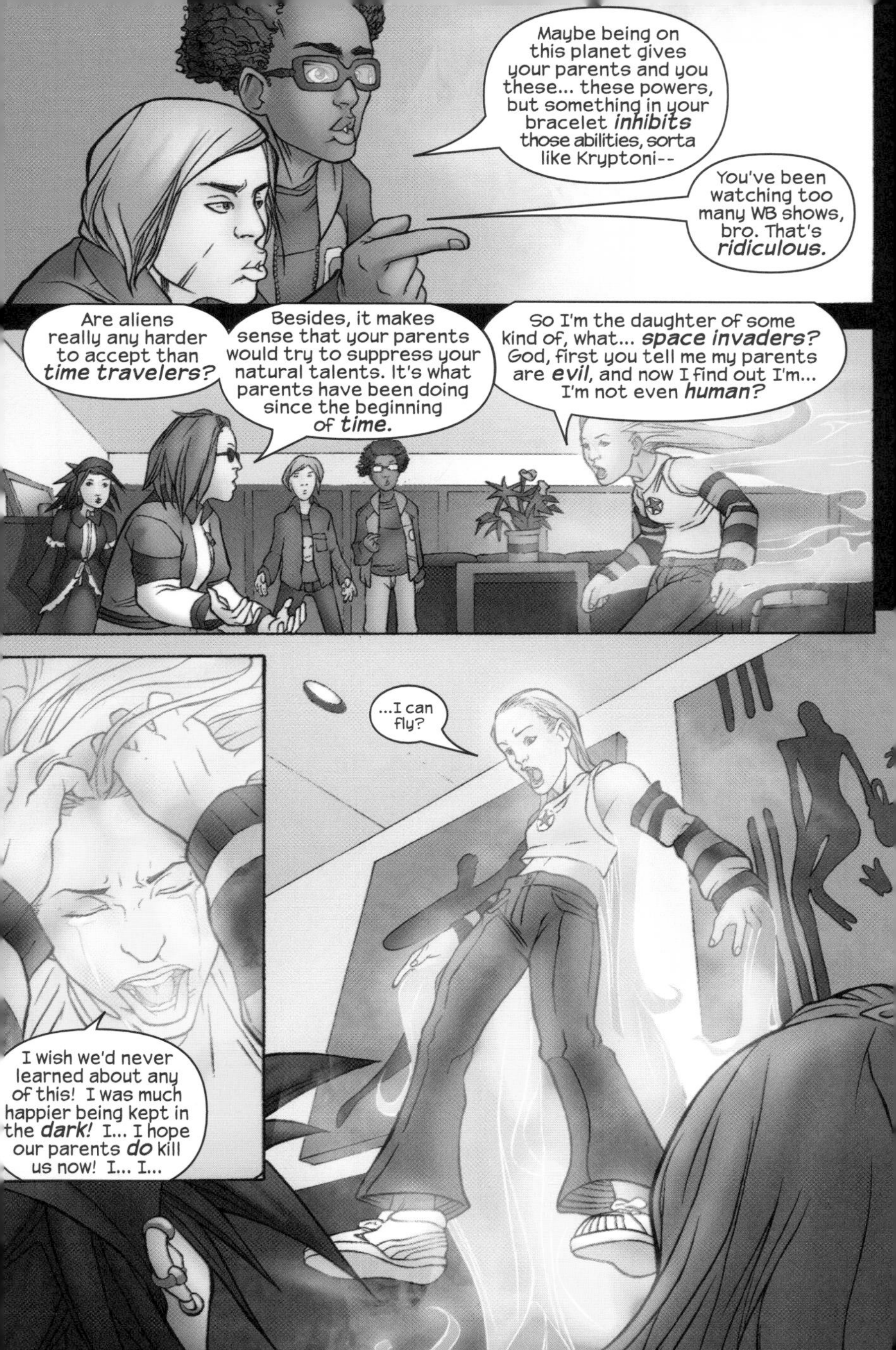
Maybe being on this planet gives your parents and you these... these powers, but something in your bracelet *inhibits* those abilities, sorta like Kryptoni--
You've been watching too many WB shows, bro. That's *ridiculous.*
Are aliens really any harder to accept than *time travelers?*
Besides, it makes sense that your parents would try to suppress your natural talents. It's what parents have been doing since the beginning of *time.*
So I'm the daughter of some kind of, what... *space invaders?* God, first you tell me my parents are *evil*, and now I find out I'm... I'm not even *human?*
I wish we'd never learned about any of this! I was much happier being kept in the *dark!* I... I hope our parents *do* kill us now! I... I...
...I can fly?

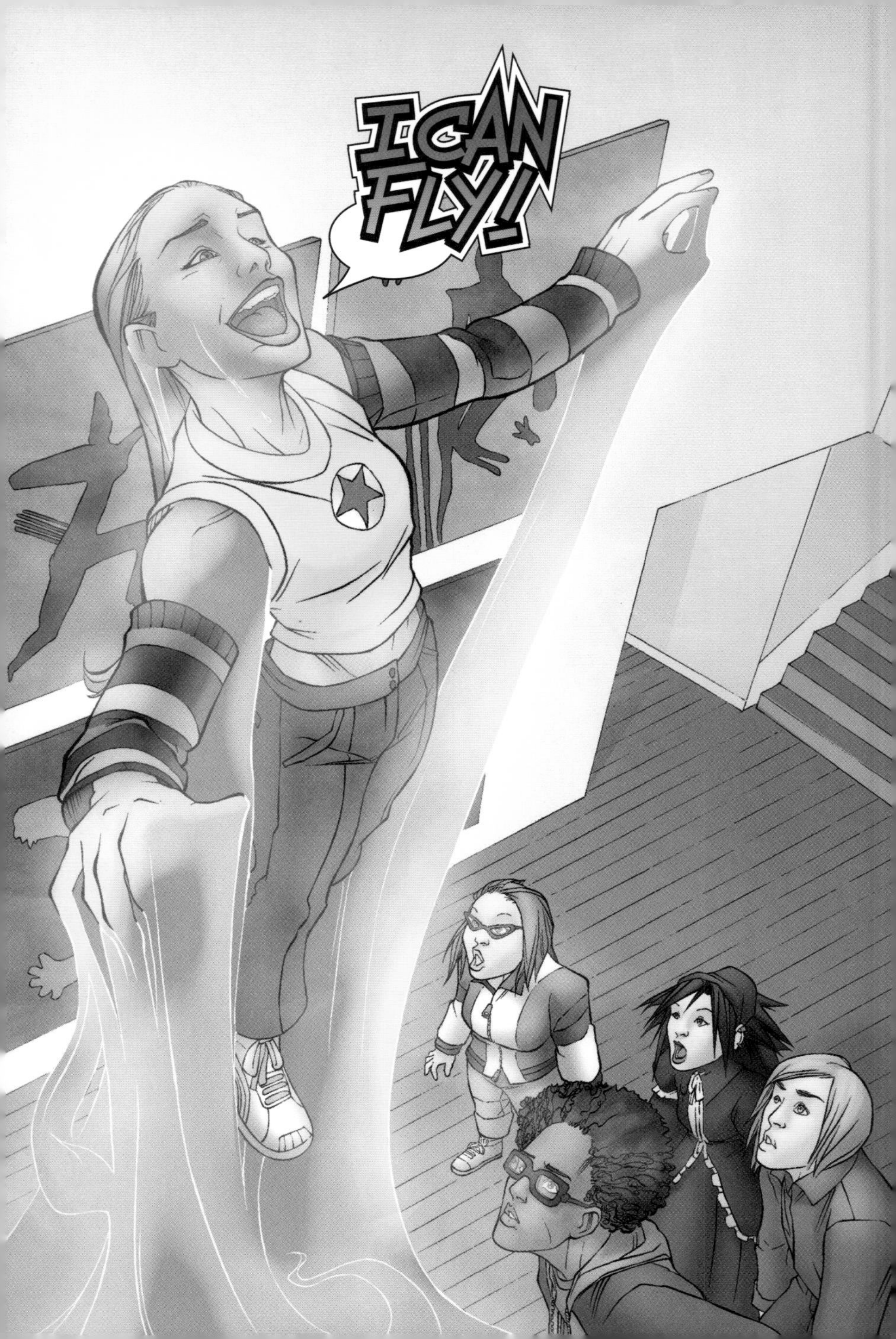
I CAN FLY!

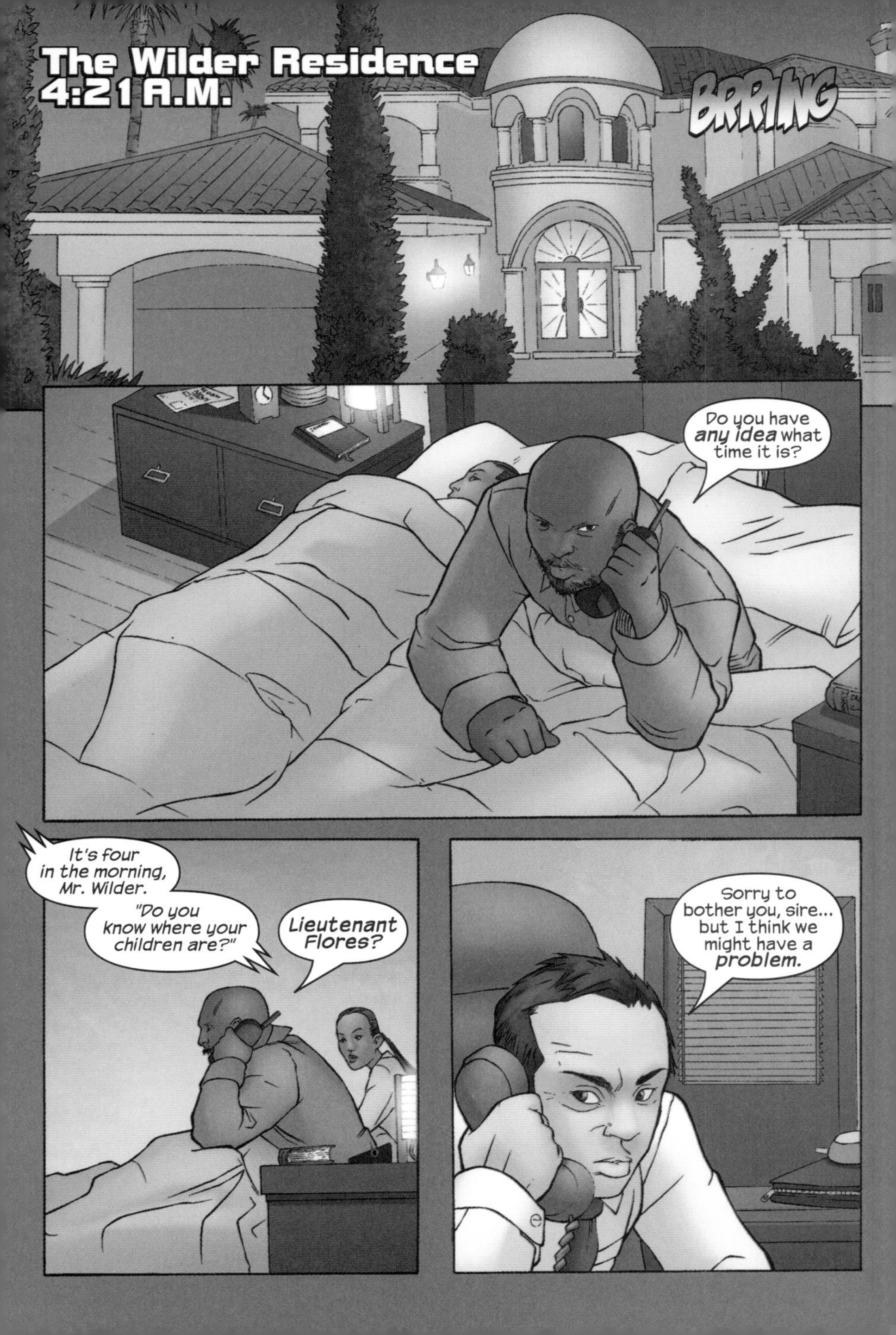
The Wilder Residence
4:21 A.M.
BRRING
Do you have any idea what time it is?
It's four in the morning, Mr. Wilder.
"Do you know where your children are?"
Lieutenant Flores?
Sorry to bother you, sire... but I think we might have a problem.

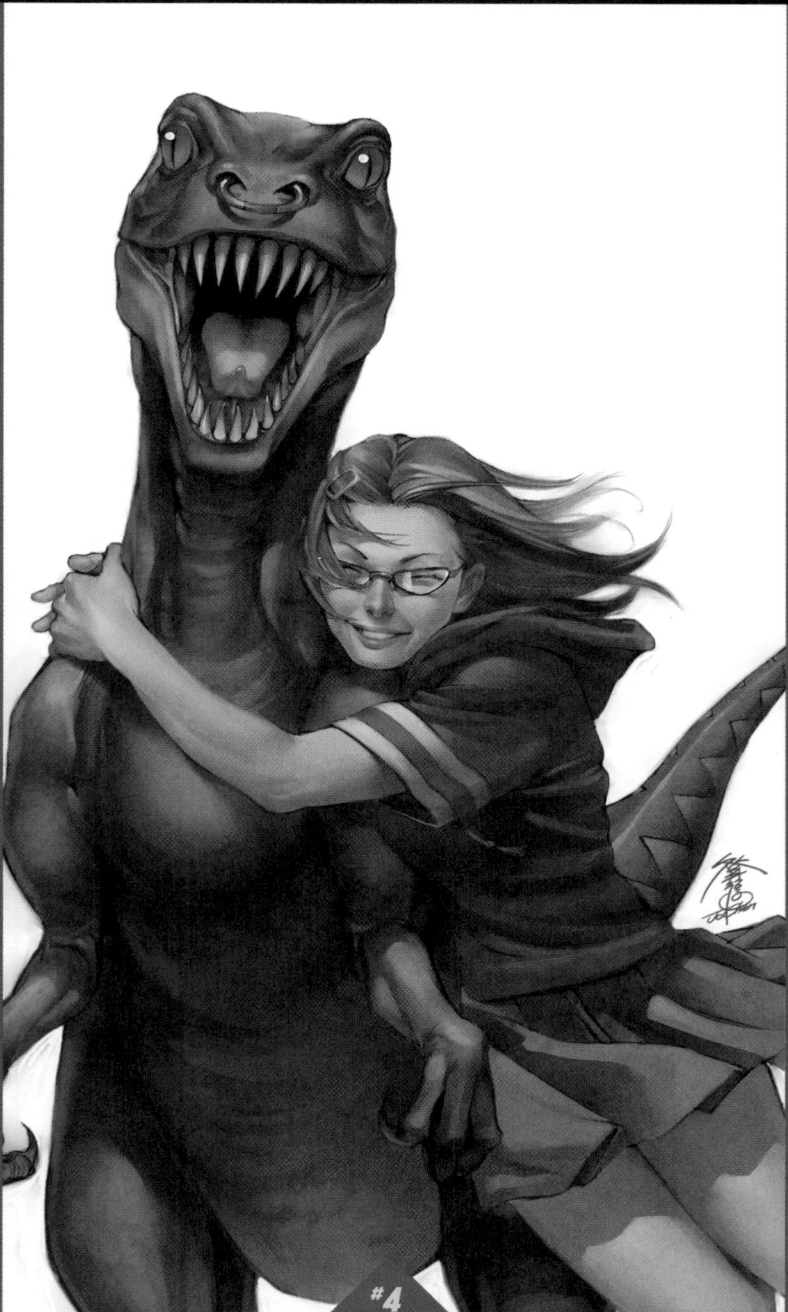
#4

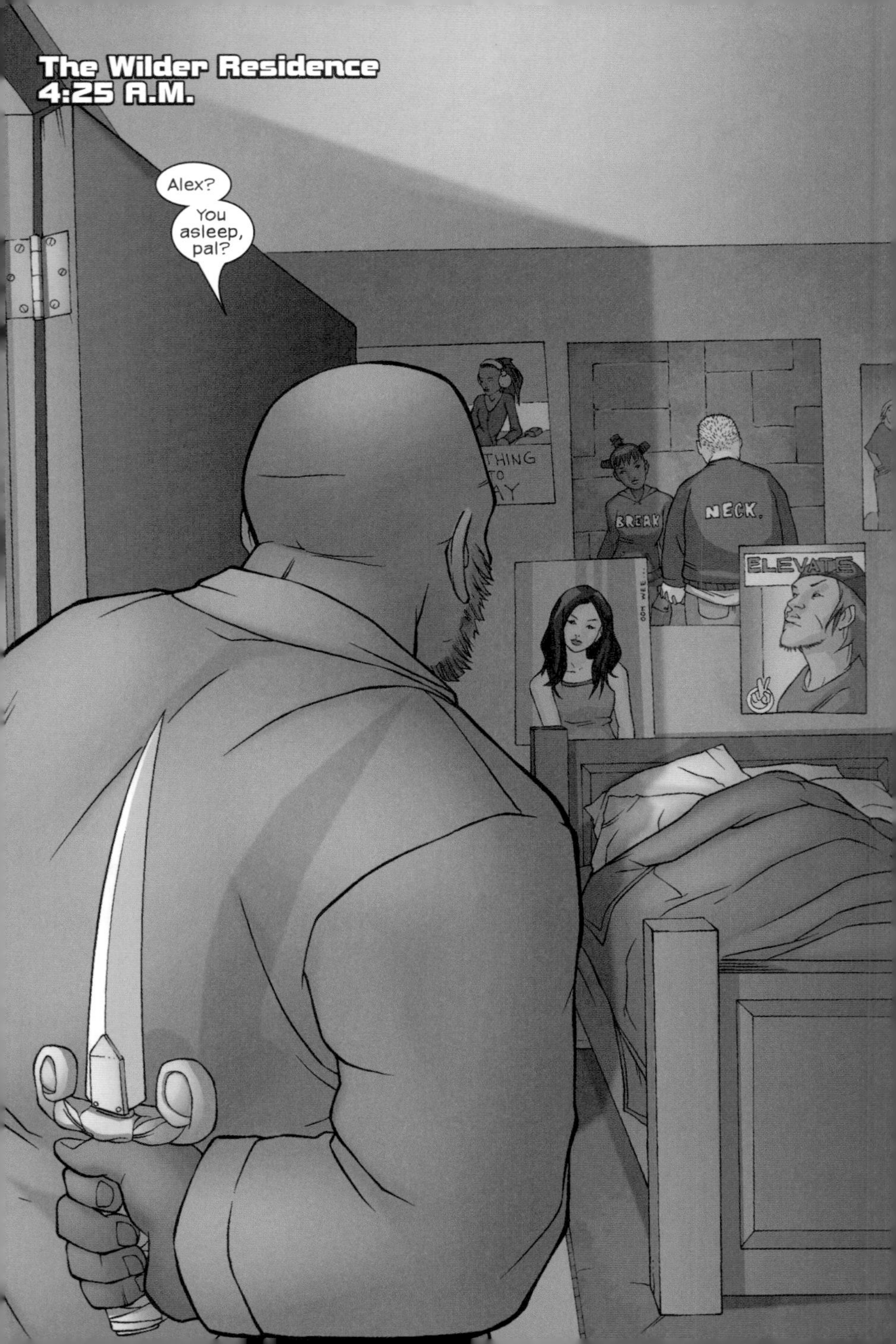
The Wilder Residence
4:25 A.M.
Alex?
You asleep, pal?
BREAK
NECK.

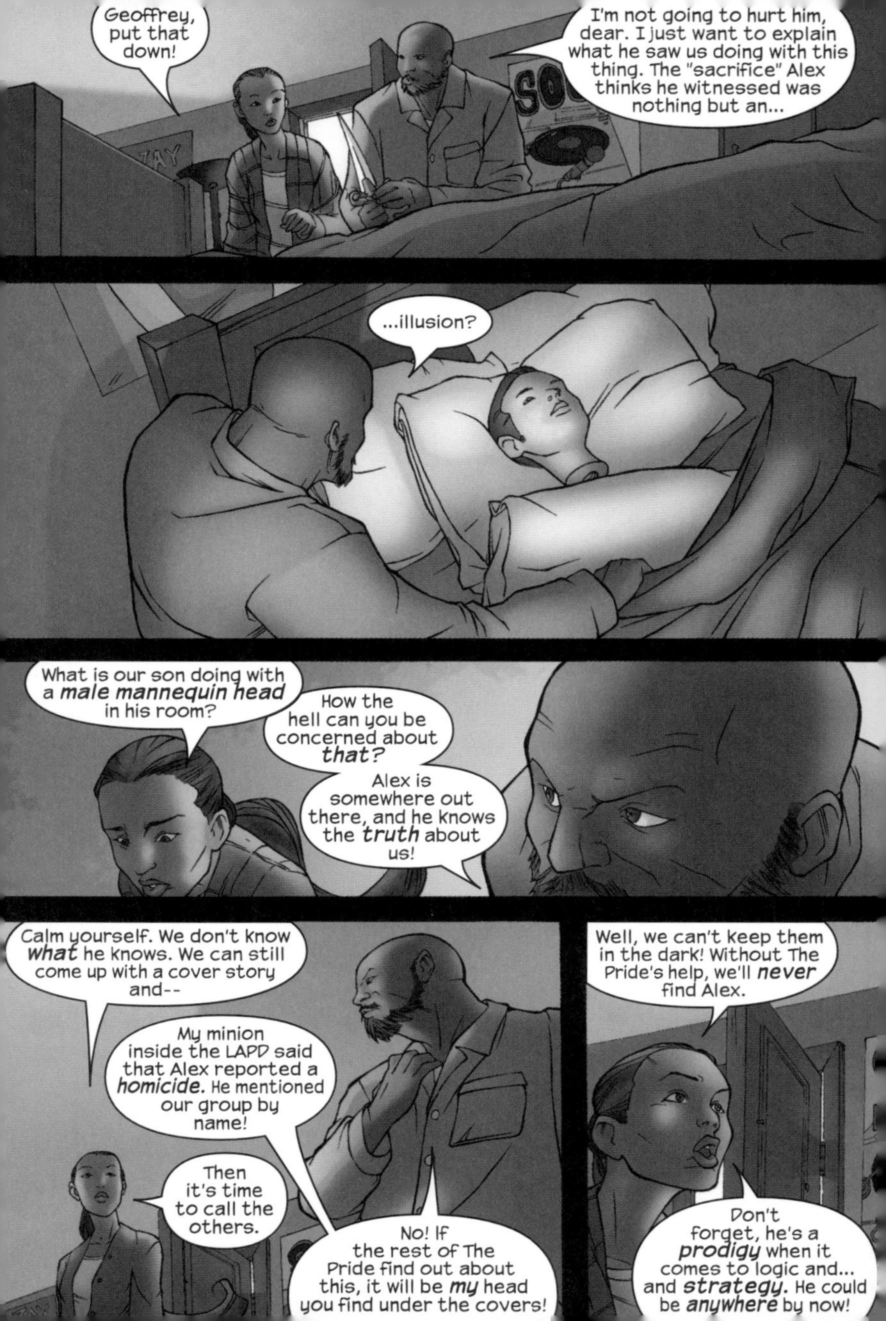
Geoffrey, put that down!
I'm not going to hurt him, dear. I just want to explain what he saw us doing with this thing. The "sacrifice" Alex thinks he witnessed was nothing but an...
...illusion?
What is our son doing with a *male mannequin head* in his room?
How the hell can you be concerned about *that?*
Alex is somewhere out there, and he knows the *truth* about us!
Calm yourself. We don't know *what* he knows. We can still come up with a cover story and--
My minion inside the LAPD said that Alex reported a *homicide.* He mentioned our group by name!
Then it's time to call the others.
No! If the rest of The Pride find out about this, it will be *my* head you find under the covers!
Well, we can't keep them in the dark! Without The Pride's help, we'll *never* find Alex.
Don't forget, he's a *prodigy* when it comes to logic and... and *strategy.* He could be *anywhere* by now!

The Dean Residence
Eleven Miles Away
4:28 A.M.
Ha ha, YEAH!
WHEEEEEEEE!
We are so dead...

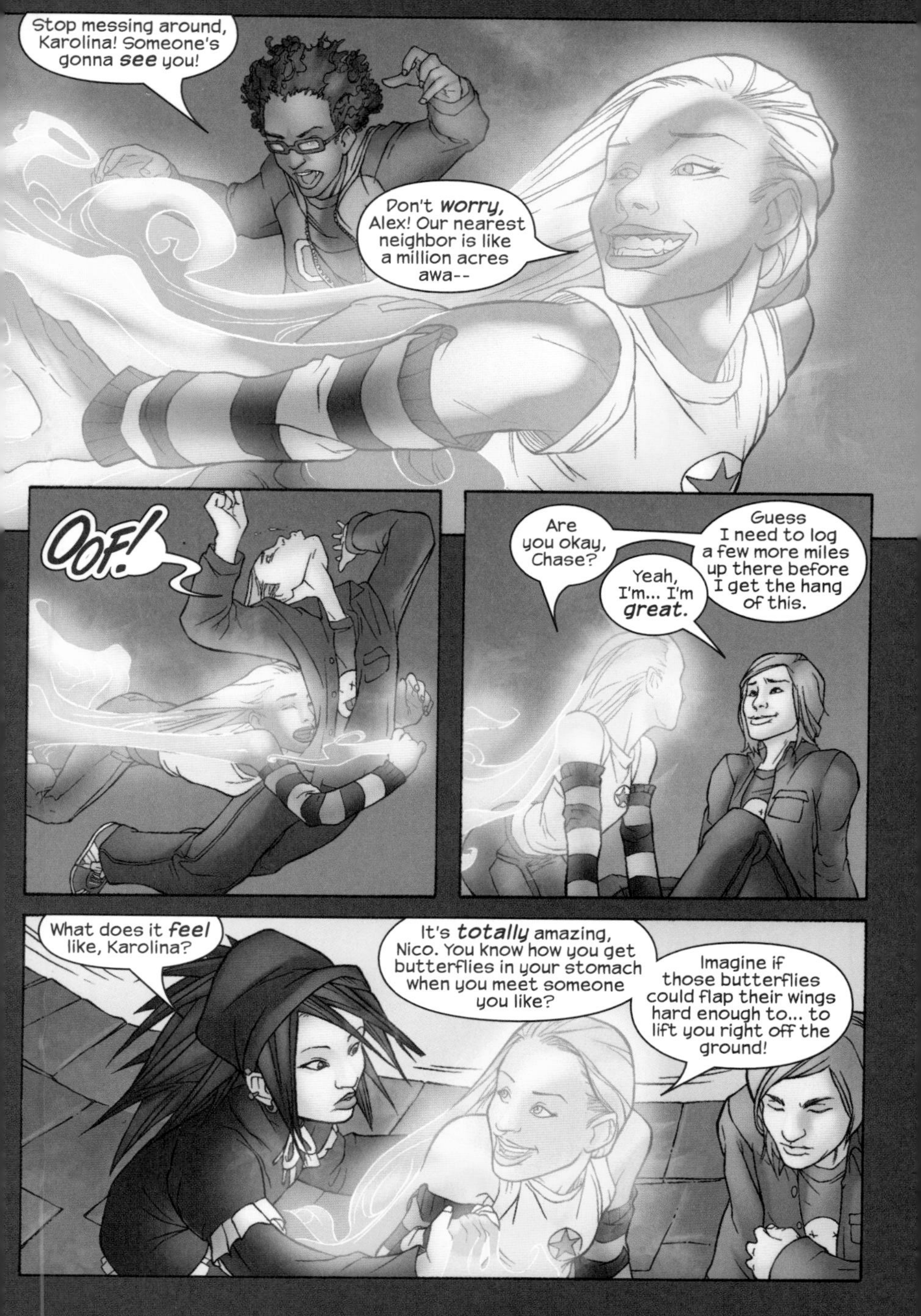
Stop messing around, Karolina! Someone's gonna see you!
Don't worry, Alex! Our nearest neighbor is like a million acres awa--
OOF!
Are you okay, Chase?
Yeah, I'm... I'm great.
Guess I need to log a few more miles up there before I get the hang of this.
What does it feel like, Karolina?
It's totally amazing, Nico. You know how you get butterflies in your stomach when you meet someone you like?
Imagine if those butterflies could flap their wings hard enough to... to lift you right off the ground!

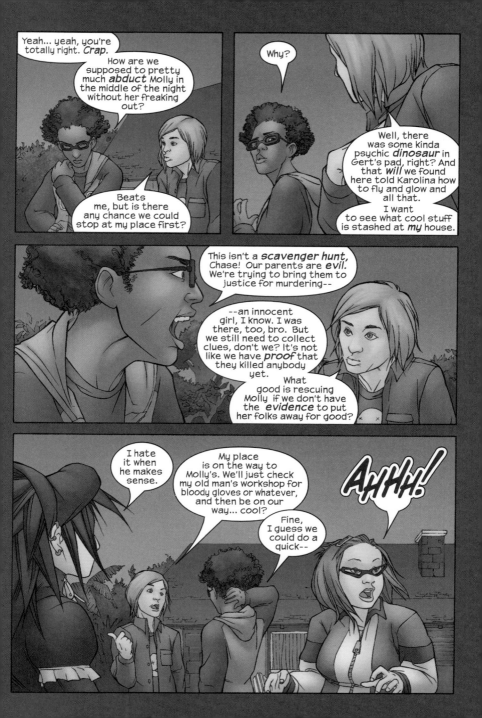

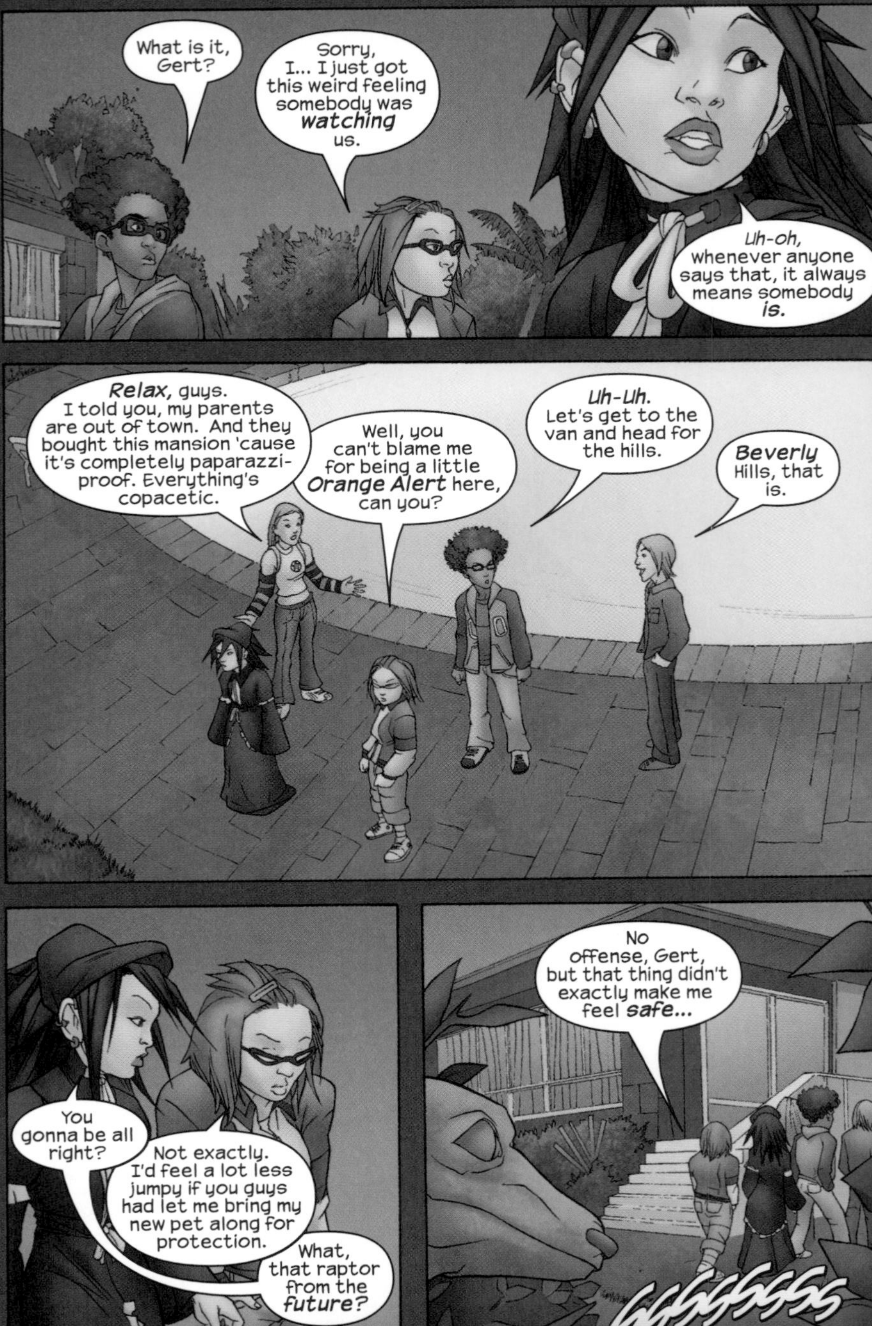
What is it, Gert?
Sorry, I... I just got this weird feeling somebody was *watching* us.
Uh-oh, whenever anyone says that, it always means somebody *is.*
Relax, guys. I told you, my parents are out of town. And they bought this mansion 'cause it's completely paparazzi-proof. Everything's copacetic.
Well, you can't blame me for being a little *Orange Alert* here, can you?
Uh-uh. Let's get to the van and head for the hills.
Beverly Hills, that is.
You gonna be all right?
Not exactly. I'd feel a lot less jumpy if you guys had let me bring my new pet along for protection.
What, that raptor from the *future?*
No offense, Gert, but that thing didn't exactly make me feel *safe...*
GGGGGGGG

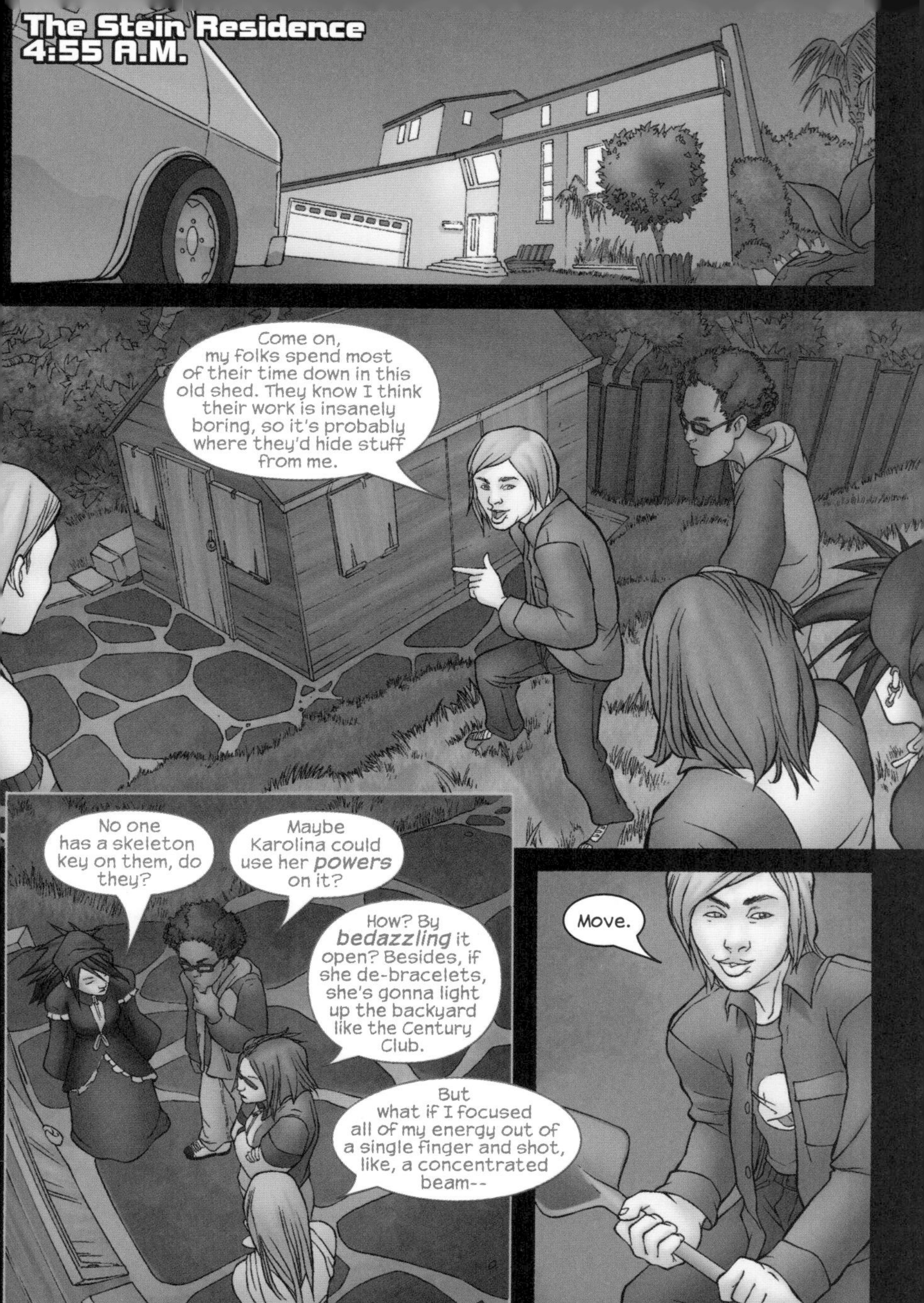
The Stein Residence 4:55 A.M.
Come on, my folks spend most of their time down in this old shed. They know I think their work is insanely boring, so it's probably where they'd hide stuff from me.
No one has a skeleton key on them, do they?
Maybe Karolina could use her *powers* on it?
How? By *bedazzling* it open? Besides, if she de-bracelets, she's gonna light up the backyard like the Century Club.
But what if I focused all of my energy out of a single finger and shot, like, a concentrated beam--
Move.

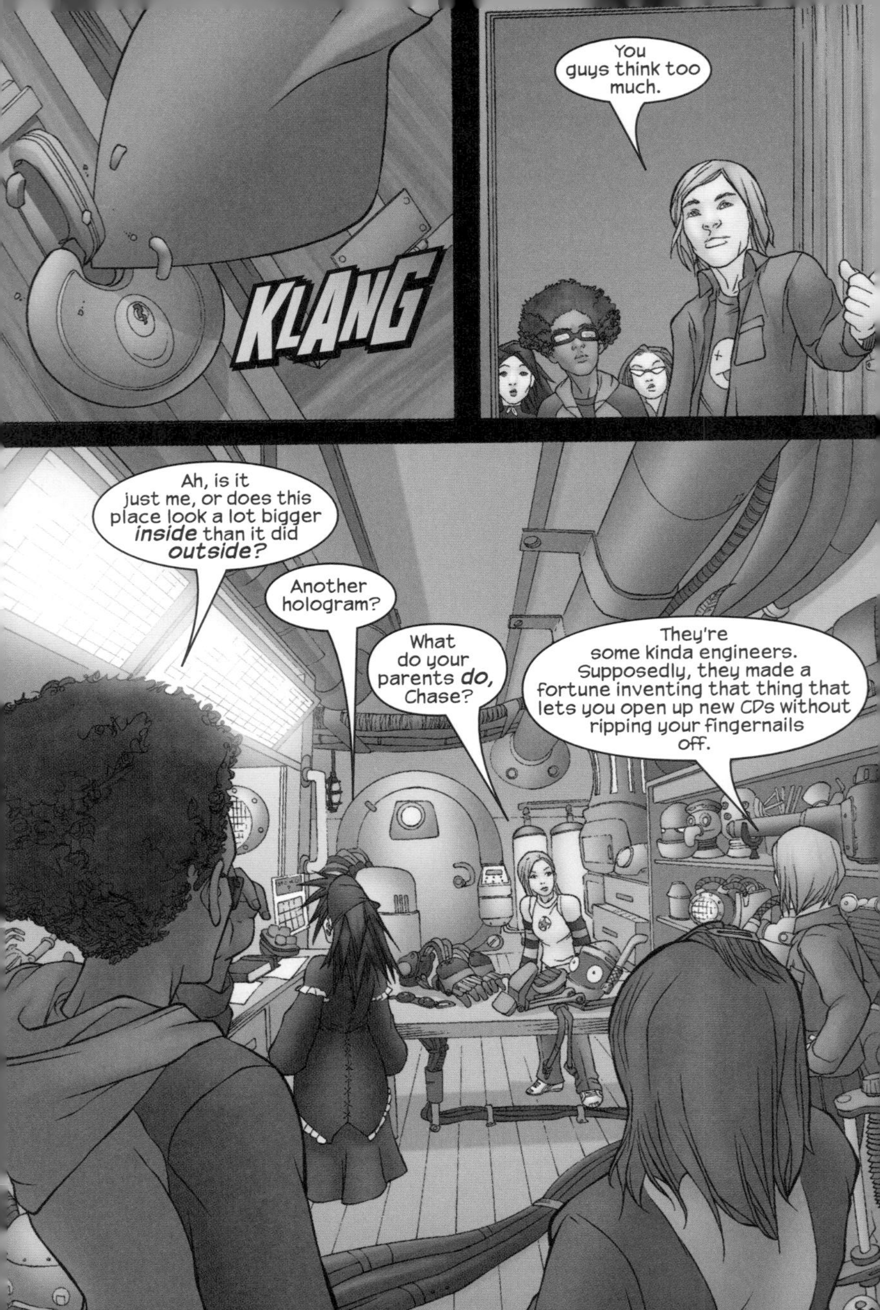
KLANG
You guys think too much.
Ah, is it just me, or does this place look a lot bigger *inside* than it did *outside?*
Another hologram?
What do your parents *do,* Chase?
They're some kinda engineers. Supposedly, they made a fortune inventing that thing that lets you open up new CDs without ripping your fingernails off.

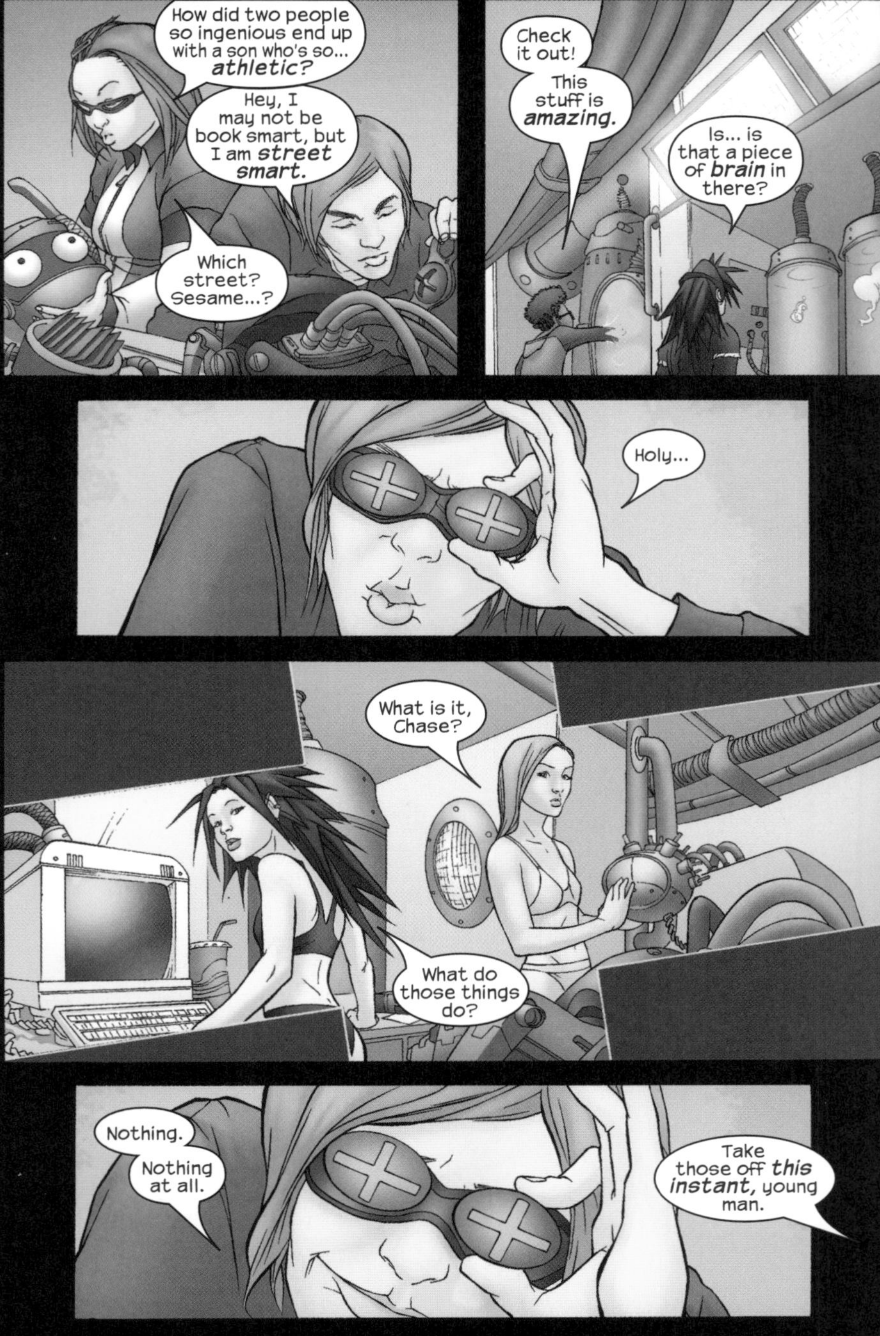

How did two people so ingenious end up with a son who's so... *athletic?*
Hey, I may not be book smart, but I am *street smart.*
Which street? Sesame...?
Check it out!
This stuff is *amazing.*
Is... is that a piece of *brain* in there?
Holy...
What is it, Chase?
What do those things do?
Nothing.
Nothing at all.
Take those off *this instant,* young man.

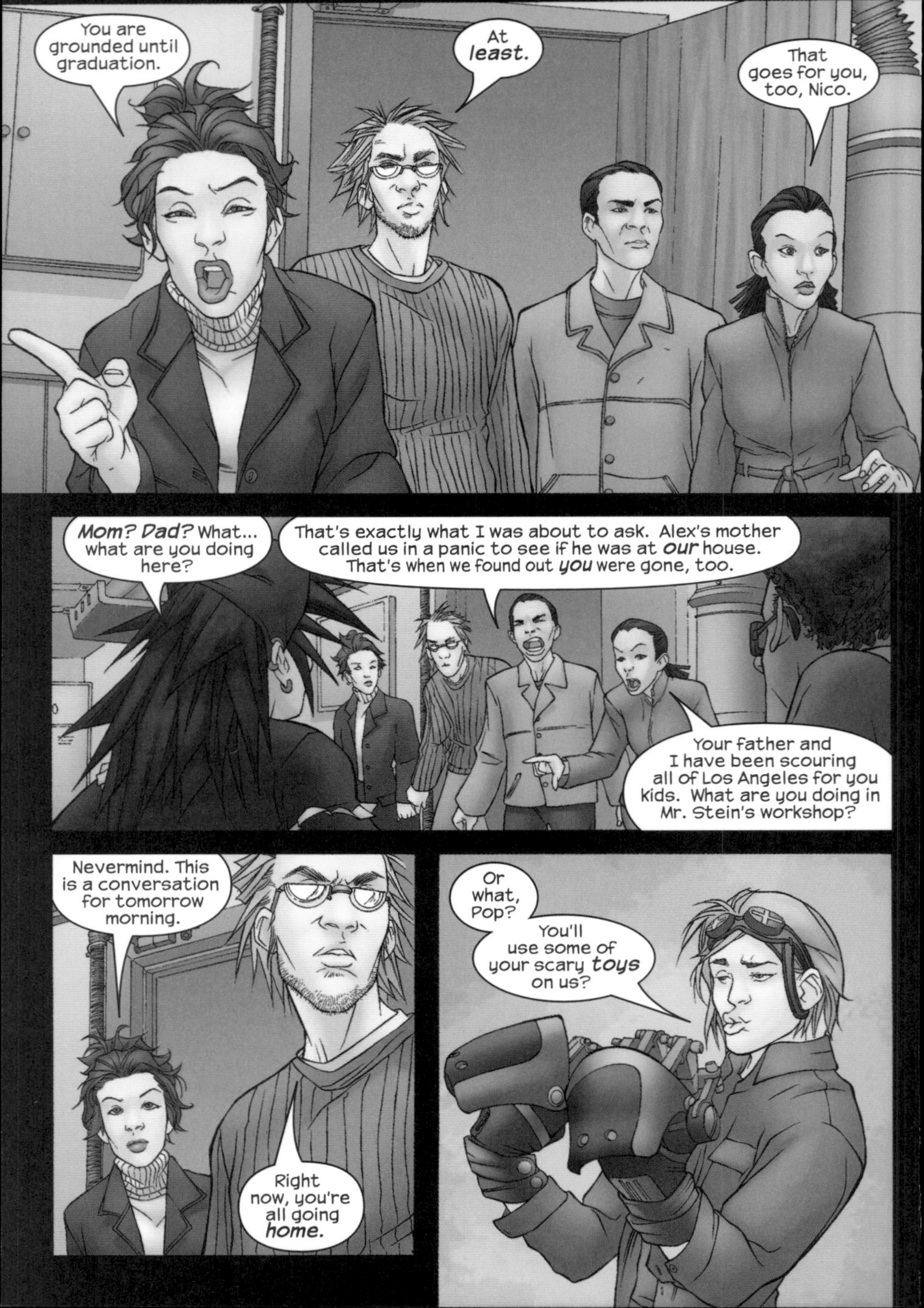
You are grounded until graduation.
At *least.*
That goes for you, too, Nico.
Mom? Dad? What... what are you doing here?
That's exactly what I was about to ask. Alex's mother called us in a panic to see if he was at *our* house. That's when we found out *you* were gone, too.
Your father and I have been scouring all of Los Angeles for you kids. What are you doing in Mr. Stein's workshop?
Nevermind. This is a conversation for tomorrow morning.
Right now, you're all going *home.*
Or what, Pop?
You'll use some of your scary *toys* on us?

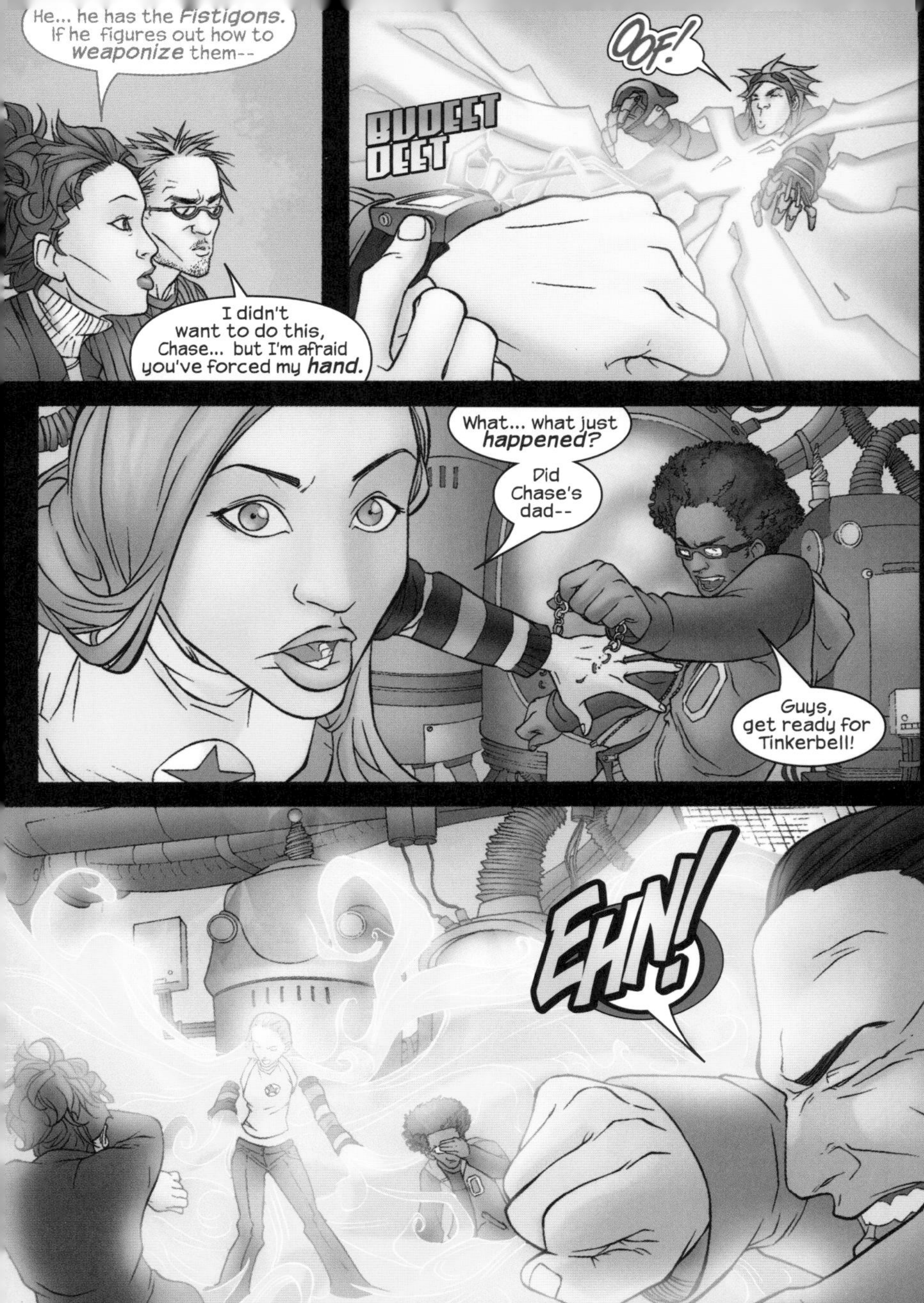
He... he has the Fistigons.
If he figures out how to weaponize them--
I didn't want to do this, Chase... but I'm afraid you've forced my hand.
BUDEET DEET
OOF!
What... what just happened?
Did Chase's dad--
Guys, get ready for Tinkerbell!
EHN!

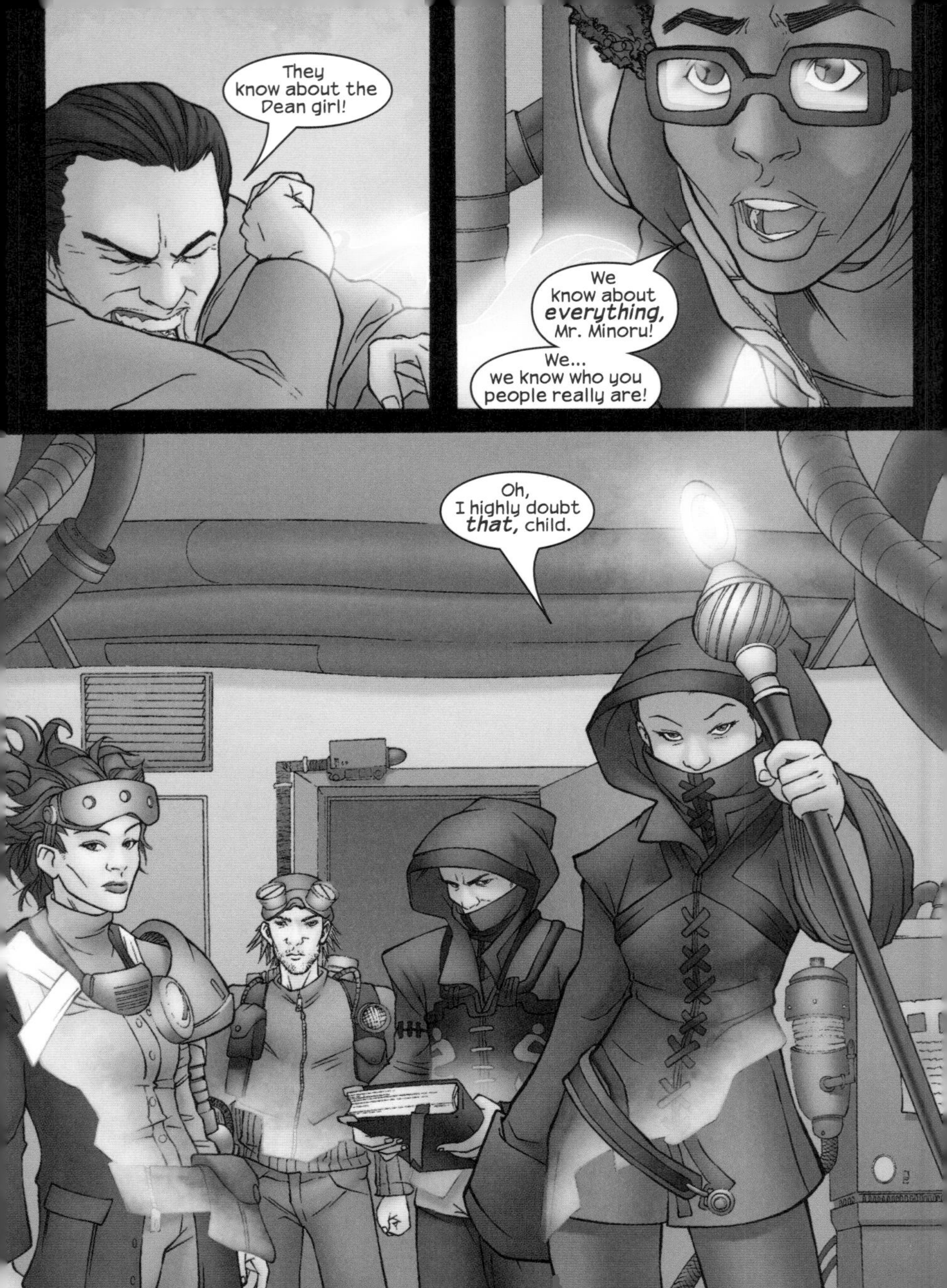
They know about the Dean girl!
We know about *everything,* Mr. Minoru!
We... we know who you people really are!
Oh, I highly doubt *that,* child.

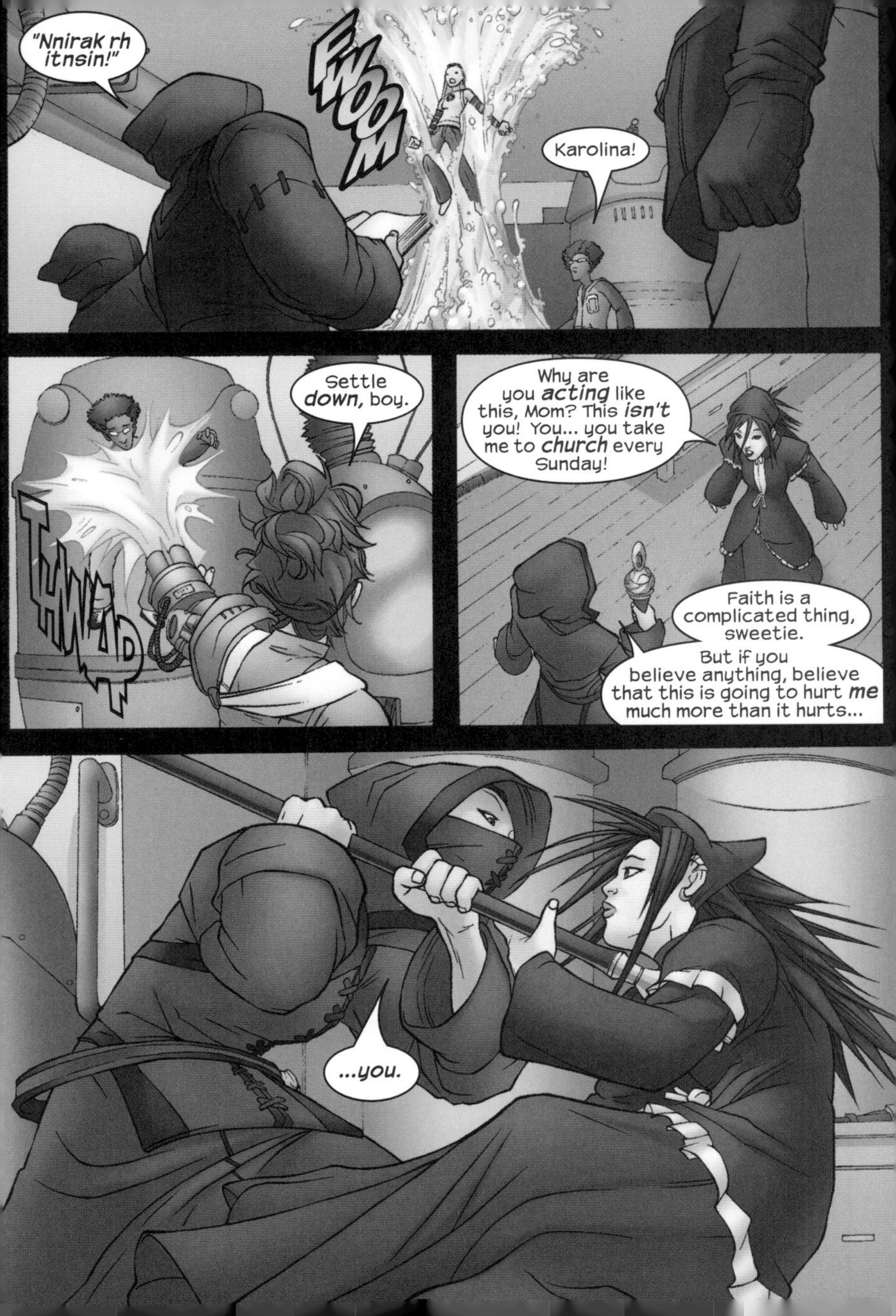
"Nnirak rh itnsin!"
FWOOM
Karolina!
Settle *down,* boy.
THWUMP
Why are you *acting* like this, Mom? This *isn't* you! You... you take me to *church* every Sunday!
Faith is a complicated thing, sweetie.
But if you believe anything, believe that this is going to hurt *me* much more than it hurts...
...you.

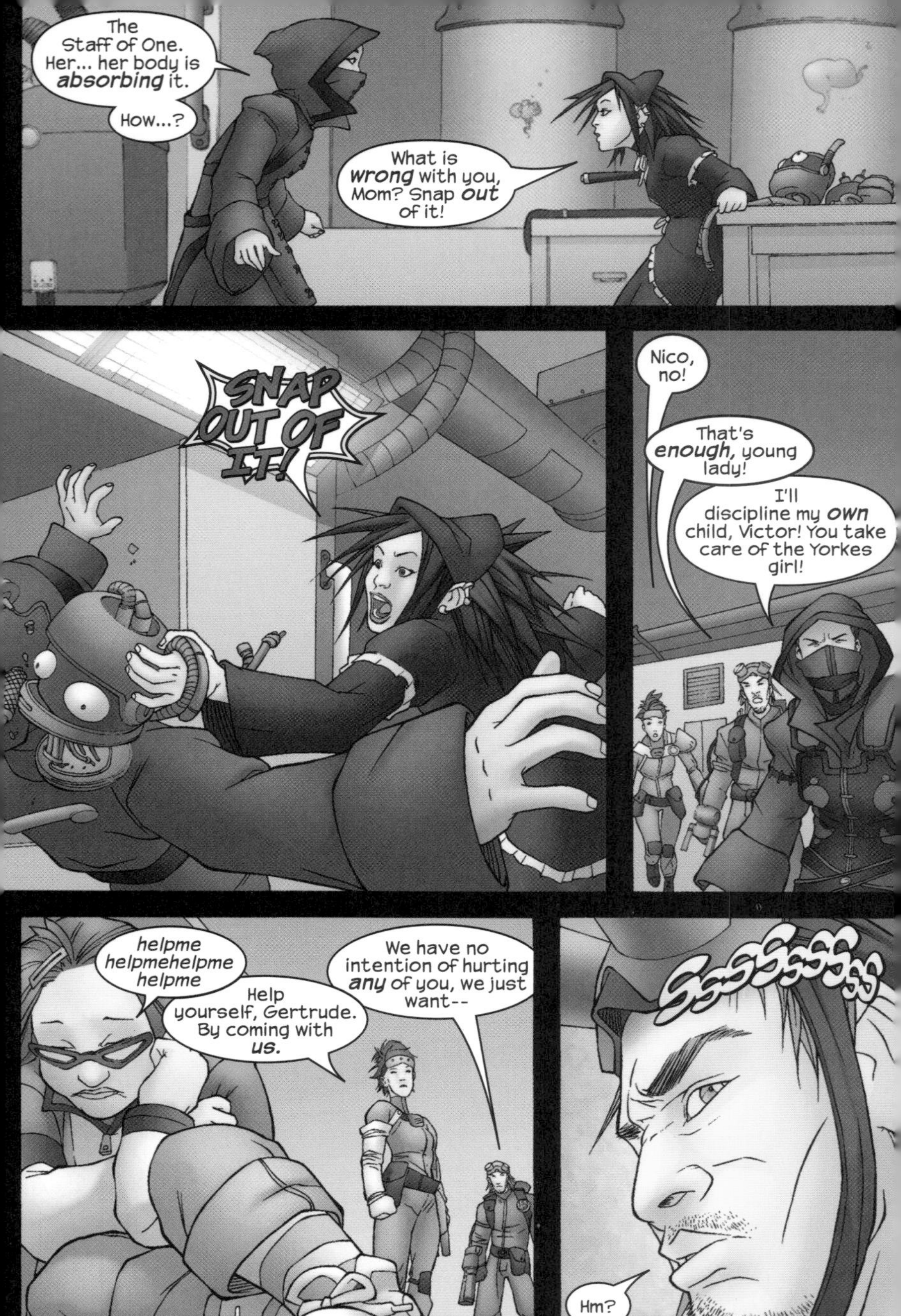
The Staff of One. Her... her body is absorbing it.
How...?
What is wrong with you, Mom? Snap out of it!
SNAP OUT OF IT!
Nico, no!
That's enough, young lady!
I'll discipline my own child, Victor! You take care of the Yorkes girl!
helpme helpmehelpme helpme
Help yourself, Gertrude. By coming with us.
We have no intention of hurting any of you, we just want--
SSSSSSSSSS
Hm?

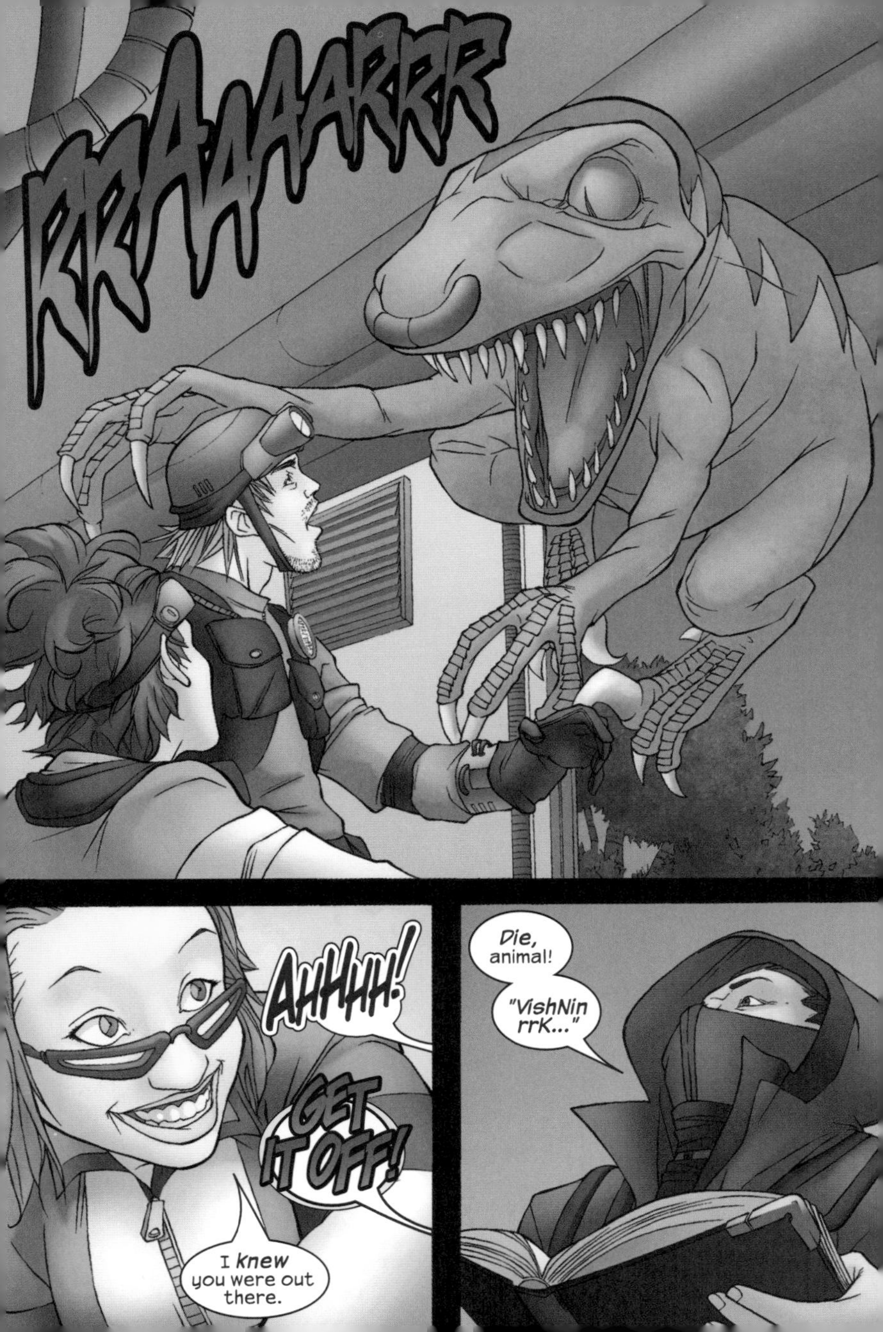
RRAAAARRR
AHHHH!
GET IT OFF!
I knew you were out there.
Die, animal!
"VishNin rrK..."

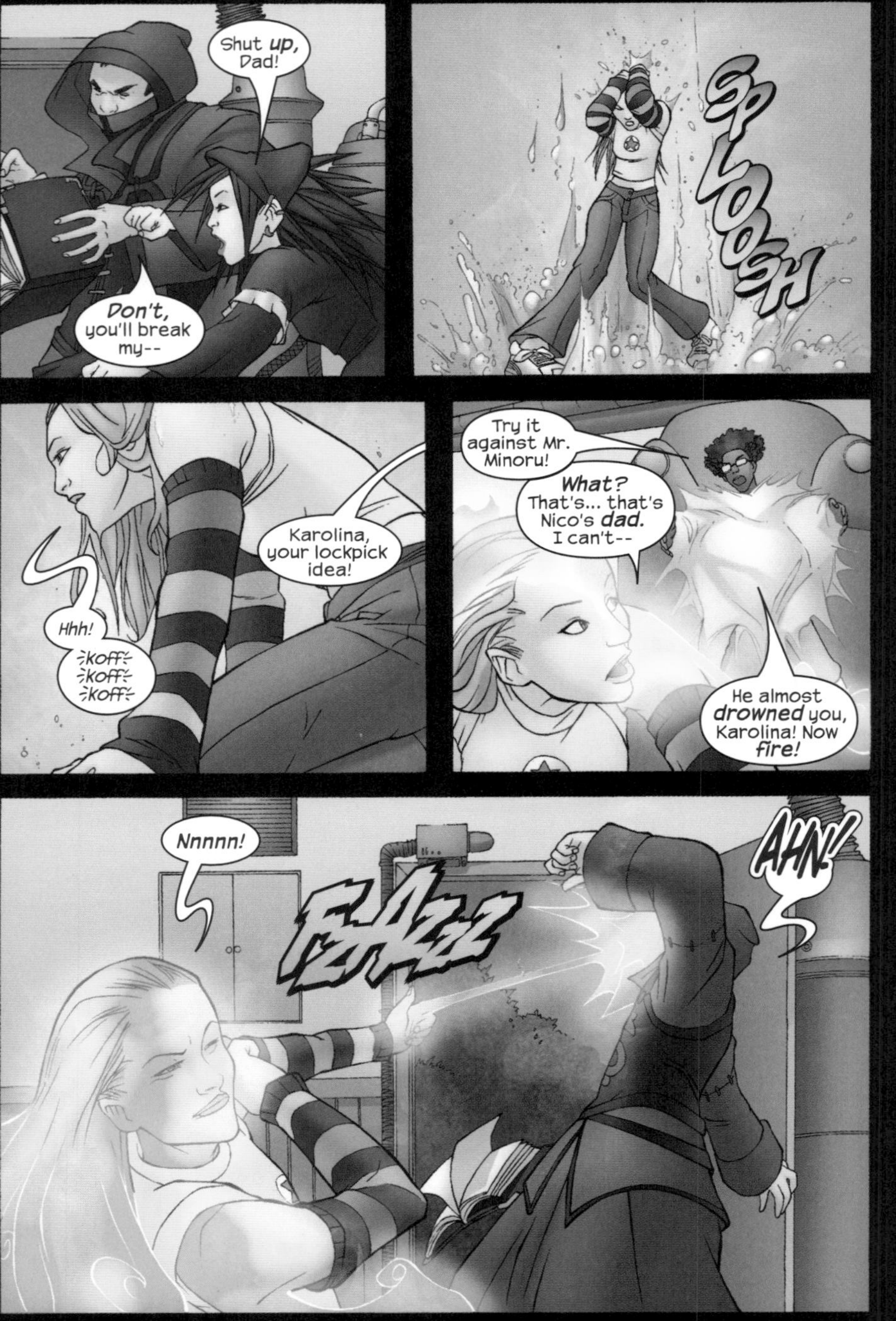
Shut up, Dad!
Don't, you'll break my--
SPLOOSH
Karolina, your lockpick idea!
Hhh! koff koff koff
Try it against Mr. Minoru!
What? That's... that's Nico's dad. I can't--
He almost drowned you, Karolina! Now fire!
Nnnnn!
FZAAZ
AHN!

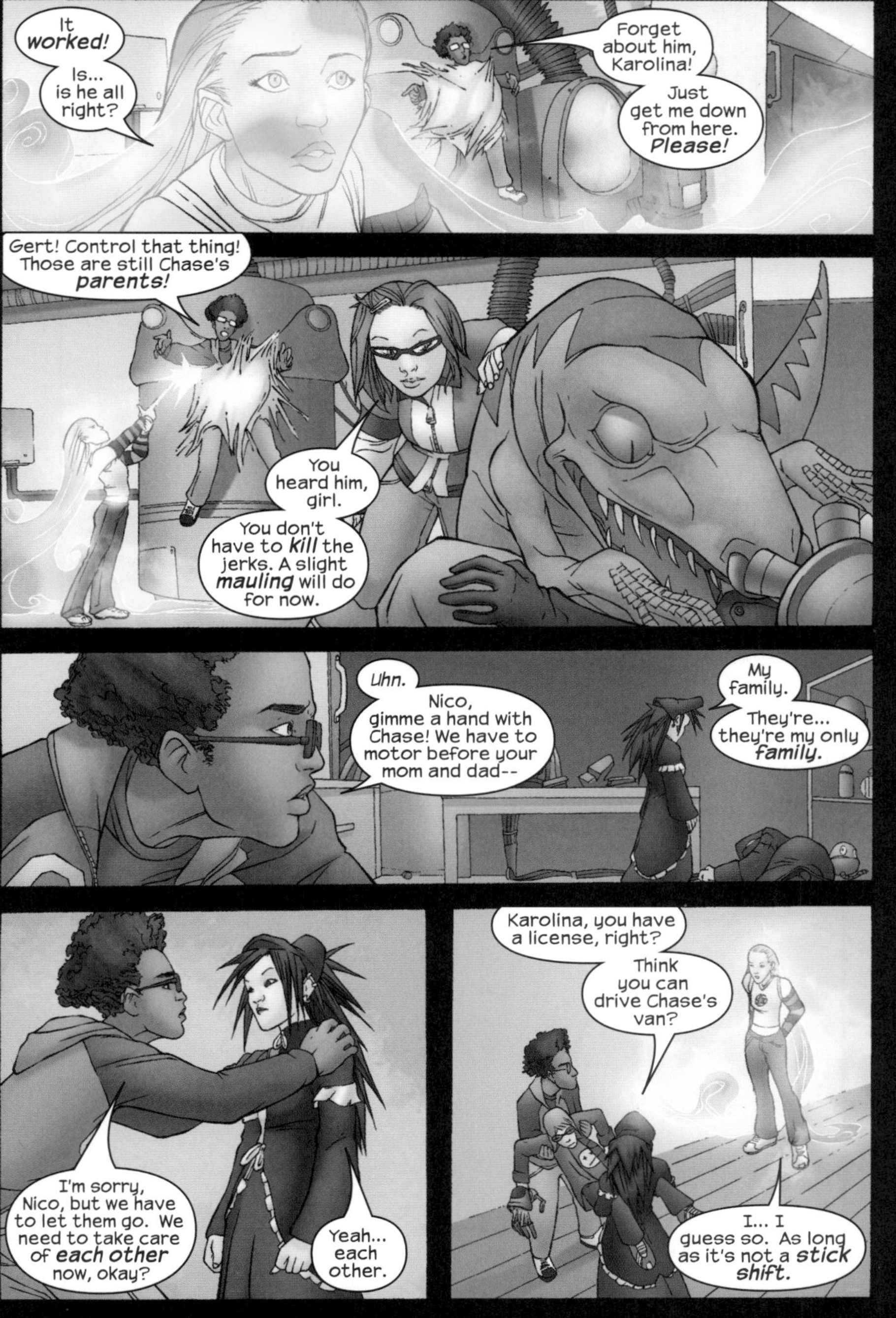
It worked!
Is... is he all right?
Forget about him, Karolina!
Just get me down from here. Please!
Gert! Control that thing! Those are still Chase's parents!
You heard him, girl.
You don't have to kill the jerks. A slight mauling will do for now.
Uhn.
Nico, gimme a hand with Chase! We have to motor before your mom and dad--
My family.
They're... they're my only family.
I'm sorry, Nico, but we have to let them go. We need to take care of each other now, okay?
Yeah... each other.
Karolina, you have a license, right?
Think you can drive Chase's van?
I... I guess so. As long as it's not a stick shift.

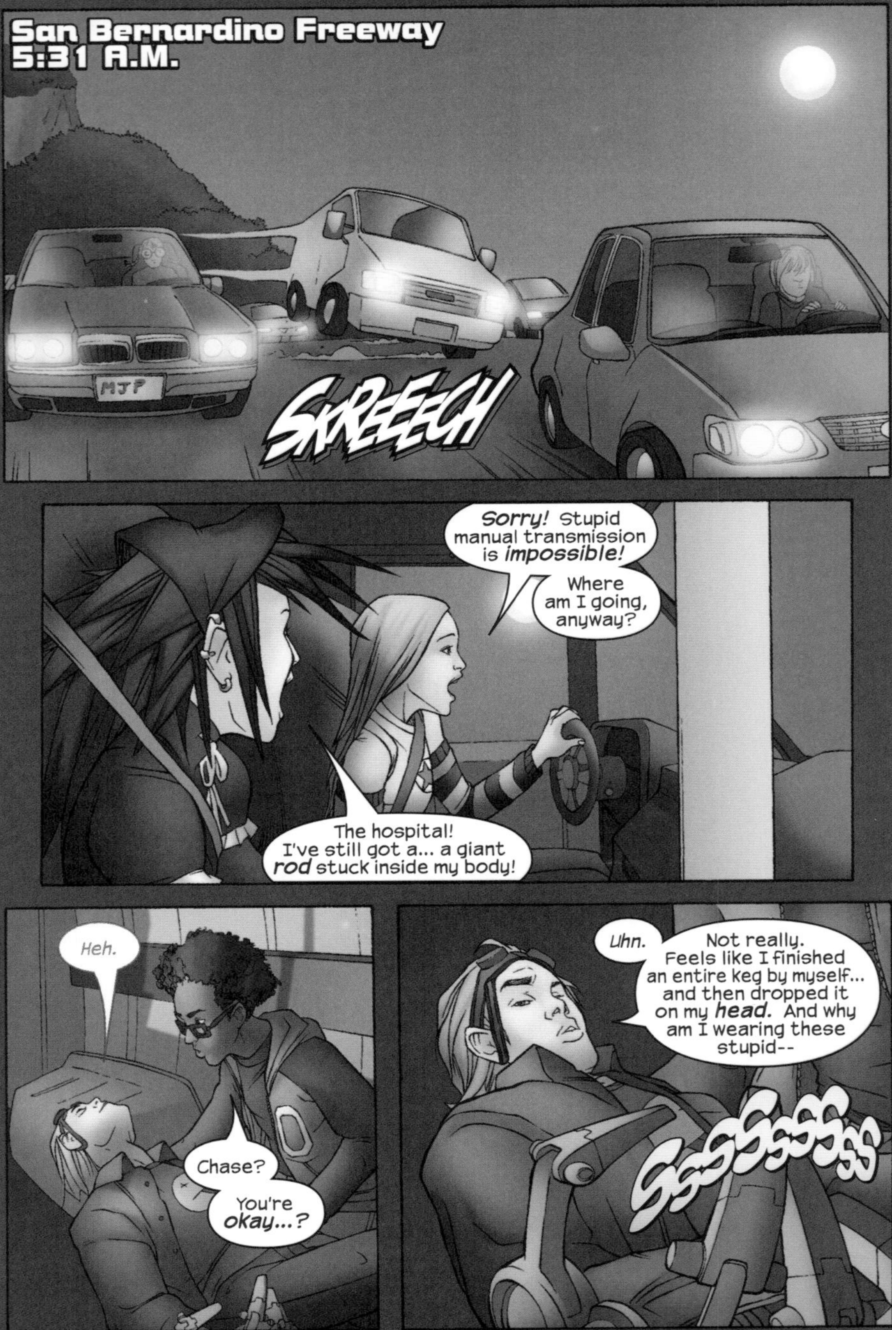
San Bernardino Freeway
5:31 A.M.
MJP
SKREEECH
Sorry! Stupid manual transmission is impossible!
Where am I going, anyway?
The hospital! I've still got a... a giant rod stuck inside my body!
Heh.
Chase?
You're okay...?
Uhn.
Not really. Feels like I finished an entire keg by myself... and then dropped it on my head. And why am I wearing these stupid--
SssSSSSSss

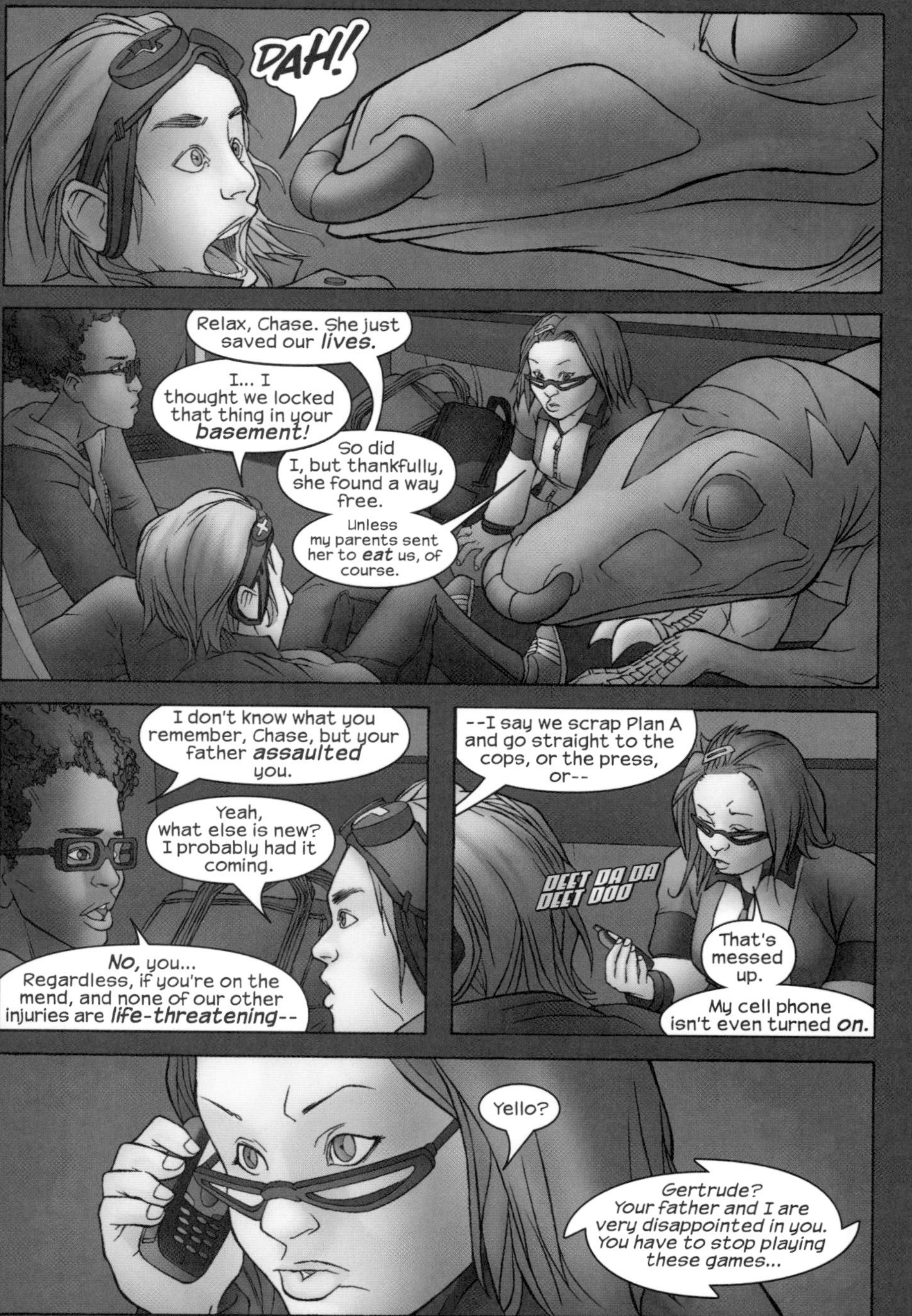
DAH!
Relax, Chase. She just saved our lives.
I... I thought we locked that thing in your basement!
So did I, but thankfully, she found a way free.
Unless my parents sent her to eat us, of course.
I don't know what you remember, Chase, but your father assaulted you.
Yeah, what else is new? I probably had it coming.
No, you... Regardless, if you're on the mend, and none of our other injuries are life-threatening--
--I say we scrap Plan A and go straight to the cops, or the press, or--
DEET DA DA DEET DOO
That's messed up.
My cell phone isn't even turned on.
Yello?
Gertrude? Your father and I are very disappointed in you. You have to stop playing these games...

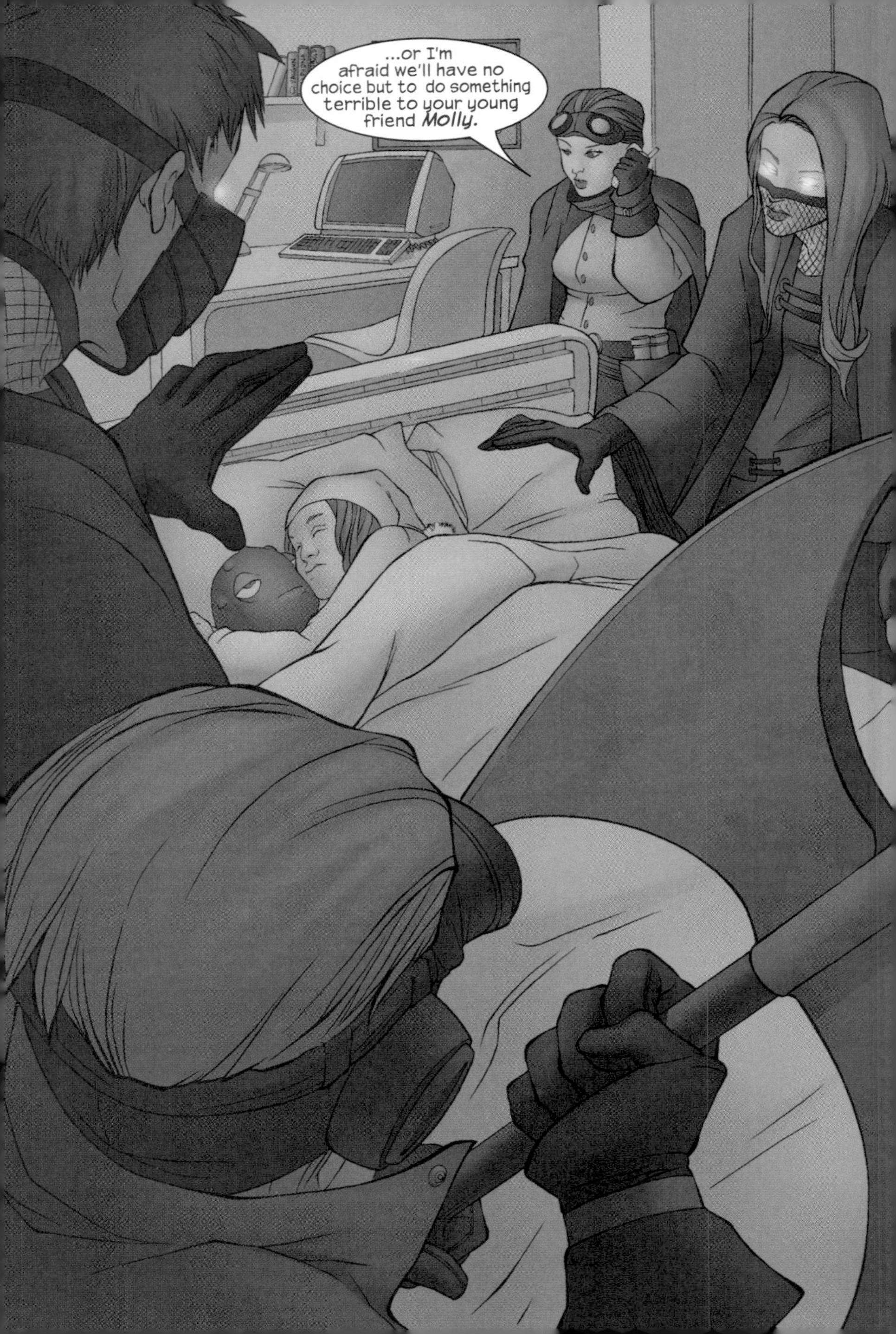
...or I'm afraid we'll have no choice but to do something terrible to your young friend Molly.

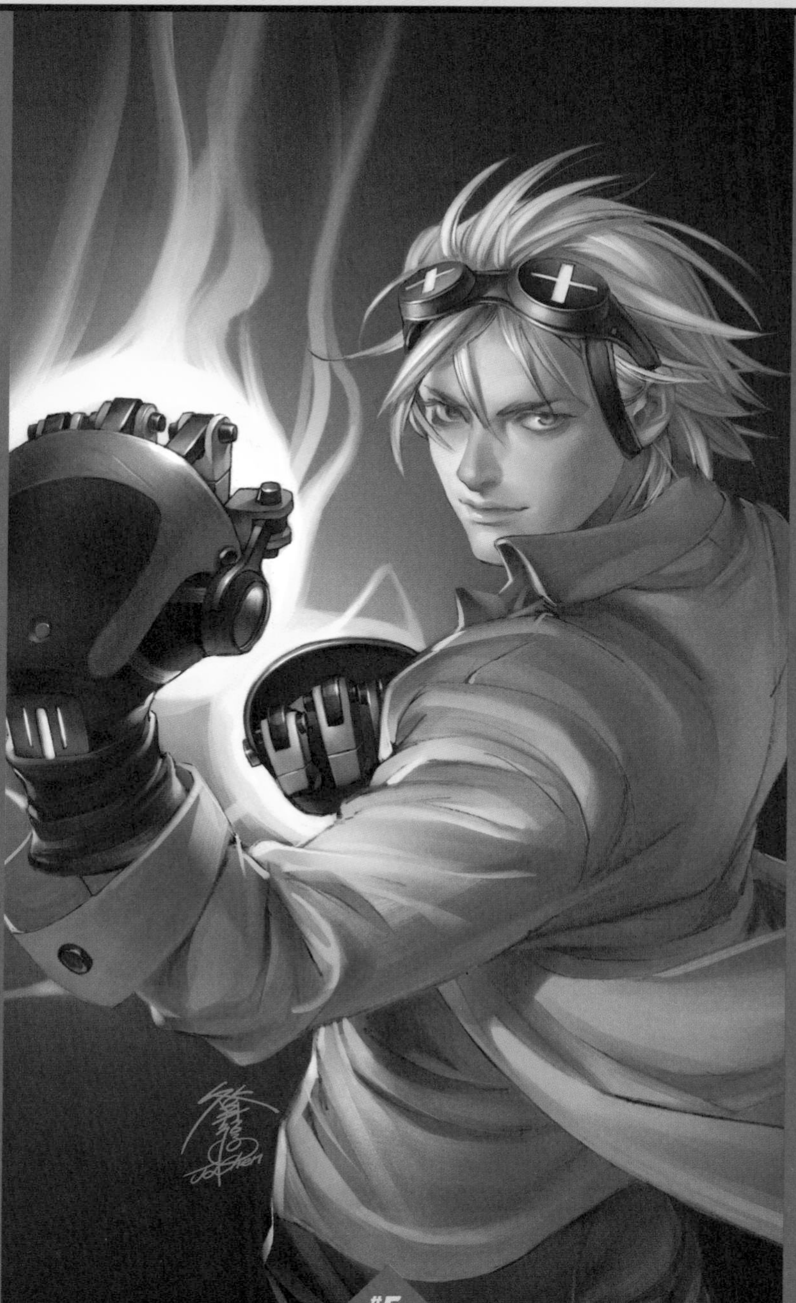

#5

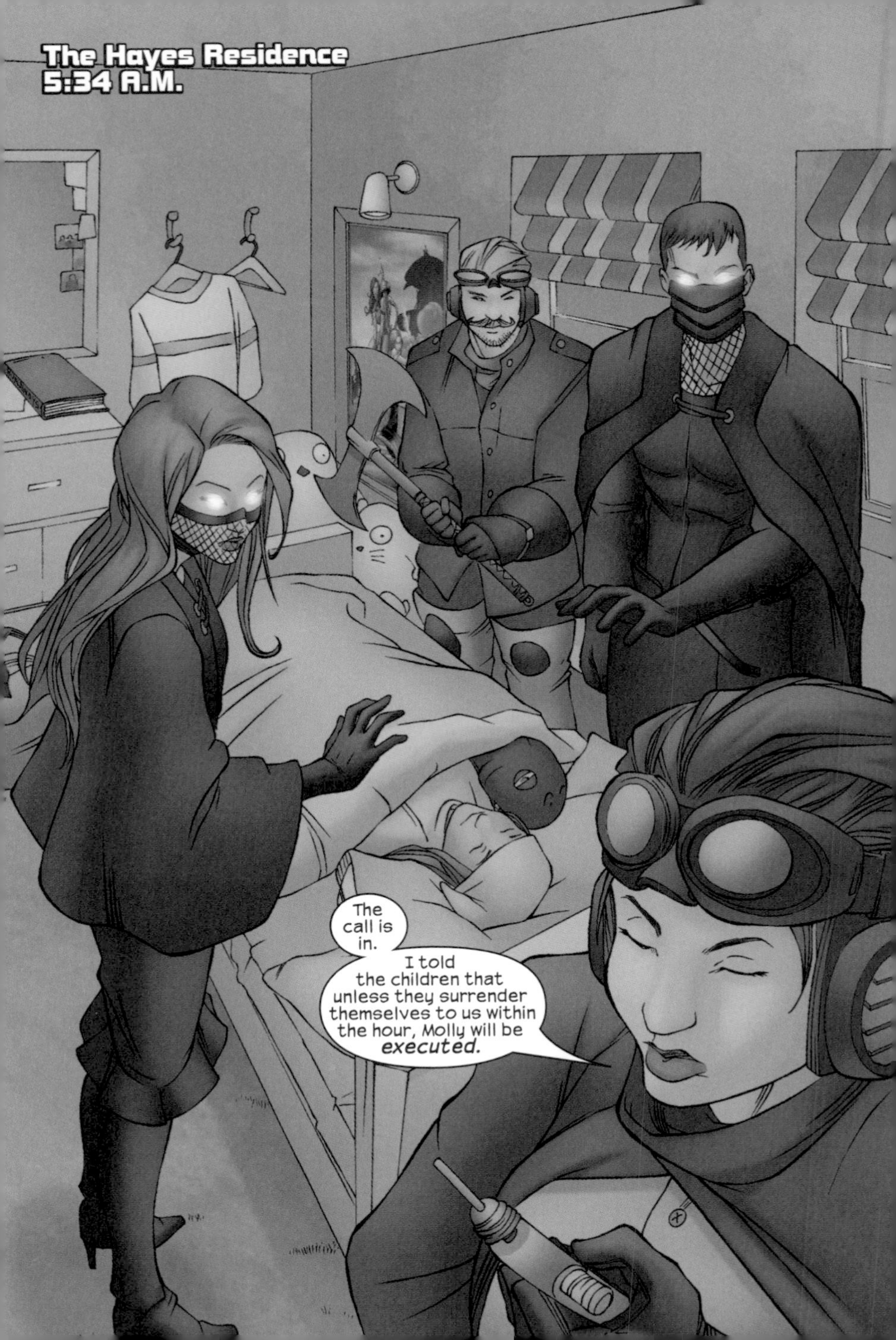
The Hayes Residence
5:34 A.M.
The call is in.
I told the children that unless they surrender themselves to us within the hour, Molly will be *executed.*

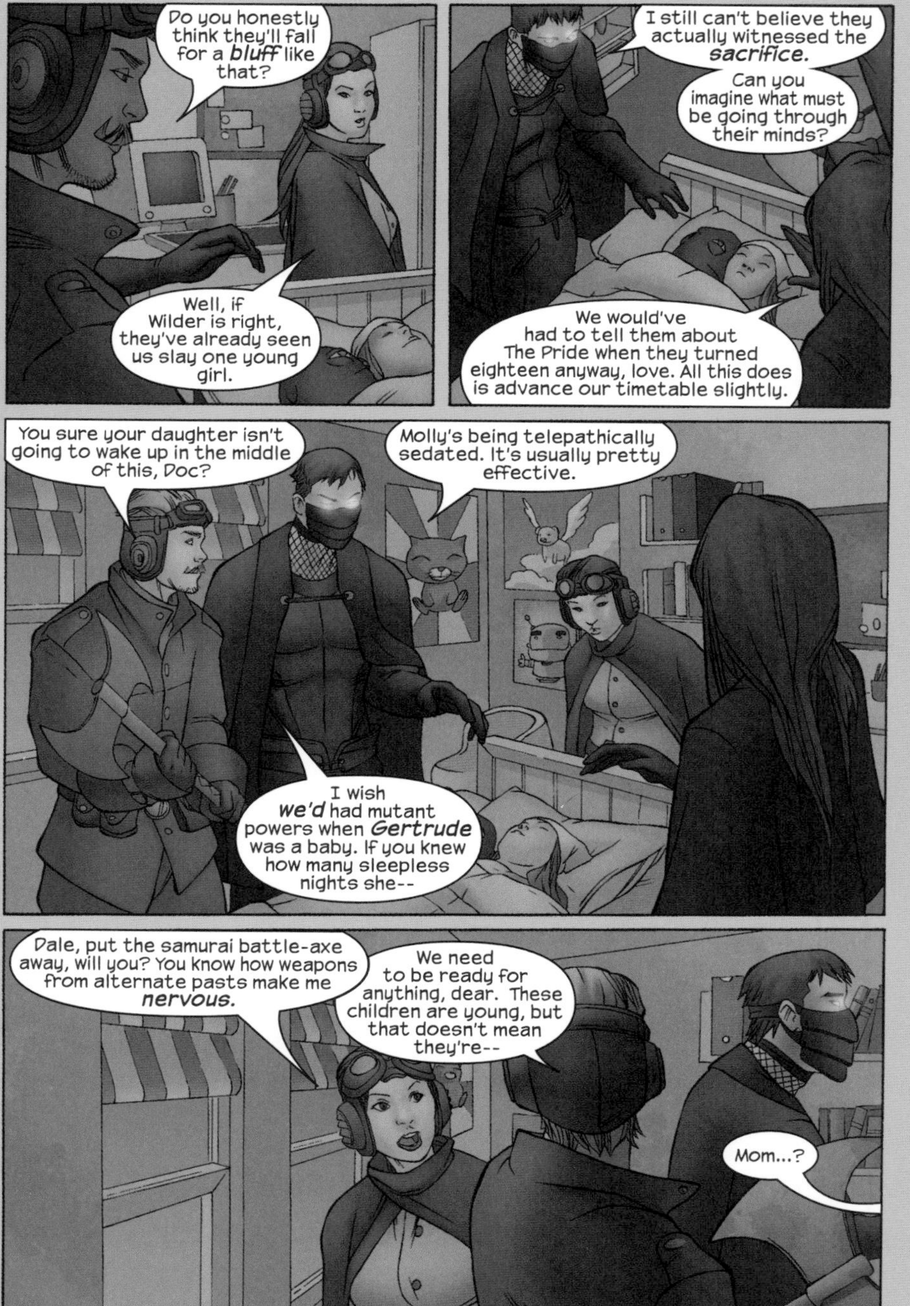
Do you honestly think they'll fall for a *bluff* like that?
Well, if Wilder is right, they've already seen us slay one young girl.
I still can't believe they actually witnessed the *sacrifice.*
Can you imagine what must be going through their minds?
We would've had to tell them about The Pride when they turned eighteen anyway, love. All this does is advance our timetable slightly.
You sure your daughter isn't going to wake up in the middle of this, Doc?
Molly's being telepathically sedated. It's usually pretty effective.
I wish *we'd* had mutant powers when *Gertrude* was a baby. If you knew how many sleepless nights she--
Dale, put the samurai battle-axe away, will you? You know how weapons from alternate pasts make me *nervous.*
We need to be ready for anything, dear. These children are young, but that doesn't mean they're--
Mom...?

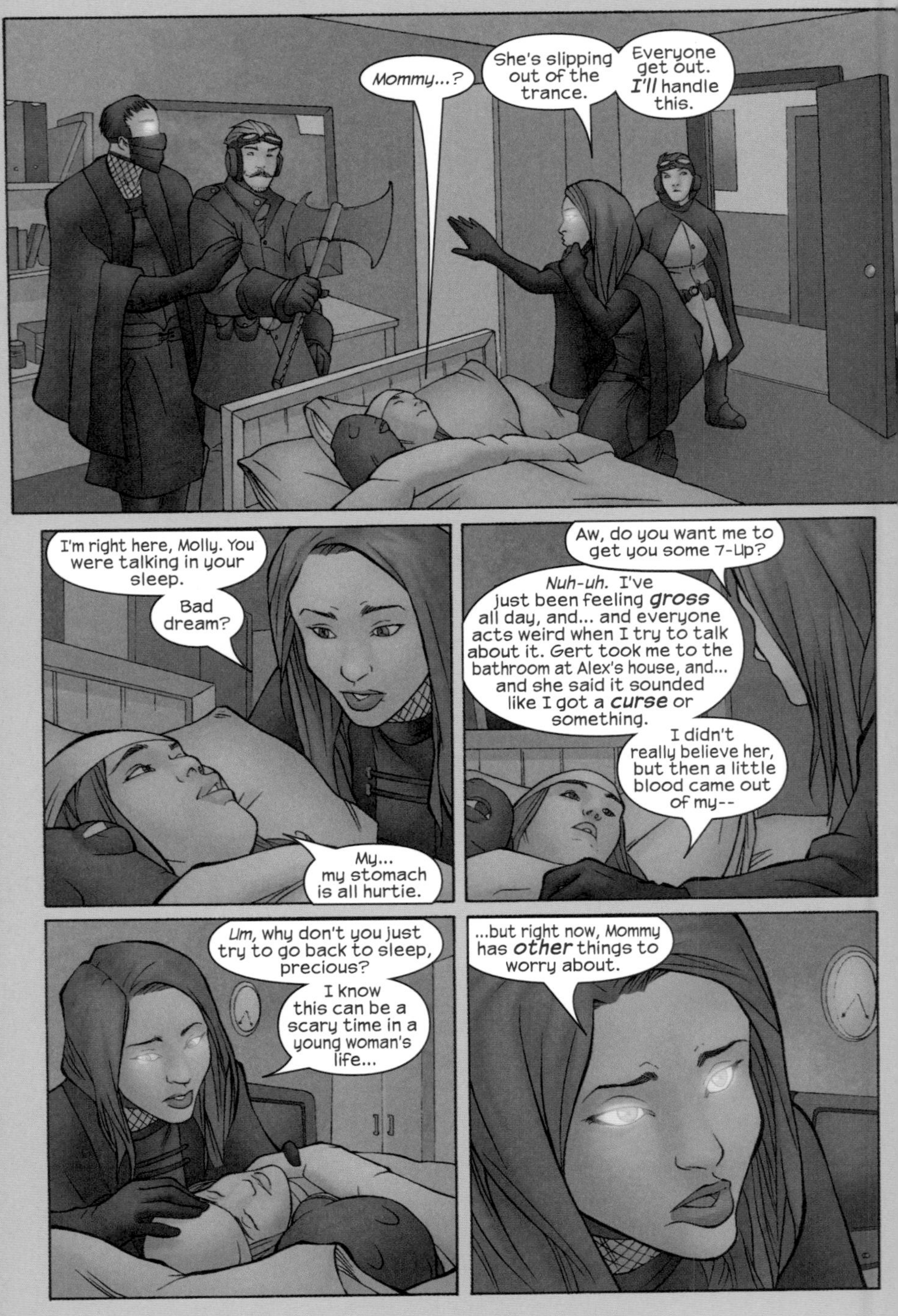

Mommy...?
She's slipping out of the trance.
Everyone get out. I'll handle this.
I'm right here, Molly. You were talking in your sleep.
Bad dream?
My... my stomach is all hurtie.
Aw, do you want me to get you some 7-Up?
Nuh-uh. I've just been feeling gross all day, and... and everyone acts weird when I try to talk about it. Gert took me to the bathroom at Alex's house, and... and she said it sounded like I got a curse or something.
I didn't really believe her, but then a little blood came out of my--
Um, why don't you just try to go back to sleep, precious?
I know this can be a scary time in a young woman's life...
...but right now, Mommy has other things to worry about.

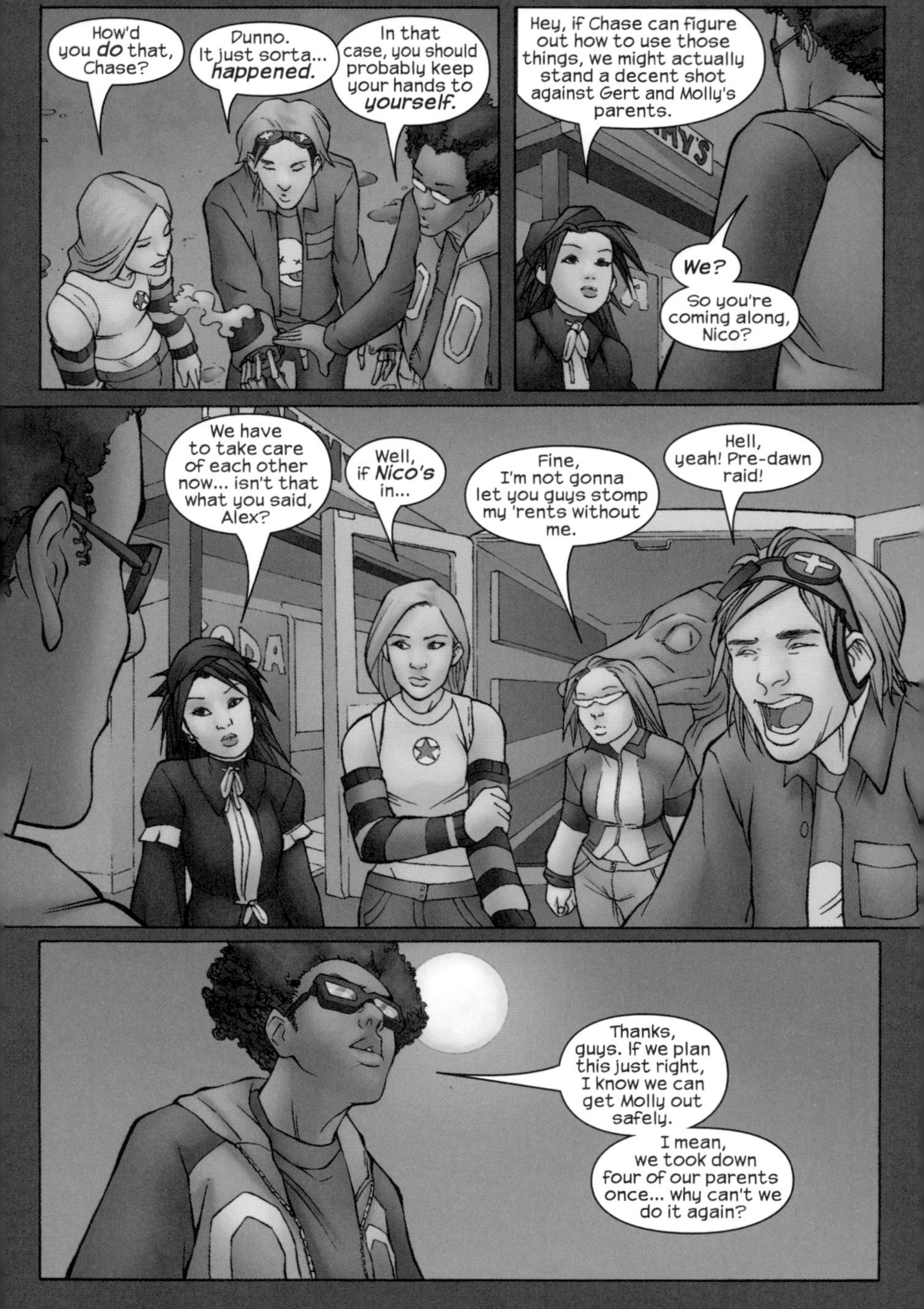
How'd you **do** that, Chase?
Dunno. It just sorta... ***happened.***
In that case, you should probably keep your hands to ***yourself.***
Hey, if Chase can figure out how to use those things, we might actually stand a decent shot against Gert and Molly's parents.
We?
So you're coming along, Nico?
We have to take care of each other now... isn't that what you said, Alex?
Well, if ***Nico's*** in...
Fine, I'm not gonna let you guys stomp my 'rents without me.
Hell, yeah! Pre-dawn raid!
Thanks, guys. If we plan this just right, I know we can get Molly out safely.
I mean, we took down four of our parents once... why can't we do it again?

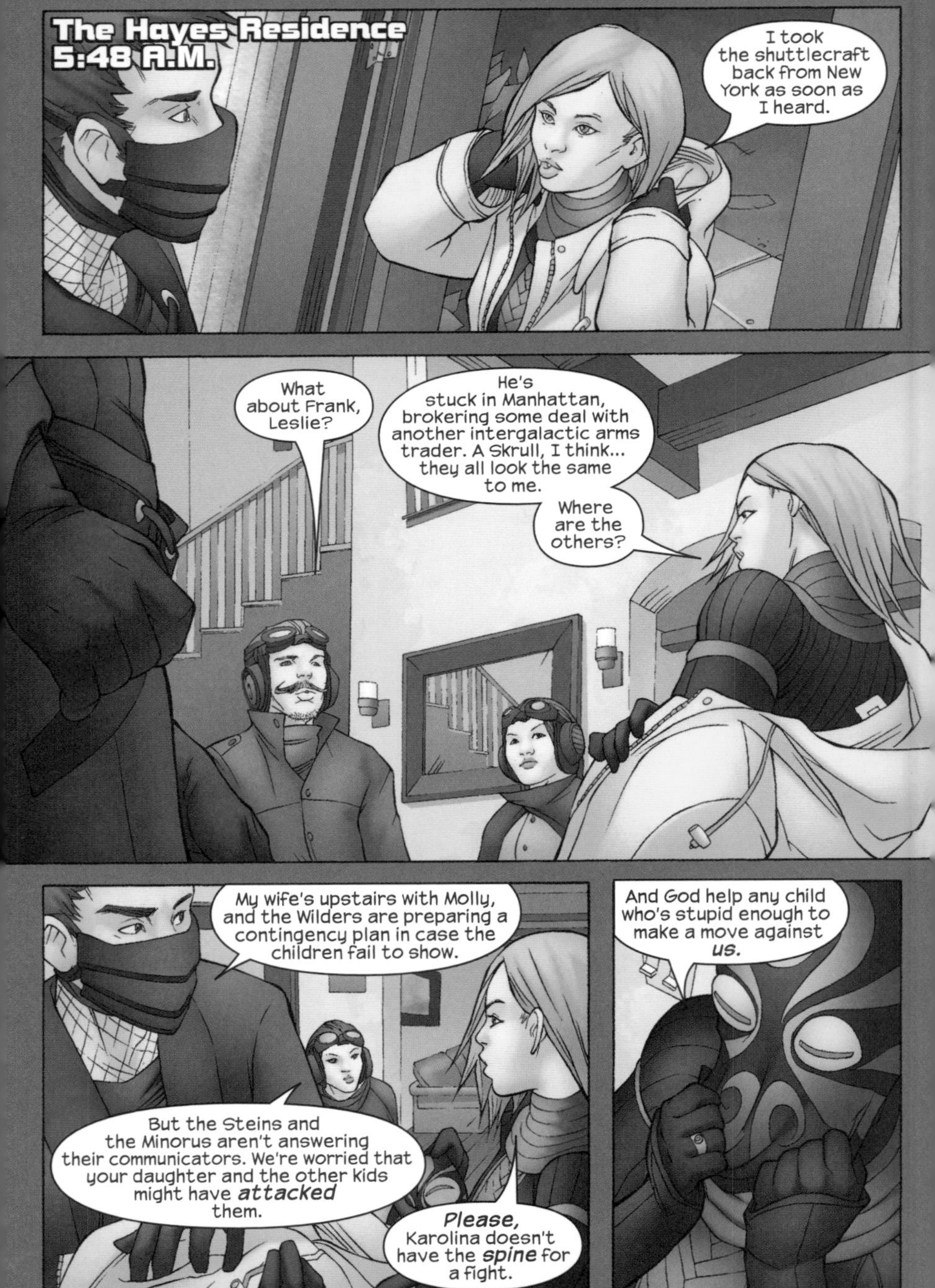
The Hayes Residence
5:48 A.M.
I took the shuttlecraft back from New York as soon as I heard.
What about Frank, Leslie?
He's stuck in Manhattan, brokering some deal with another intergalactic arms trader. A Skrull, I think... they all look the same to me.
Where are the others?
My wife's upstairs with Molly, and the Wilders are preparing a contingency plan in case the children fail to show.
But the Steins and the Minorus aren't answering their communicators. We're worried that your daughter and the other kids might have attacked them.
Please, Karolina doesn't have the spine for a fight.
And God help any child who's stupid enough to make a move against us.

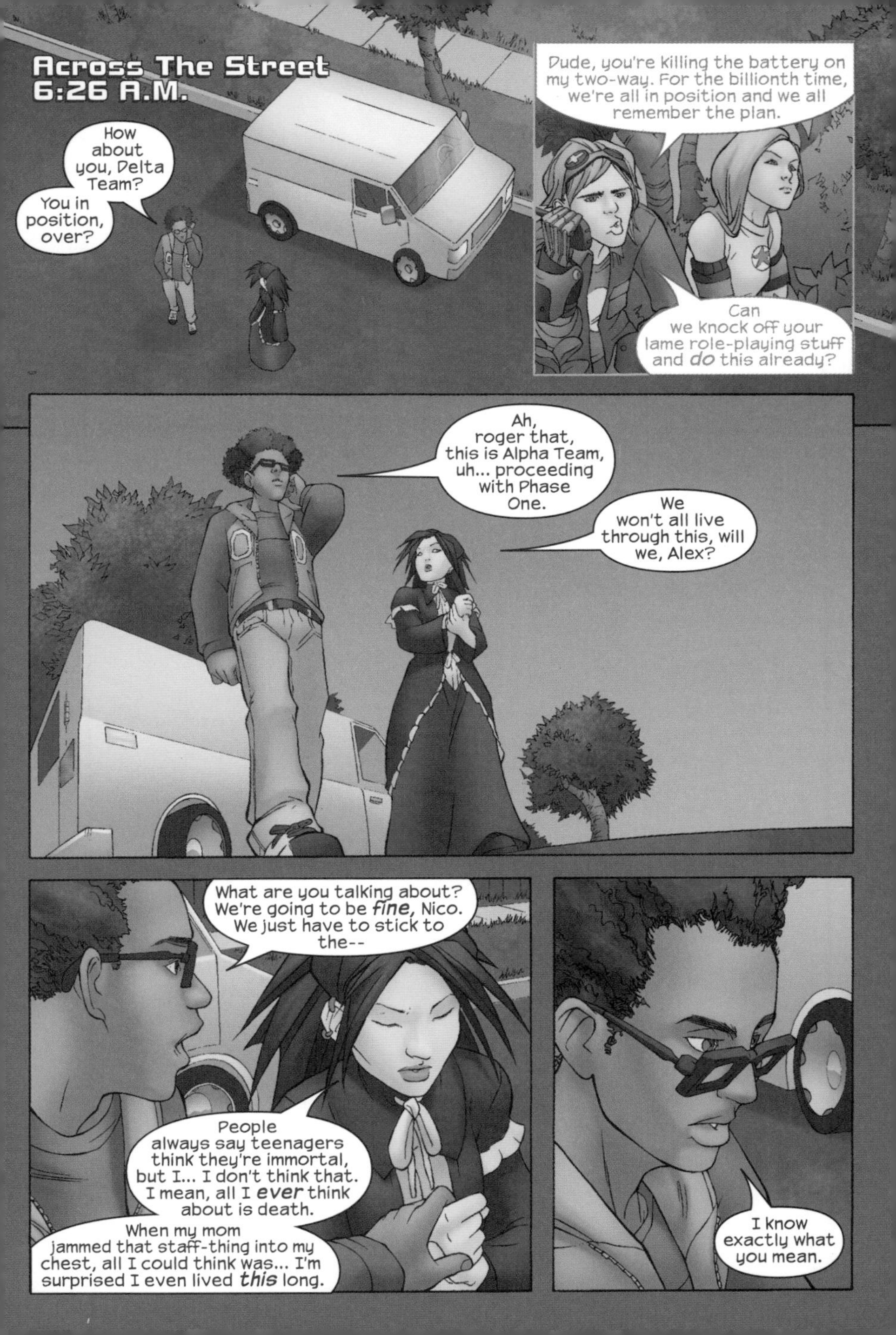
Across The Street
6:26 A.M.
How about you, Delta Team? You in position, over?
Dude, you're killing the battery on my two-way. For the billionth time, we're all in position and we all remember the plan.
Can we knock off your lame role-playing stuff and do this already?
Ah, roger that, this is Alpha Team, uh... proceeding with Phase One.
We won't all live through this, will we, Alex?
What are you talking about? We're going to be fine, Nico. We just have to stick to the--
People always say teenagers think they're immortal, but I... I don't think that. I mean, all I ever think about is death.
When my mom jammed that staff-thing into my chest, all I could think was... I'm surprised I even lived this long.
I know exactly what you mean.

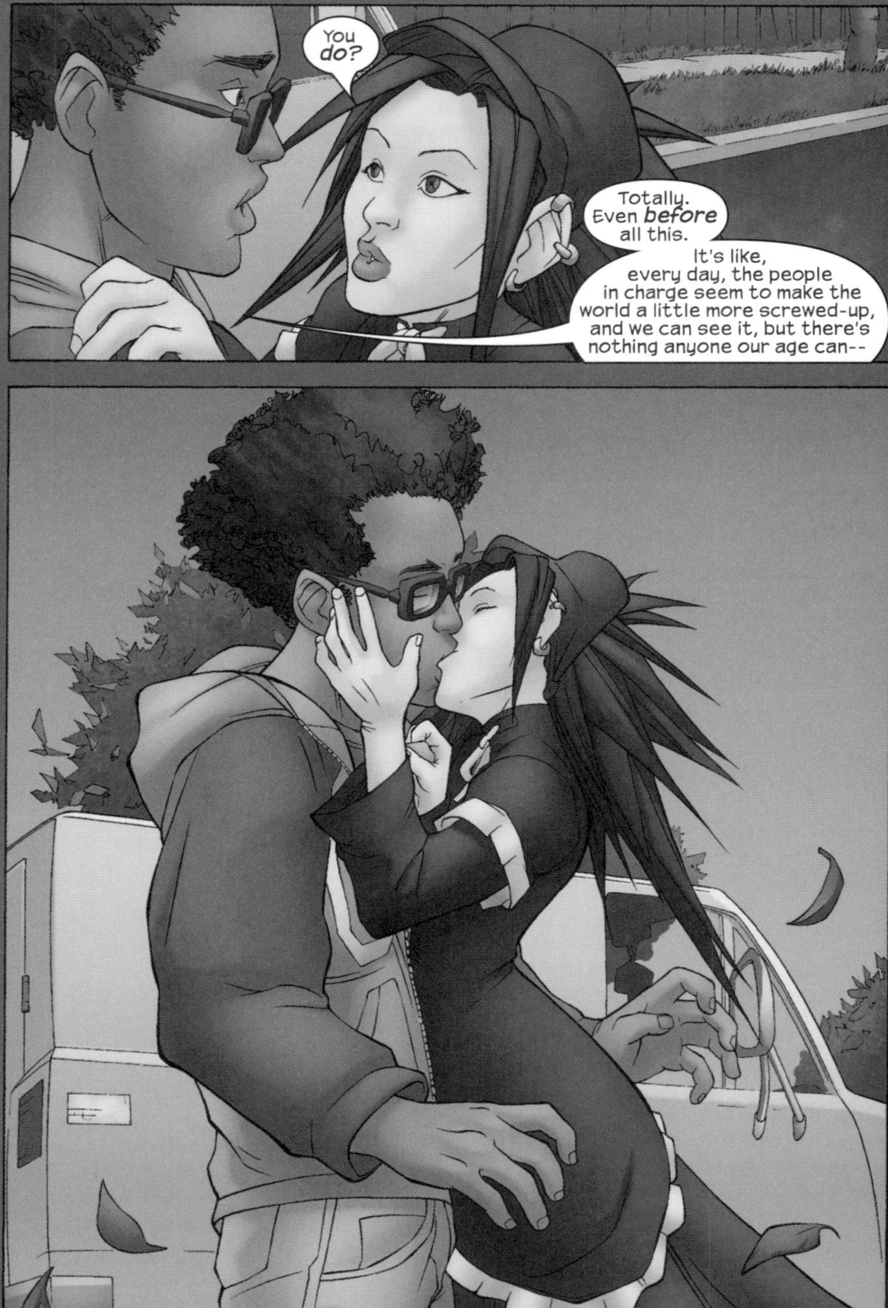
You *do*?
Totally. Even ***before*** all this.
It's like, every day, the people in charge seem to make the world a little more screwed-up, and we can see it, but there's nothing anyone our age can--

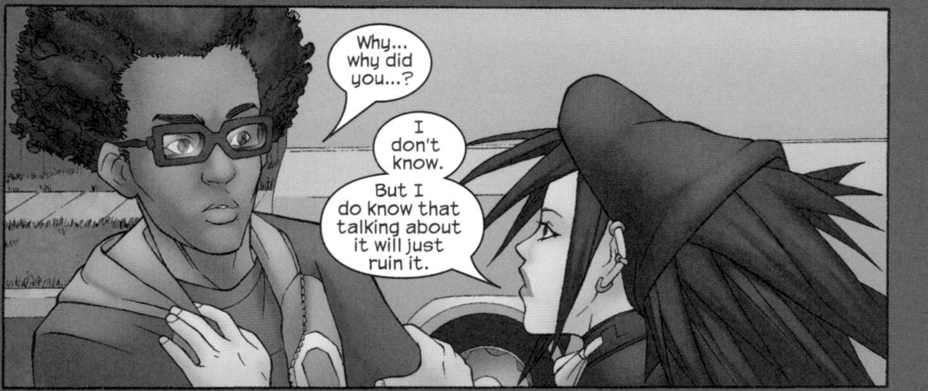
Why... why did you...?
I don't know.
But I do know that talking about it will just ruin it.
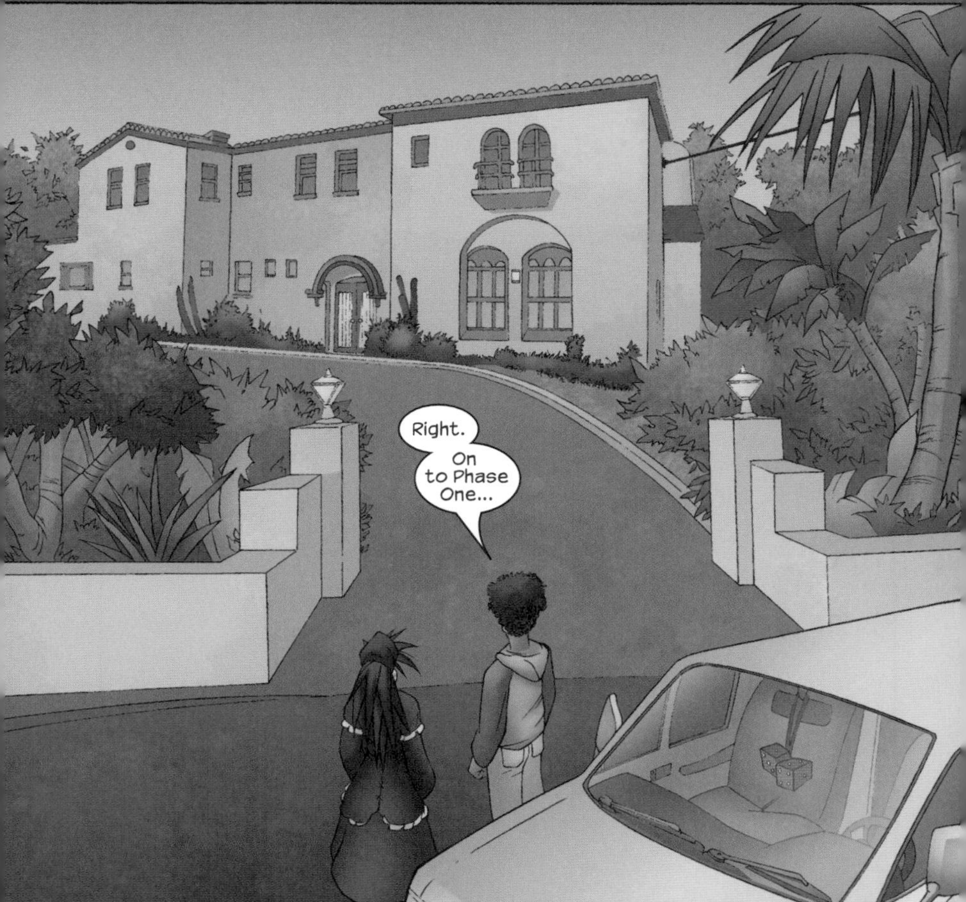
Right.
On to Phase One...

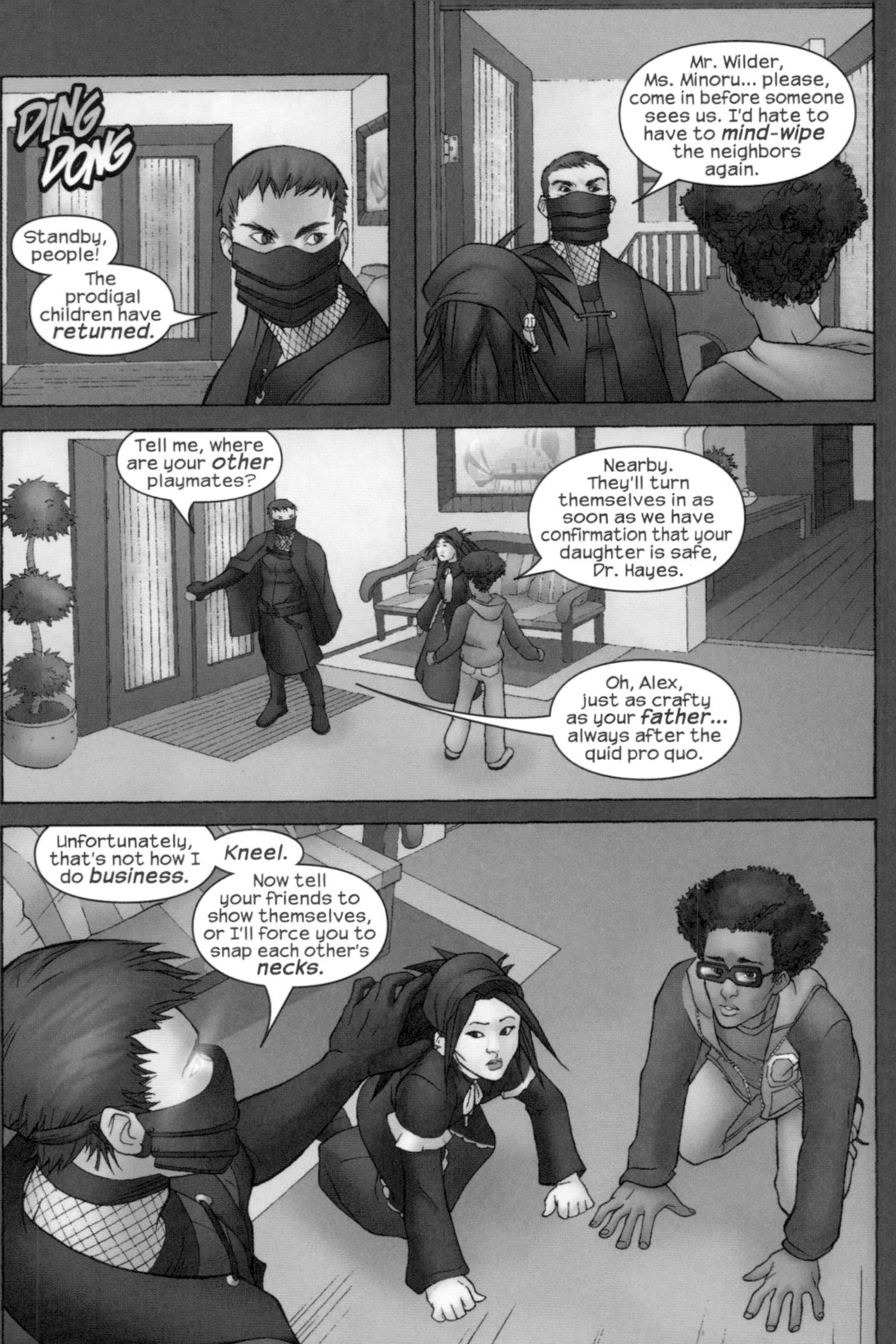
DING DONG
Standby, people!
The prodigal children have returned.
Mr. Wilder, Ms. Minoru... please, come in before someone sees us. I'd hate to have to mind-wipe the neighbors again.
Tell me, where are your other playmates?
Nearby. They'll turn themselves in as soon as we have confirmation that your daughter is safe, Dr. Hayes.
Oh, Alex, just as crafty as your father... always after the quid pro quo.
Unfortunately, that's not how I do business.
Kneel.
Now tell your friends to show themselves, or I'll force you to snap each other's necks.

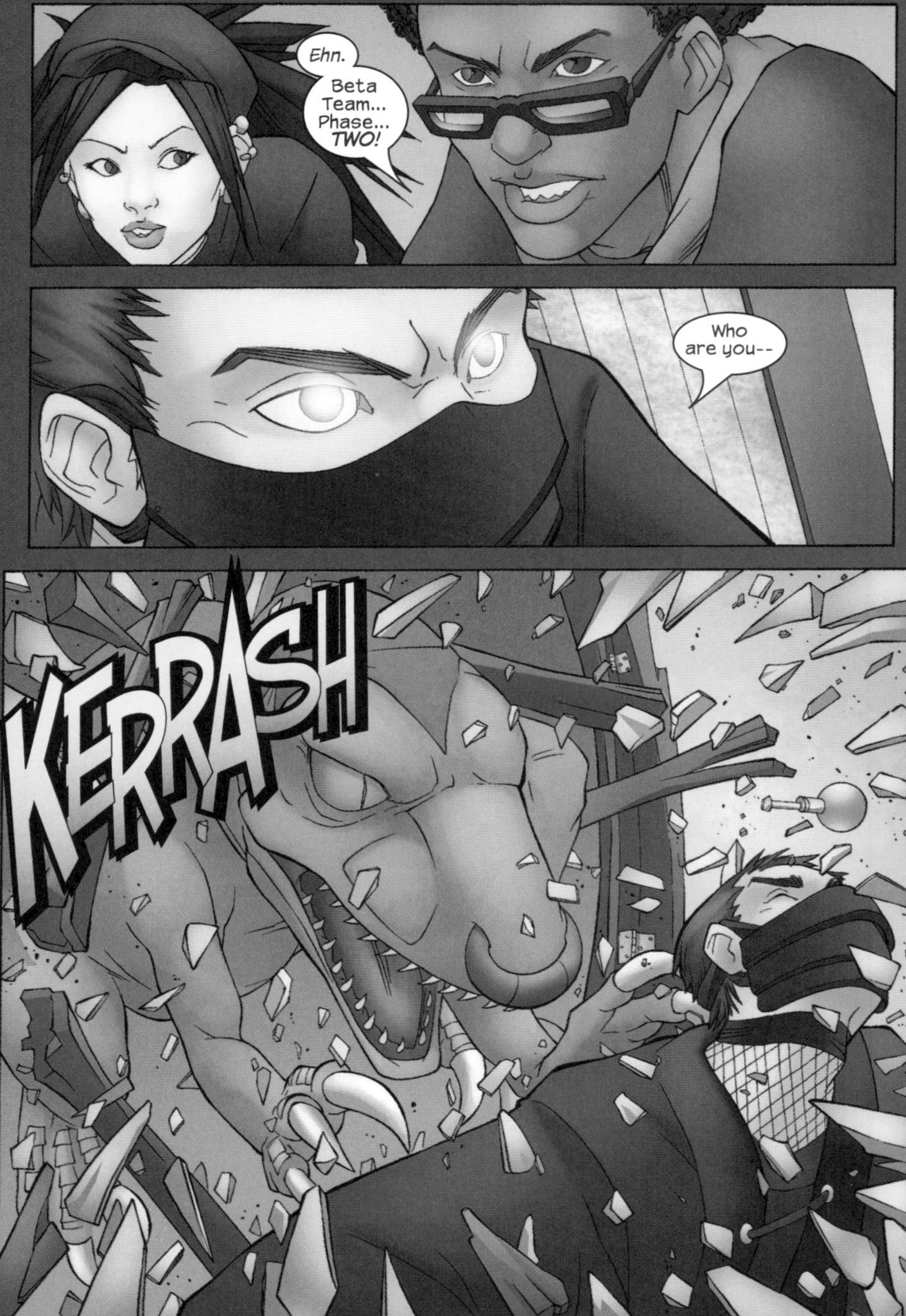
Ehn.
Beta Team... Phase... TWO!
Who are you--
KERRASH

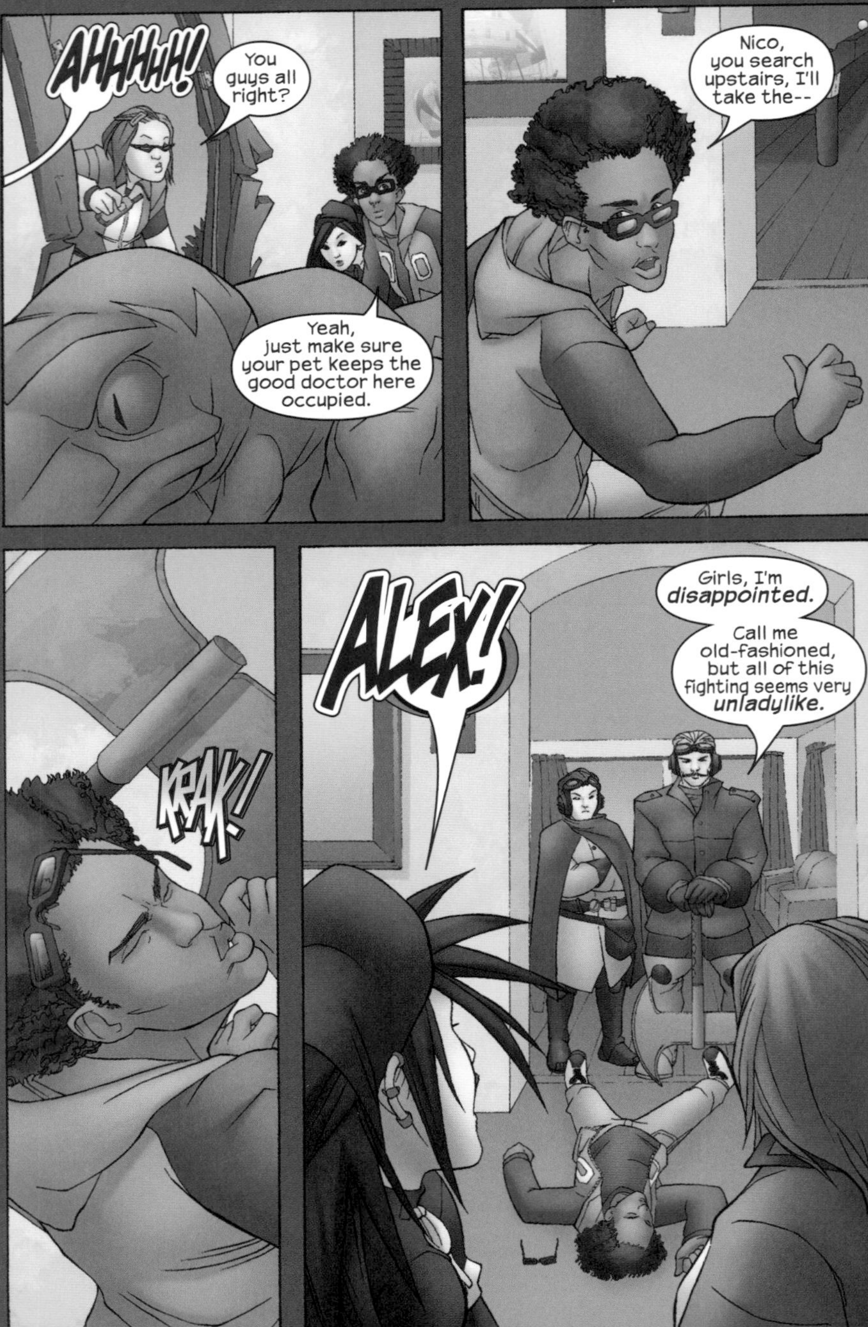
AHHHHH!
You guys all right?
Yeah, just make sure your pet keeps the good doctor here occupied.
Nico, you search upstairs, I'll take the--
KRAK!
ALEX!
Girls, I'm *disappointed.*
Call me old-fashioned, but all of this fighting seems very *unladylike.*

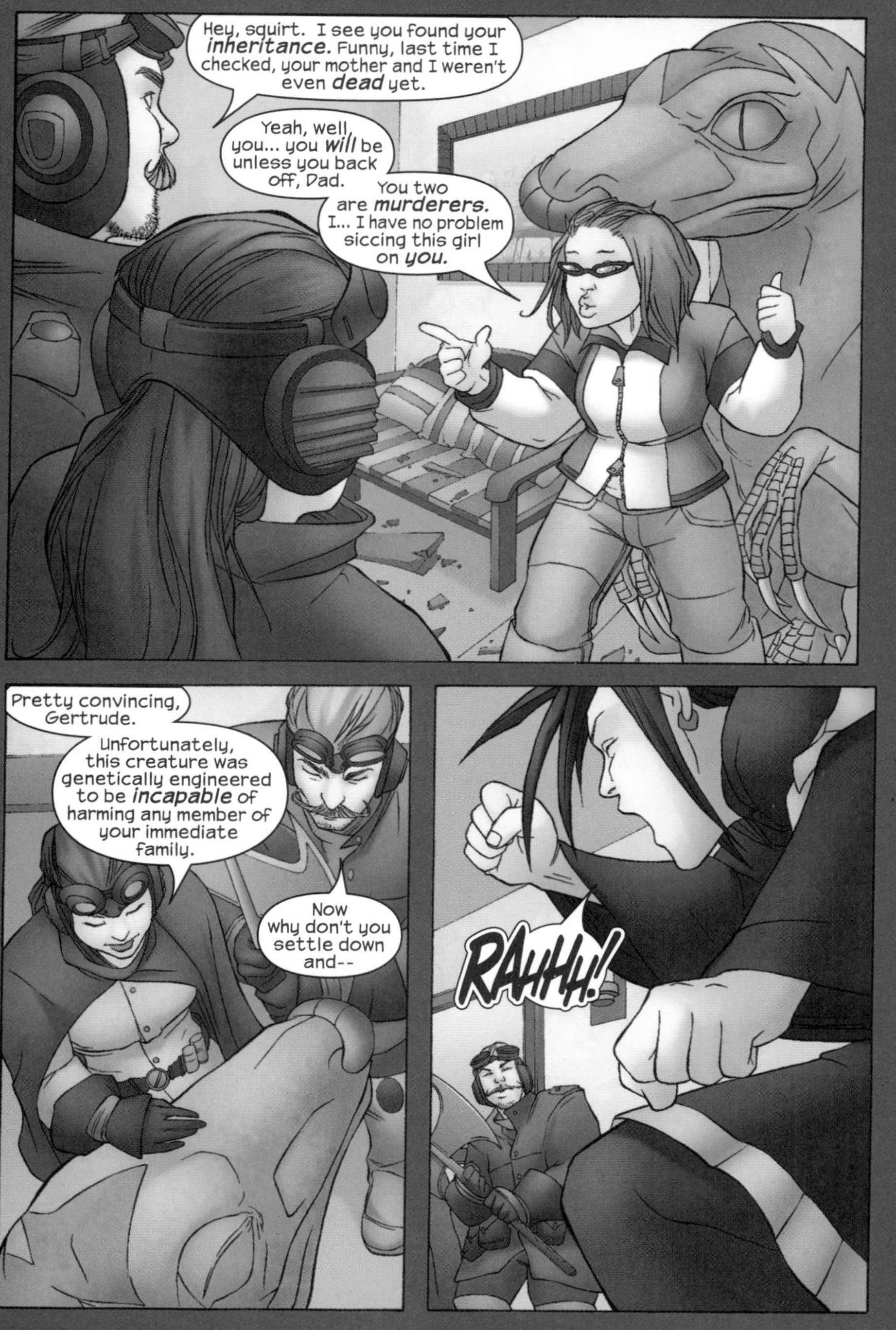
Hey, squirt. I see you found your inheritance. Funny, last time I checked, your mother and I weren't even dead yet.
Yeah, well, you... you will be unless you back off, Dad.
You two are murderers. I... I have no problem siccing this girl on you.
Pretty convincing, Gertrude.
Unfortunately, this creature was genetically engineered to be incapable of harming any member of your immediate family.
Now why don't you settle down and--
RAHHH!

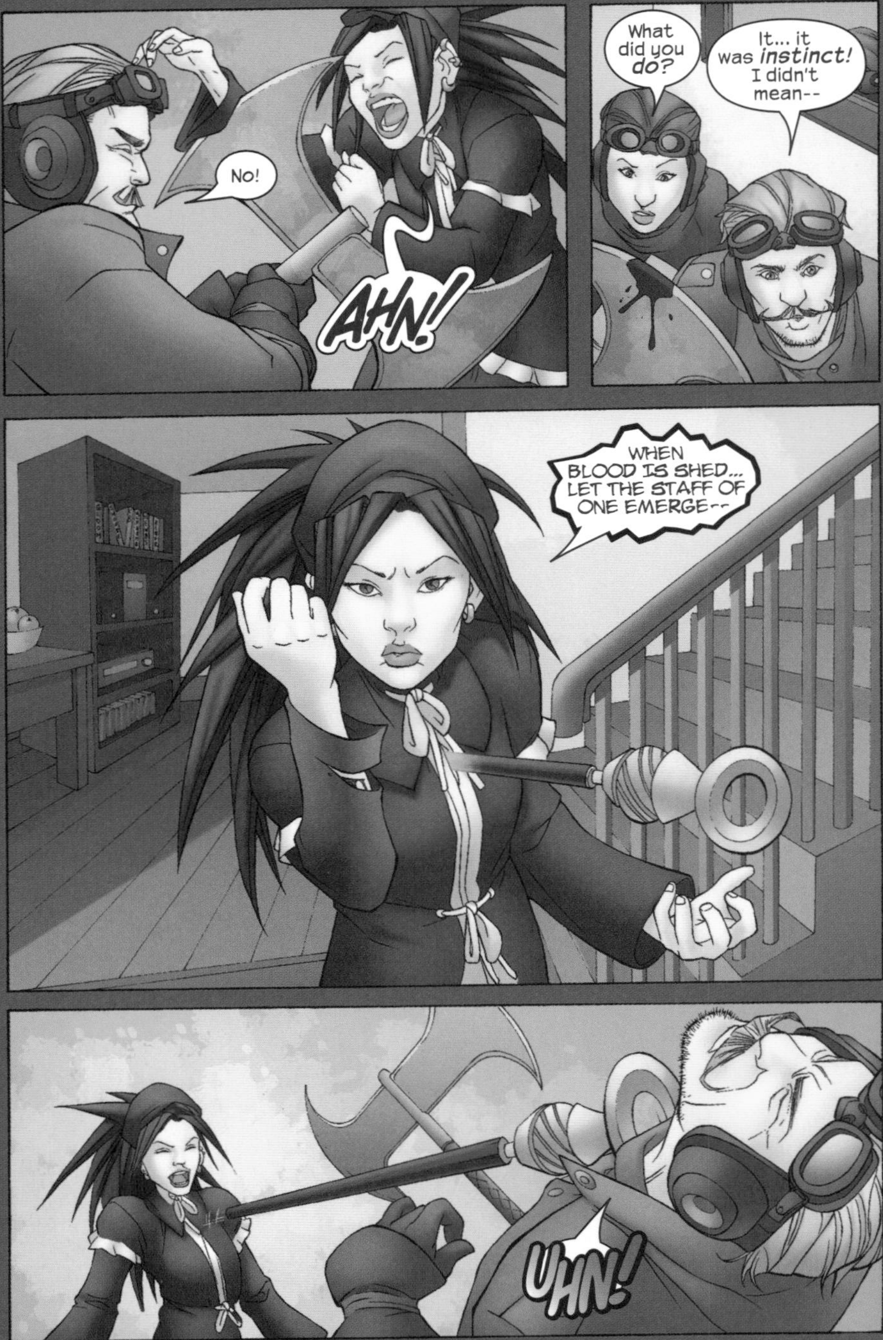
No!
AHN!
What did you do?
It... it was instinct! I didn't mean--
WHEN BLOOD IS SHED... LET THE STAFF OF ONE EMERGE--
UHN!

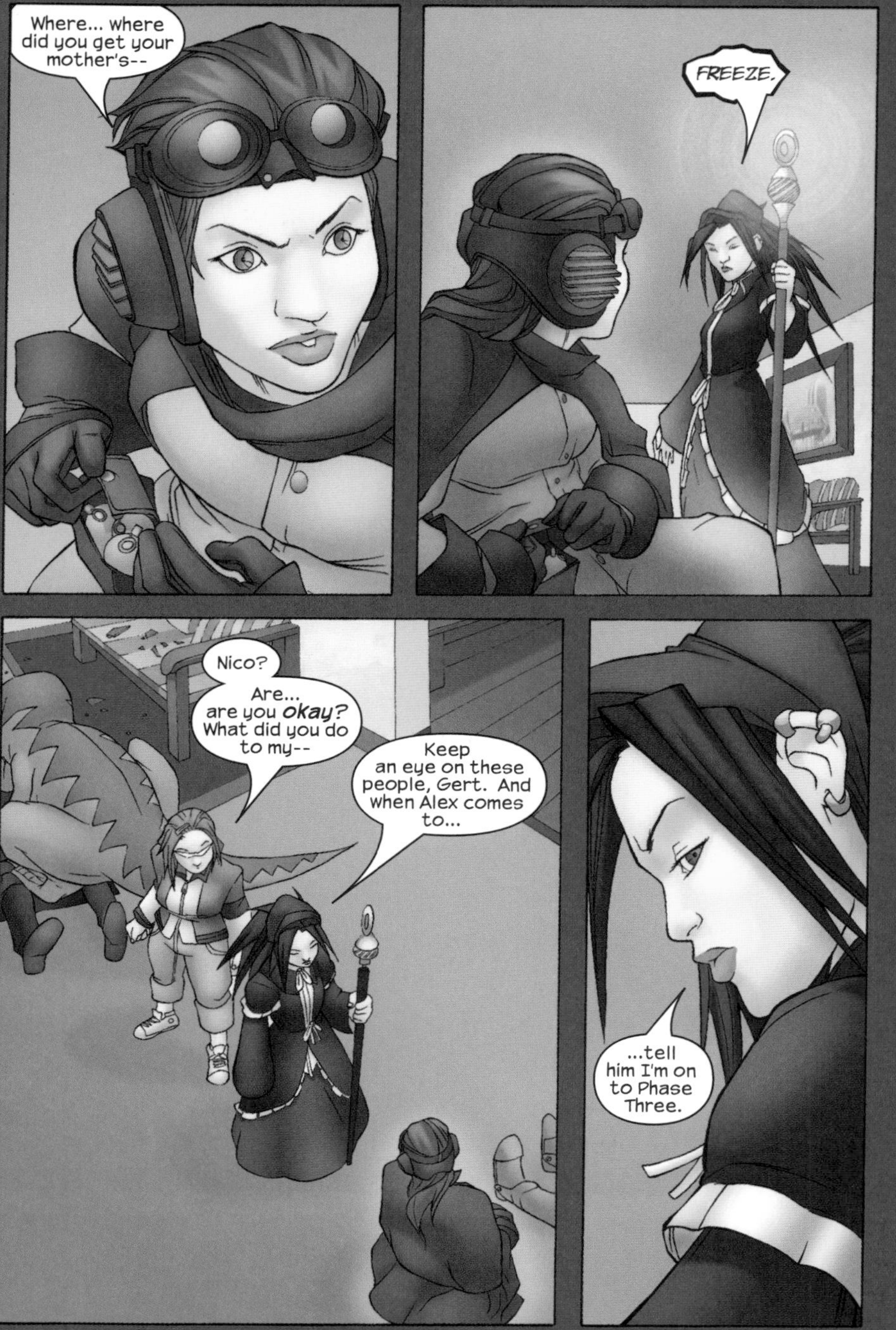
Where... where did you get your mother's--
FREEZE.
Nico?
Are... are you okay? What did you do to my--
Keep an eye on these people, Gert. And when Alex comes to...
...tell him I'm on to Phase Three.

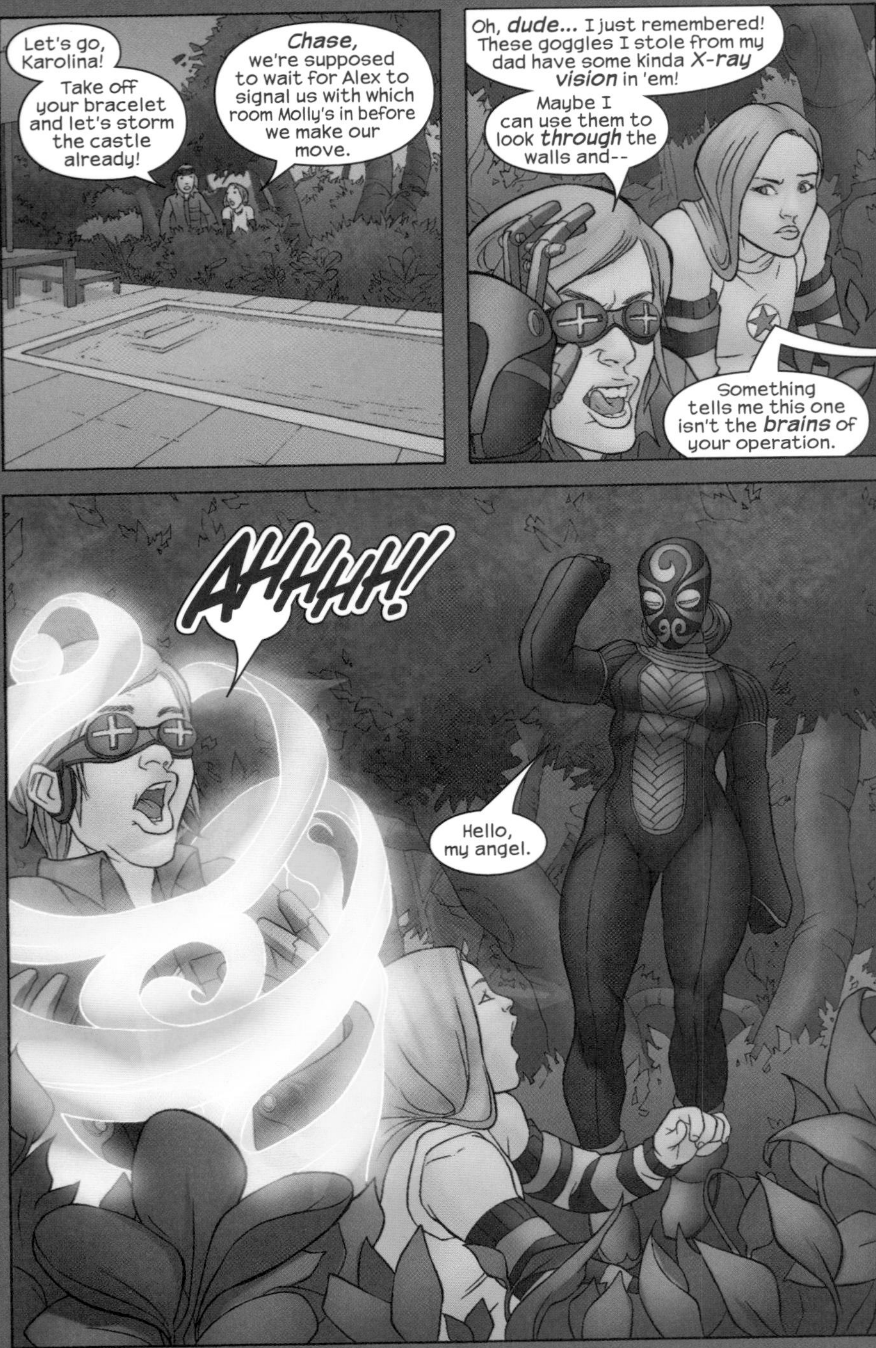
Let's go, Karolina!
Take off your bracelet and let's storm the castle already!
Chase, we're supposed to wait for Alex to signal us with which room Molly's in before we make our move.
Oh, *dude...* I just remembered! These goggles I stole from my dad have some kinda *X-ray vision* in 'em!
Maybe I can use them to look *through* the walls and--
Something tells me this one isn't the *brains* of your operation.
AHHHH!
Hello, my angel.

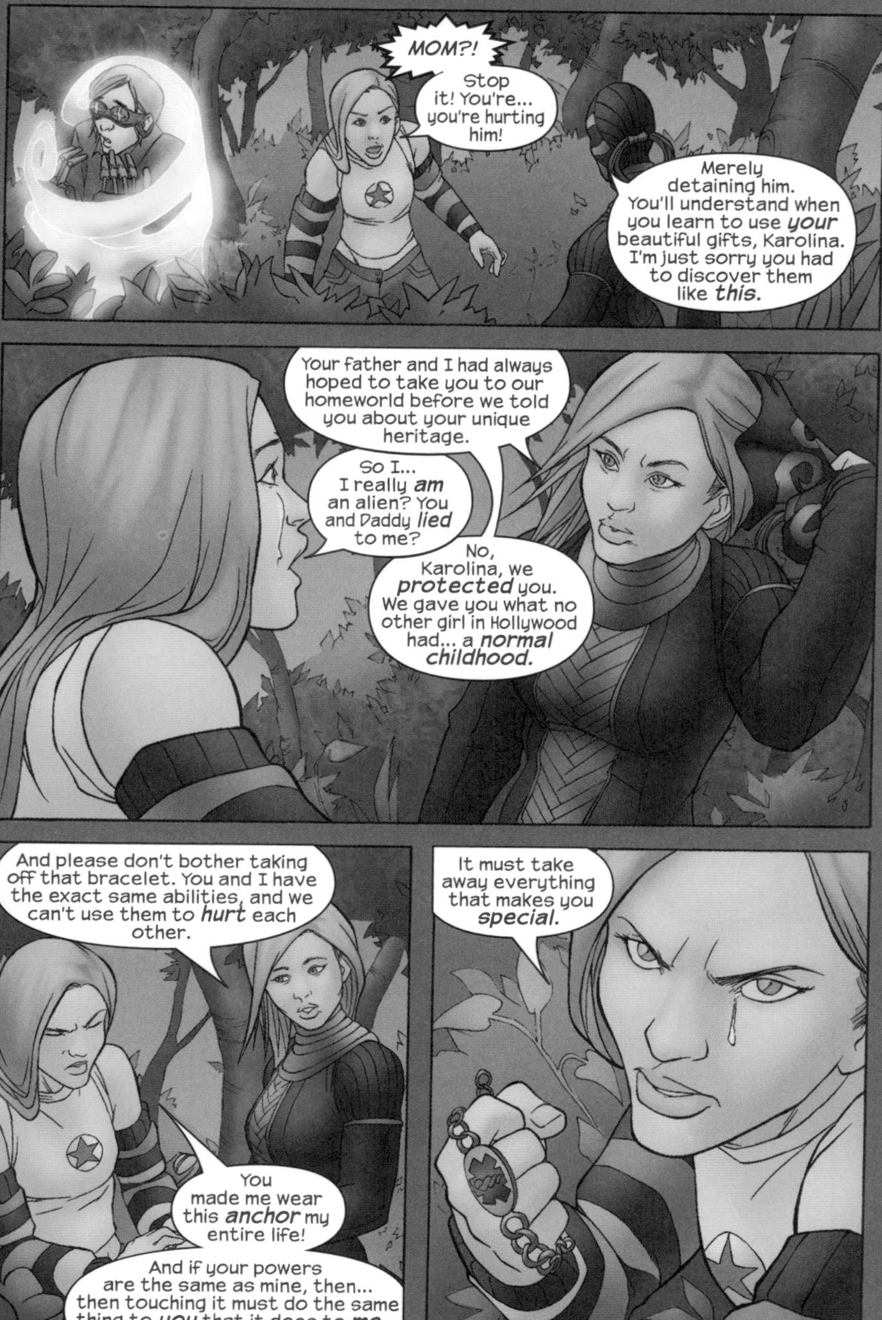
MOM?!
Stop it! You're... you're hurting him!
Merely detaining him. You'll understand when you learn to use your beautiful gifts, Karolina. I'm just sorry you had to discover them like this.
Your father and I had always hoped to take you to our homeworld before we told you about your unique heritage.
So I... I really am an alien? You and Daddy lied to me?
No, Karolina, we protected you. We gave you what no other girl in Hollywood had... a normal childhood.
And please don't bother taking off that bracelet. You and I have the exact same abilities, and we can't use them to hurt each other.
You made me wear this anchor my entire life!
And if your powers are the same as mine, then... then touching it must do the same thing to you that it does to me.
It must take away everything that makes you special.

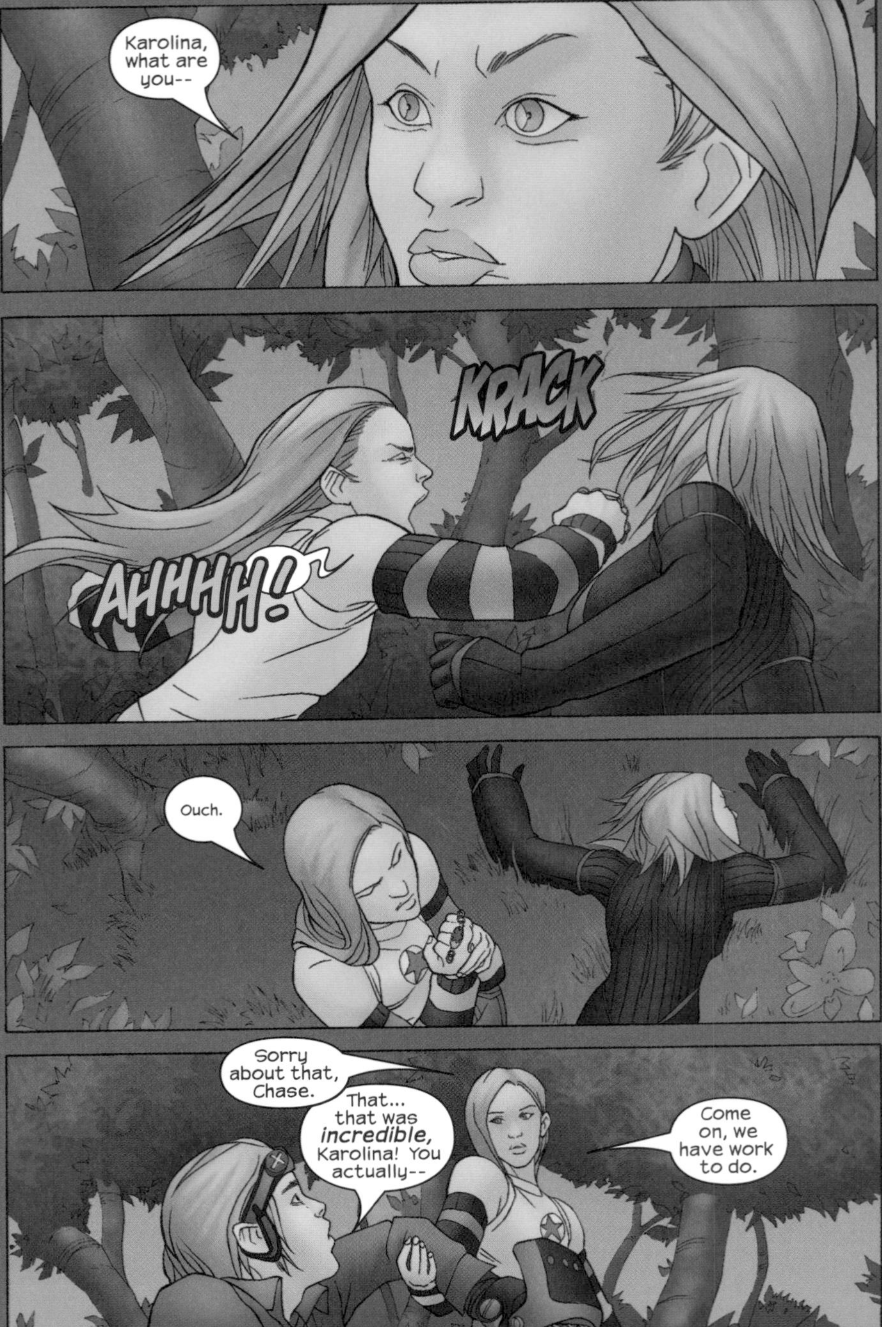
Karolina, what are you--
KRACK
AHHHH!
Ouch.
Sorry about that, Chase.
That... that was *incredible,* Karolina! You actually--
Come on, we have work to do.

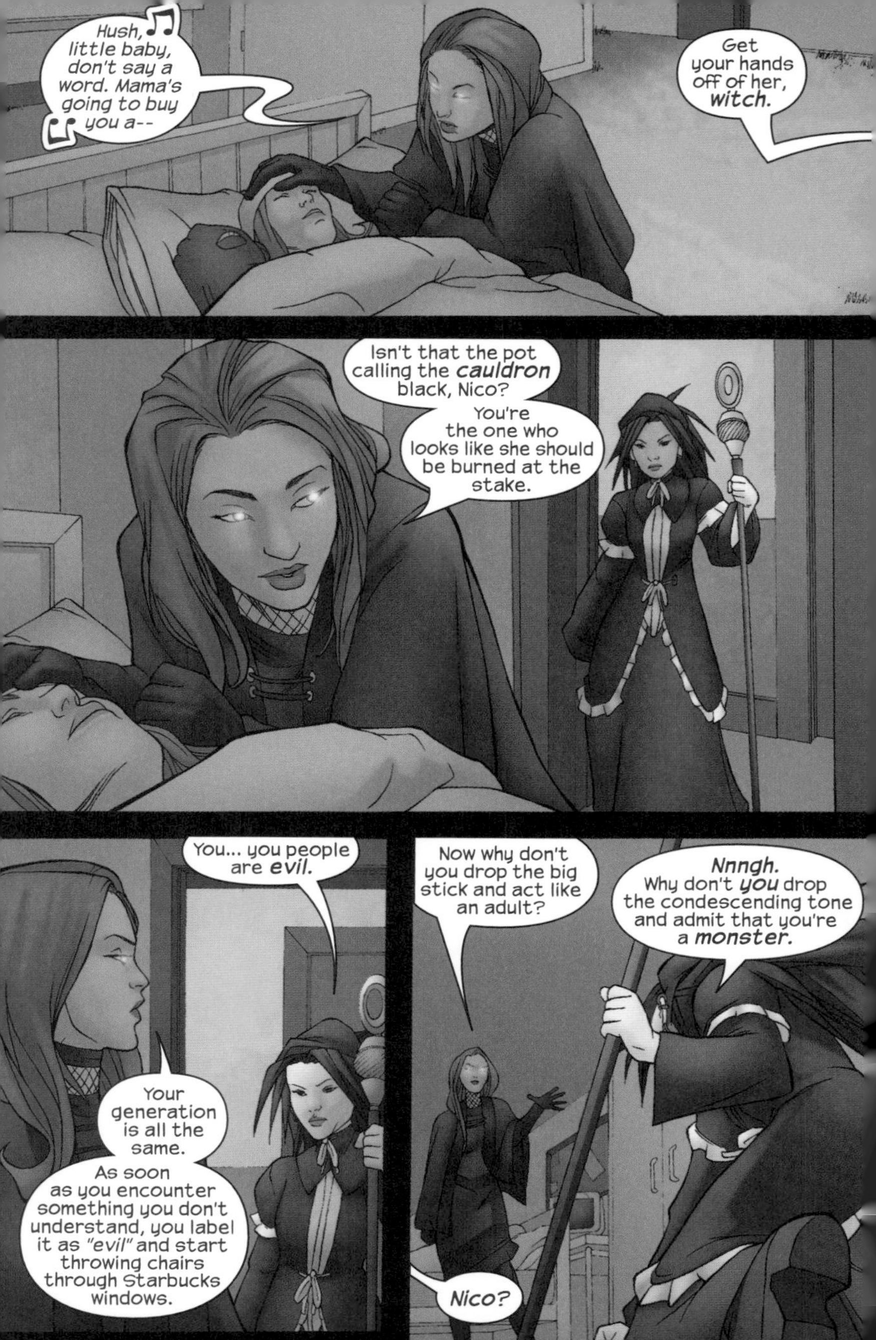
Hush, little baby, don't say a word. Mama's going to buy you a--
Get your hands off of her, *witch.*
Isn't that the pot calling the *cauldron* black, Nico?
You're the one who looks like she should be burned at the stake.
You... you people are *evil.*
Your generation is all the same.
As soon as you encounter something you don't understand, you label it as "*evil*" and start throwing chairs through Starbucks windows.
Now why don't you drop the big stick and act like an adult?
Nnngh. Why don't *you* drop the condescending tone and admit that you're a *monster.*
Nico?

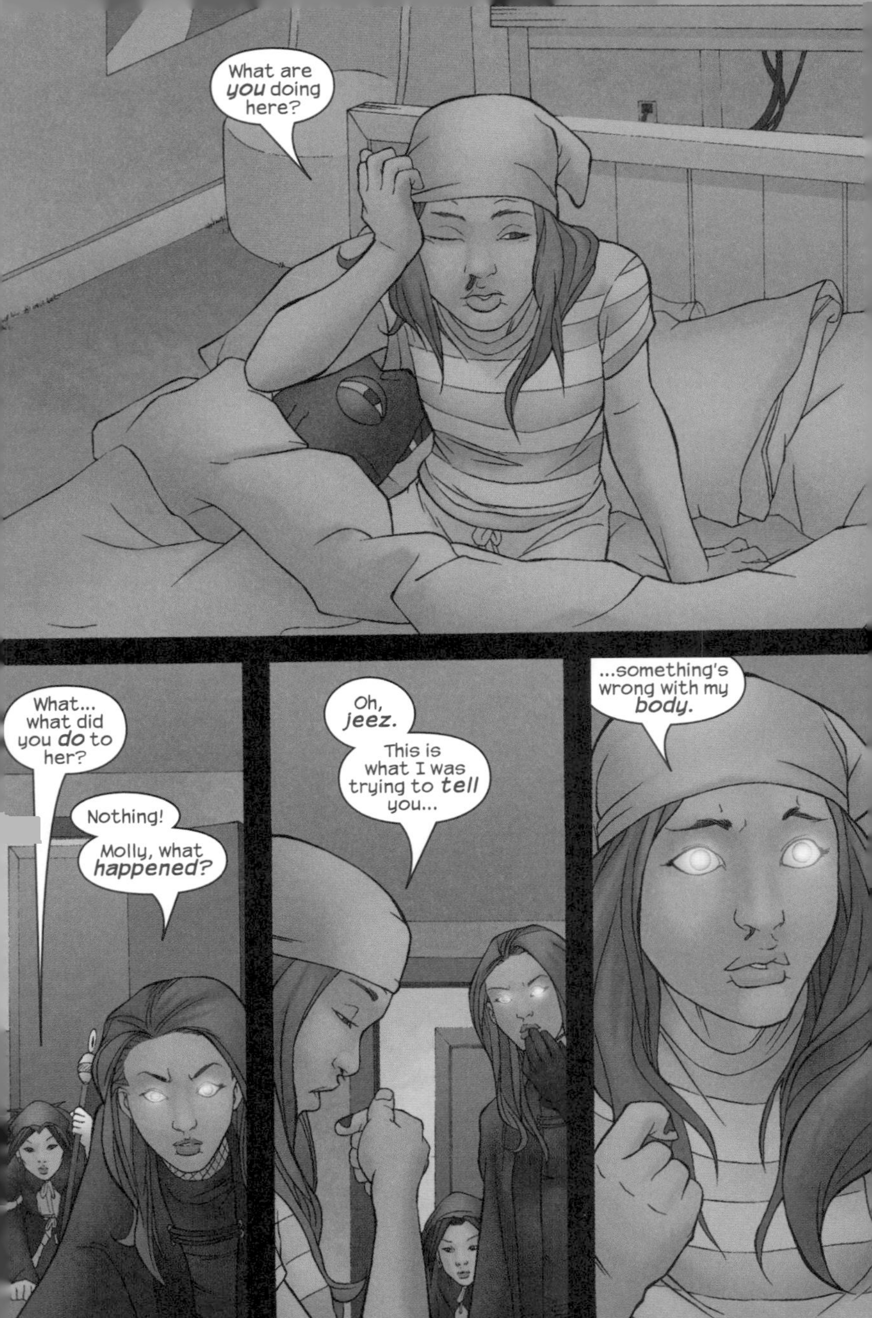
What are *you* doing here?
What... what did you *do* to her?
Nothing!
Molly, what *happened?*
Oh, *jeez.*
This is what I was trying to *tell* you...
...something's wrong with my *body.*

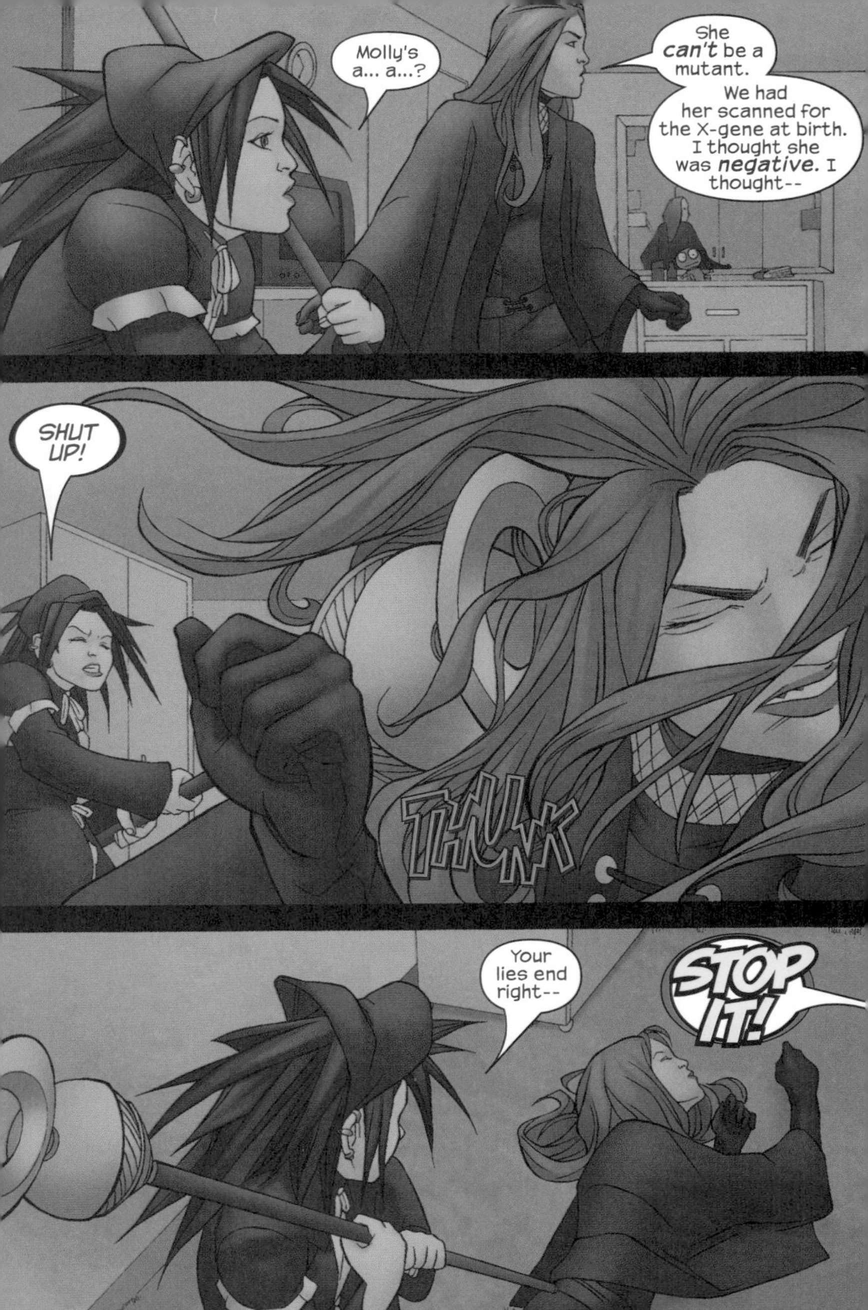
Molly's a... a...?
She can't be a mutant.
We had her scanned for the X-gene at birth. I thought she was negative. I thought--
SHUT UP!
THUNK
Your lies end right--
STOP IT!

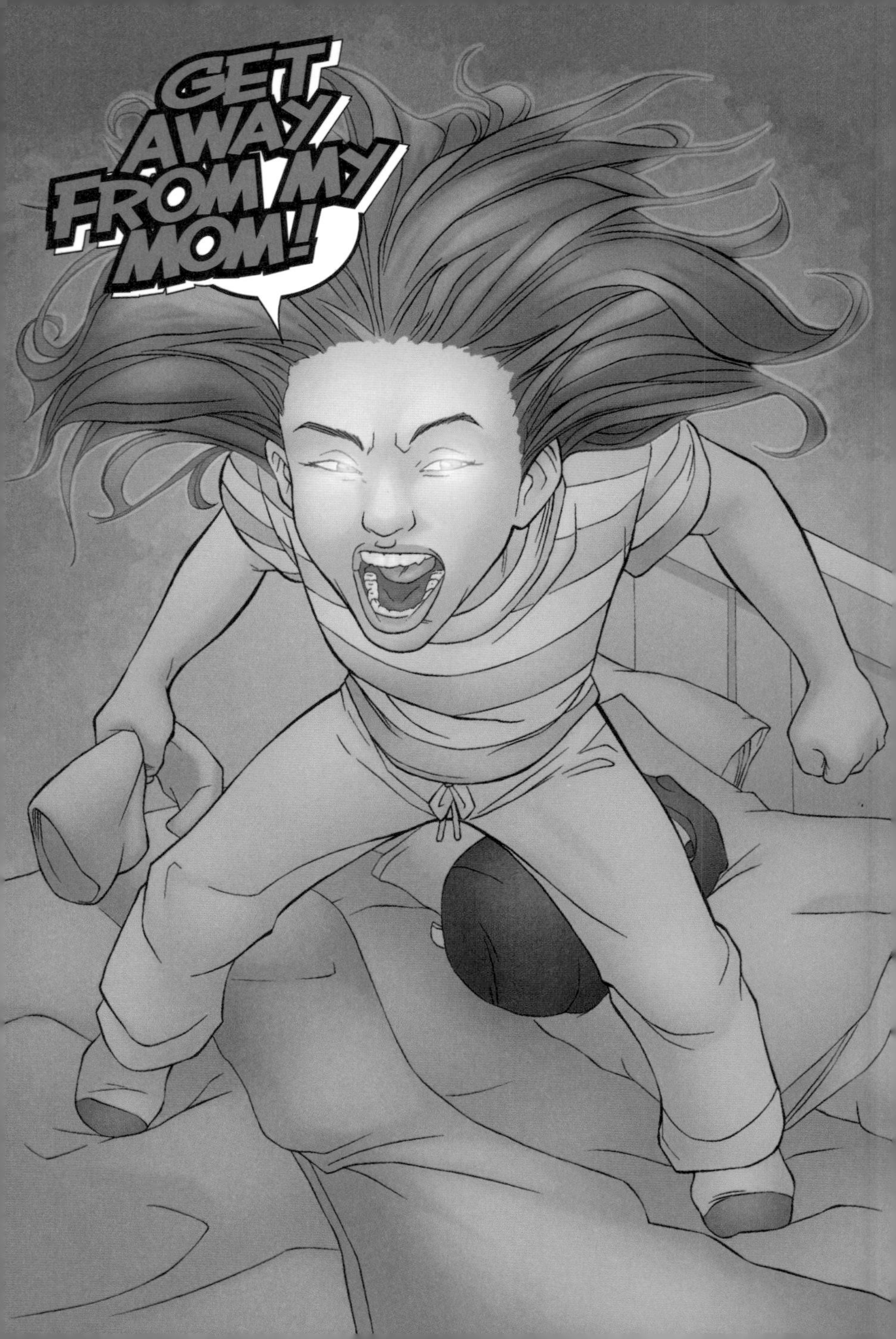
GET AWAY FROM MY MOM!!

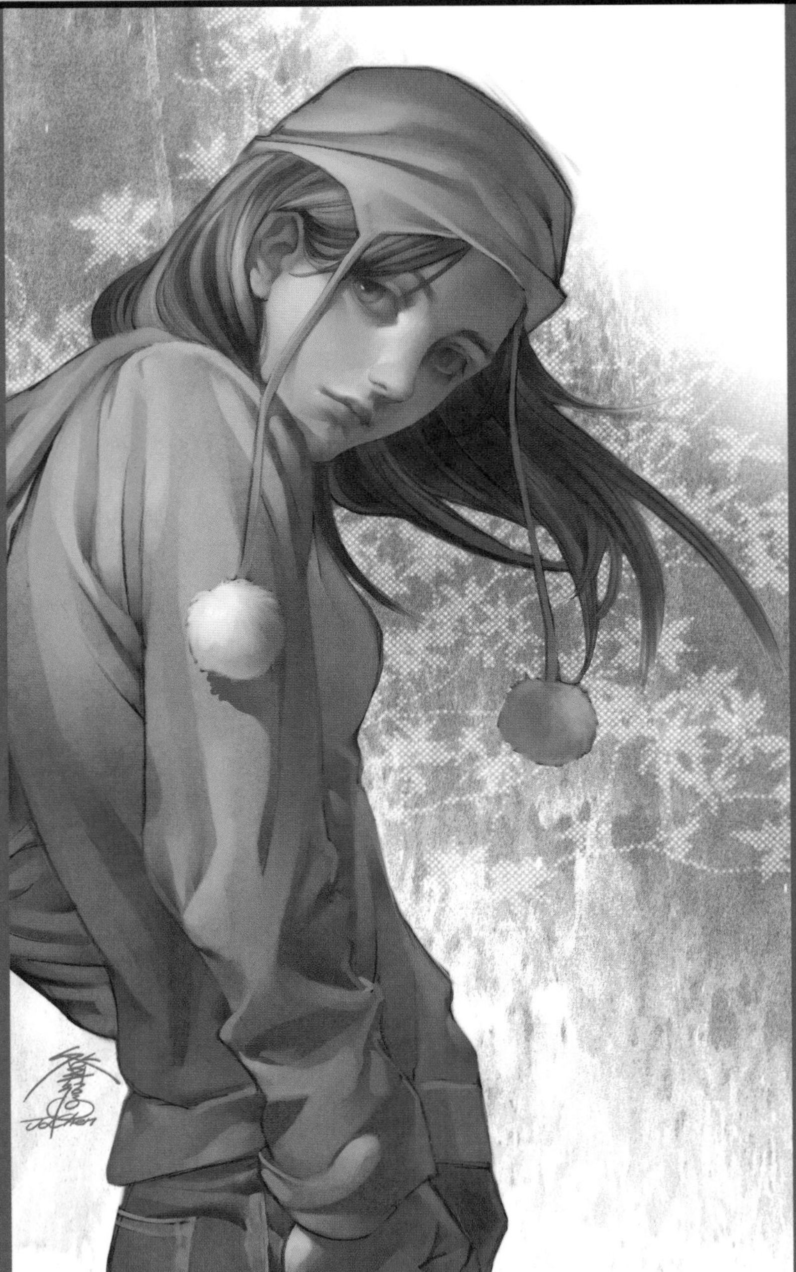
#6

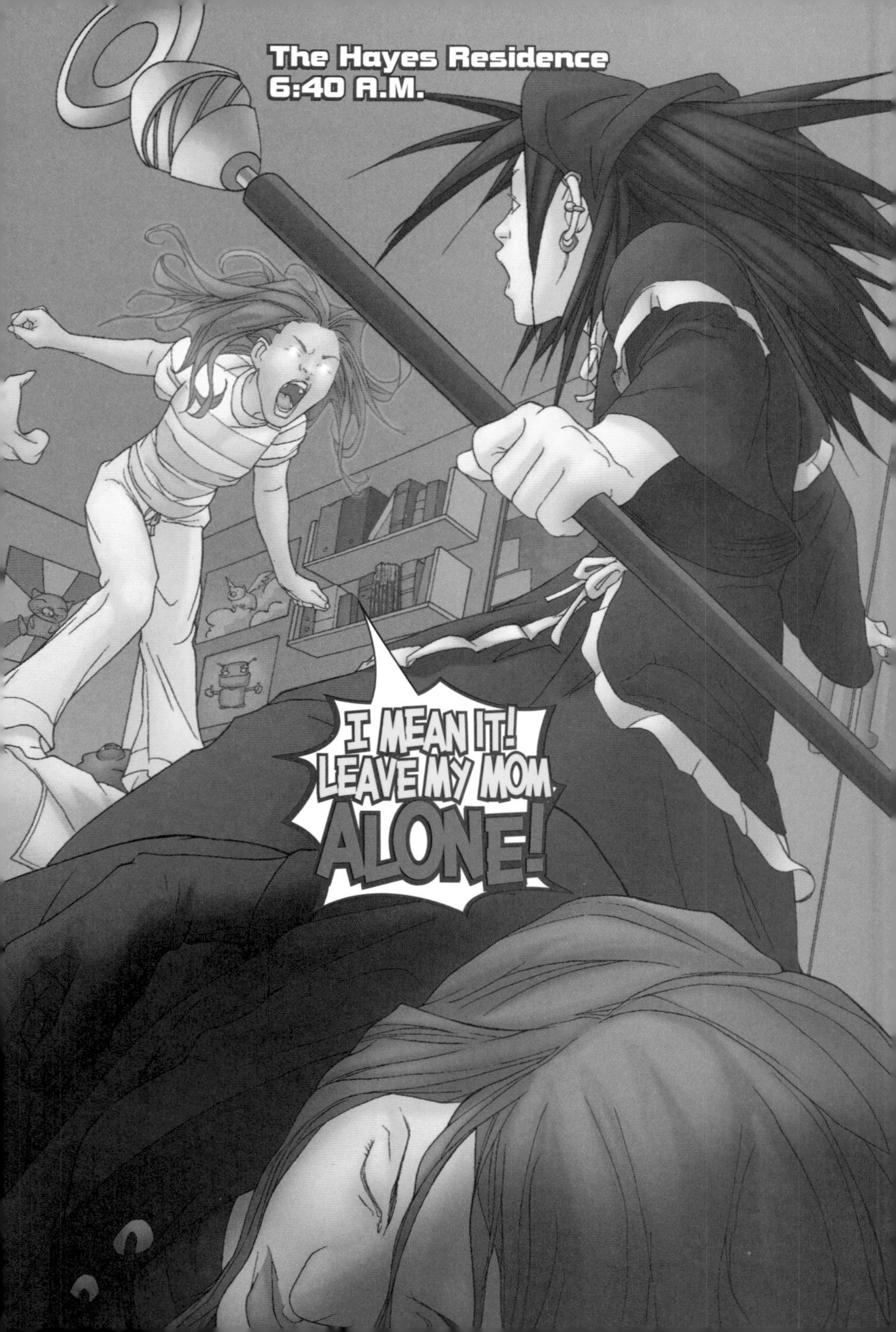
The Hayes Residence
6:40 A.M.
I MEAN IT! LEAVE MY MOM ALONE!

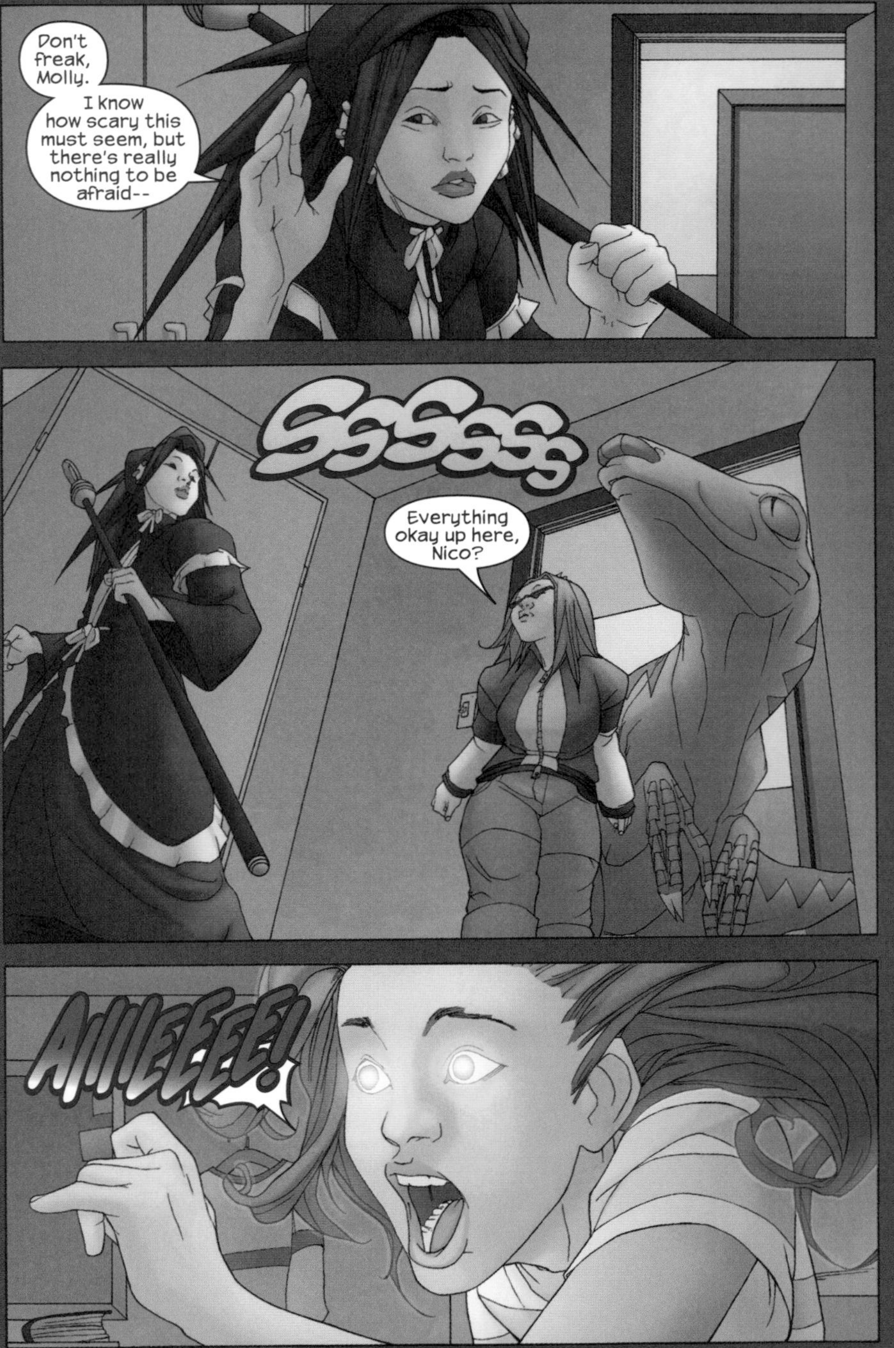
Don't freak, Molly.
I know how scary this must seem, but there's really nothing to be afraid--
SSSSSS
Everything okay up here, Nico?
AIIIEEEE!

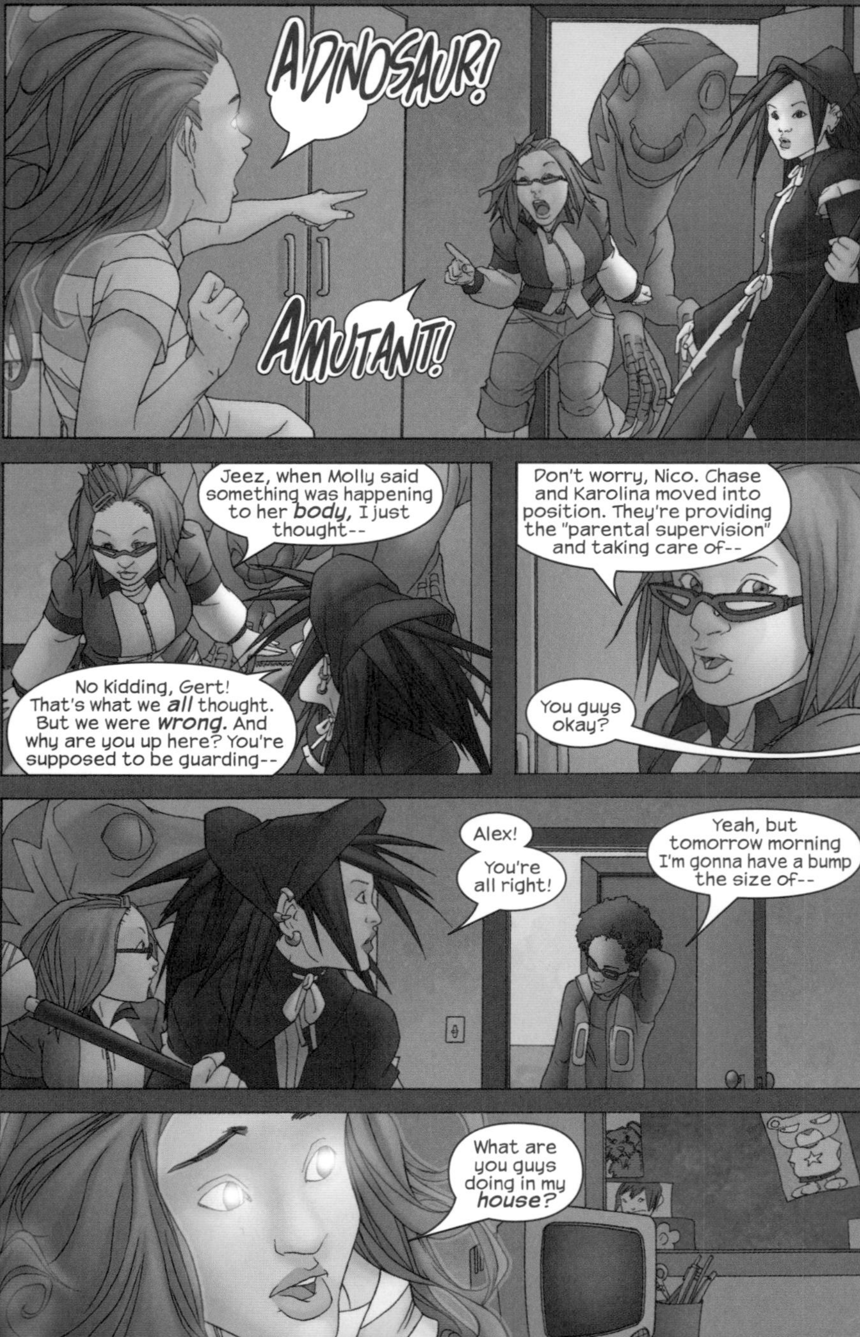
A DINOSAUR!
A MUTANT!
Jeez, when Molly said something was happening to her *body,* I just thought--
No kidding, Gert! That's what we *all* thought. But we were *wrong.* And why are you up here? You're supposed to be guarding--
Don't worry, Nico. Chase and Karolina moved into position. They're providing the "parental supervision" and taking care of--
You guys okay?
Alex!
You're all right!
Yeah, but tomorrow morning I'm gonna have a bump the size of--
What are you guys doing in my *house?*

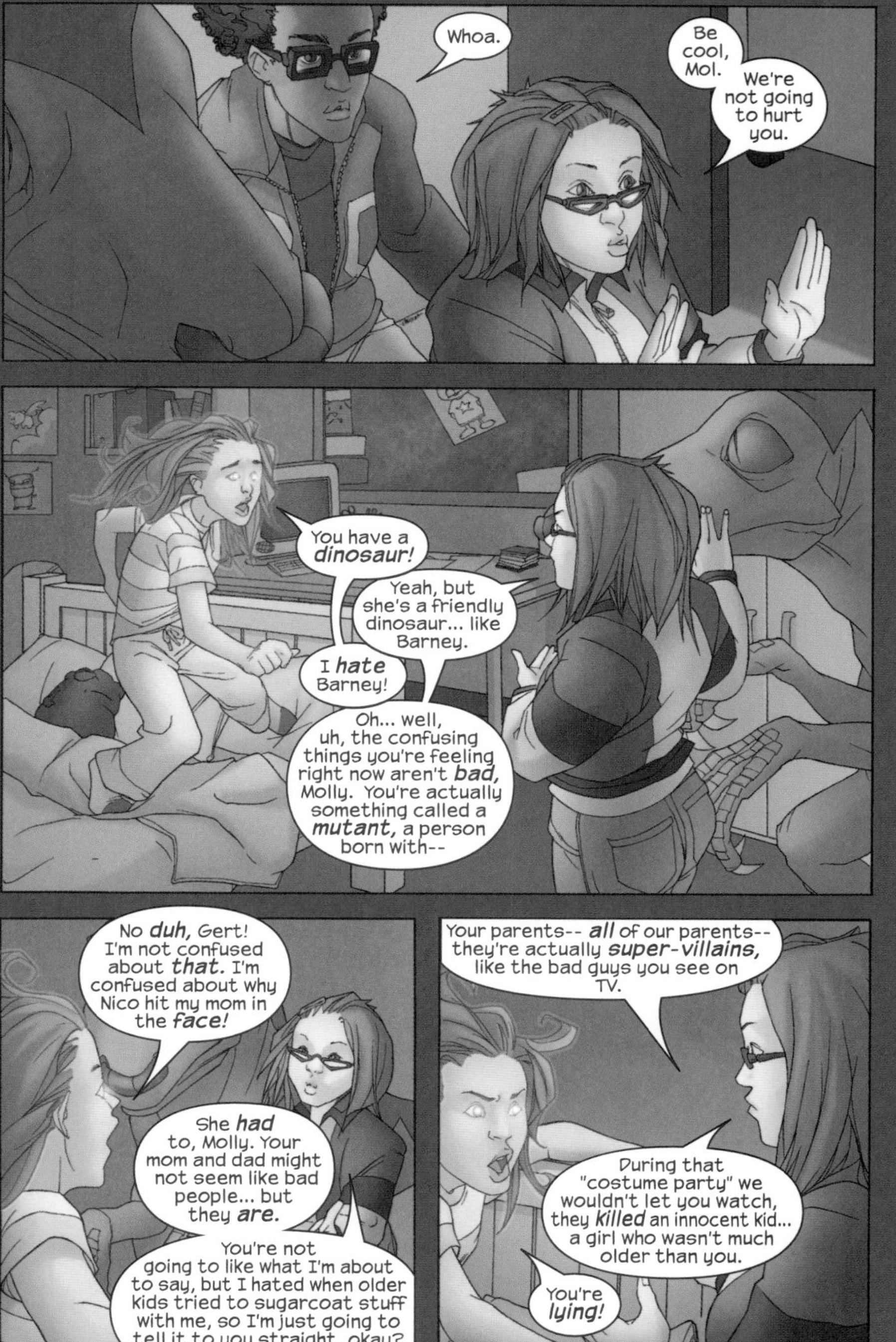
Whoa.
Be cool, Mol.
We're not going to hurt you.
You have a *dinosaur!*
Yeah, but she's a friendly dinosaur... like Barney.
I *hate* Barney!
Oh... well, uh, the confusing things you're feeling right now aren't *bad,* Molly. You're actually something called a *mutant,* a person born with--
No *duh,* Gert! I'm not confused about *that.* I'm confused about why Nico hit my mom in the *face!*
She *had* to, Molly. Your mom and dad might not seem like bad people... but they *are.*
You're not going to like what I'm about to say, but I hated when older kids tried to sugarcoat stuff with me, so I'm just going to tell it to you straight, okay?
Your parents-- *all* of our parents-- they're actually *super-villains,* like the bad guys you see on TV.
During that "costume party" we wouldn't let you watch, they *killed* an innocent kid... a girl who wasn't much older than you.
You're *lying!*

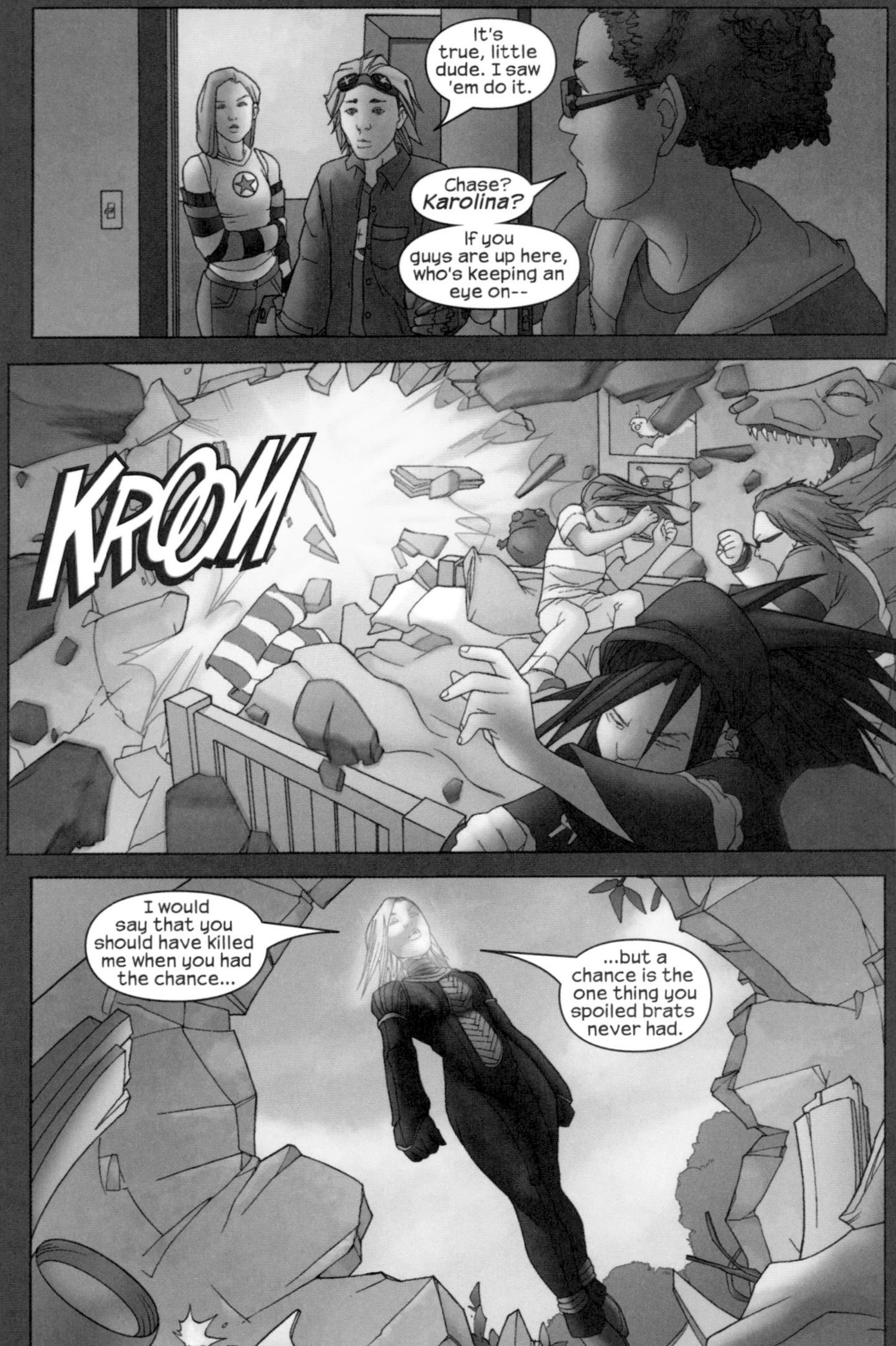
It's true, little dude. I saw 'em do it.
Chase? Karolina?
If you guys are up here, who's keeping an eye on--
KROOM
I would say that you should have killed me when you had the chance...
...but a chance is the one thing you spoiled brats never had.

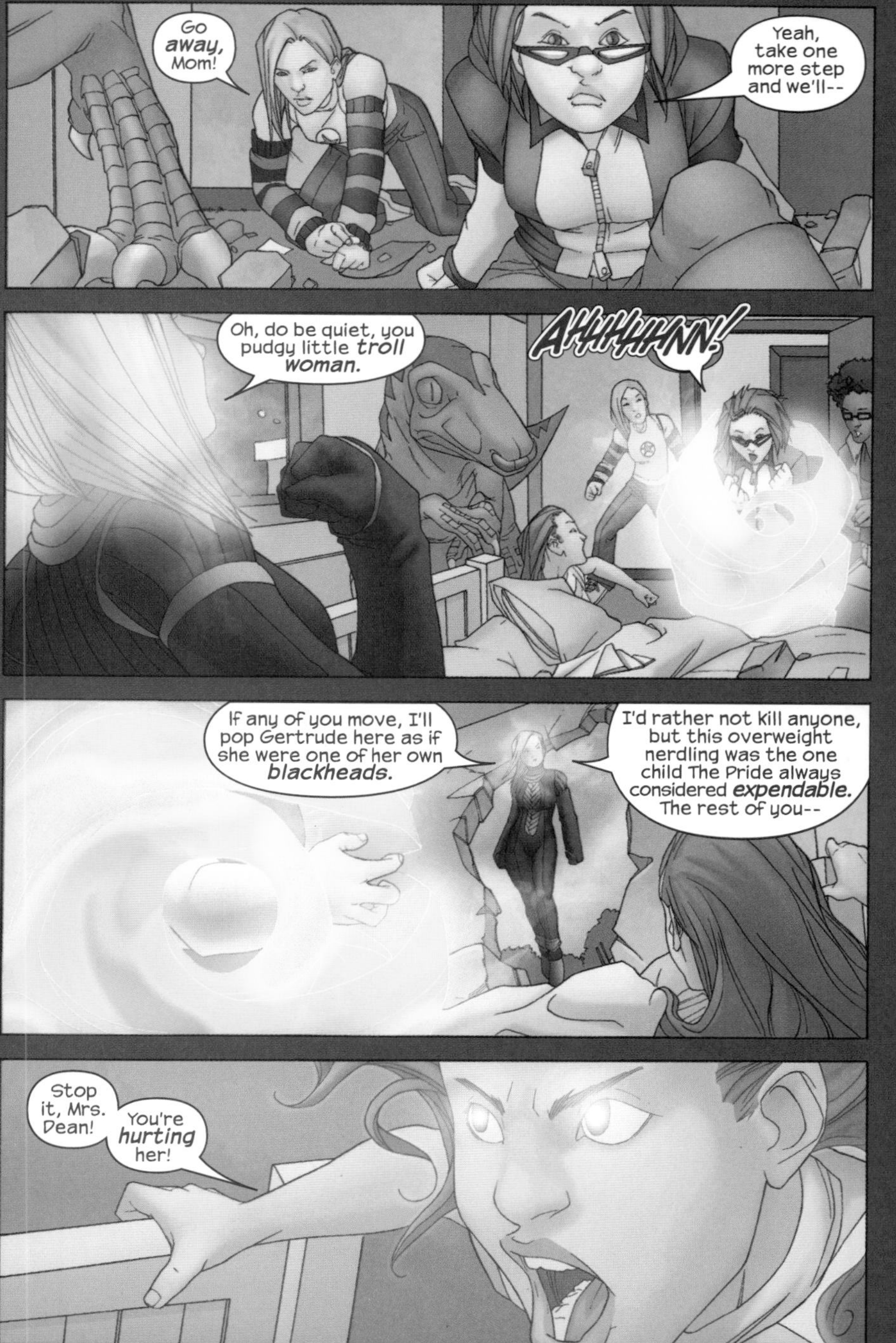
Go away, Mom!
Yeah, take one more step and we'll--
Oh, do be quiet, you pudgy little troll woman.
AHHHHHNN!
If any of you move, I'll pop Gertrude here as if she were one of her own blackheads.
I'd rather not kill anyone, but this overweight nerdling was the one child The Pride always considered expendable. The rest of you--
Stop it, Mrs. Dean!
You're hurting her!

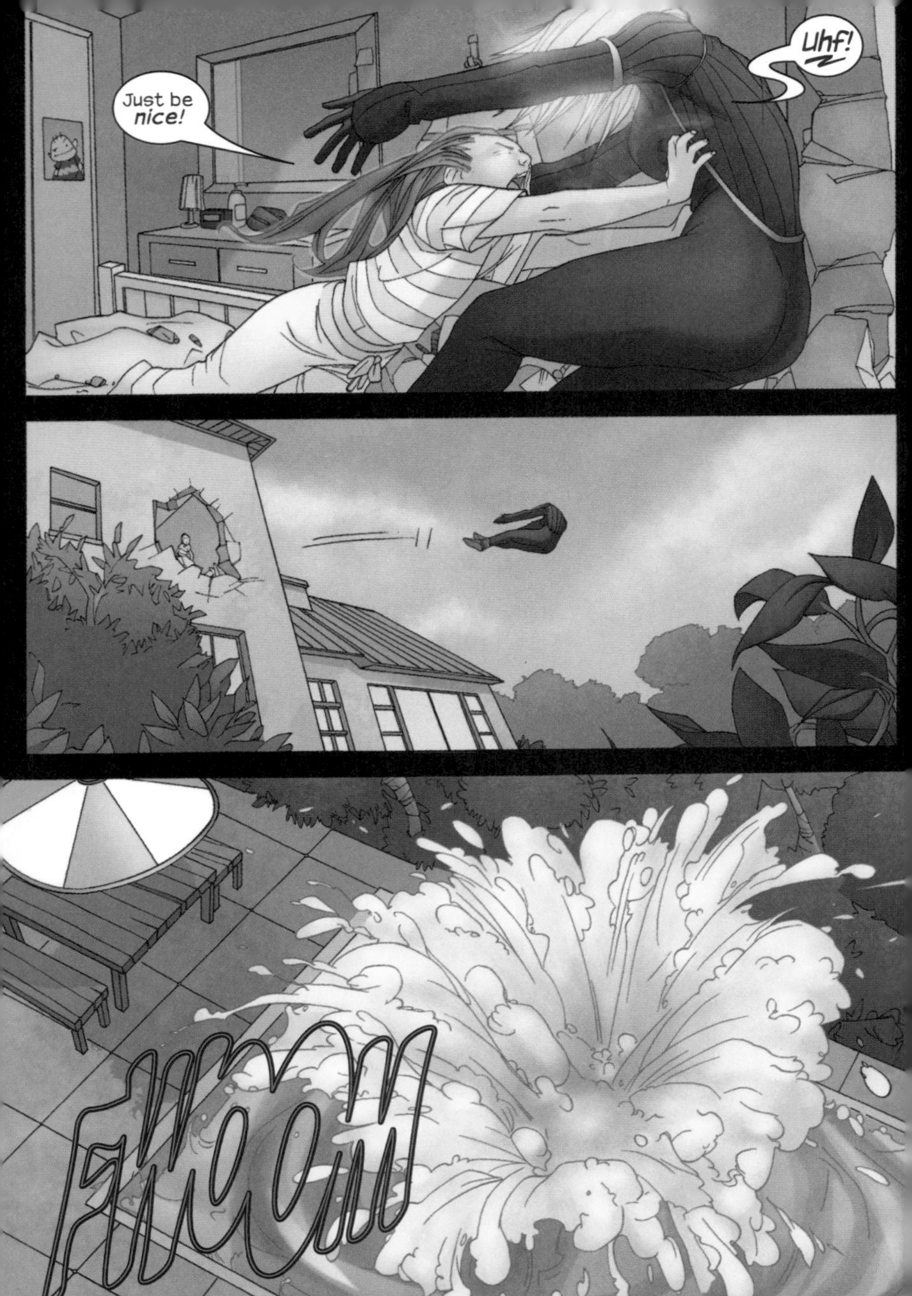
Just be nice!
Uhf!

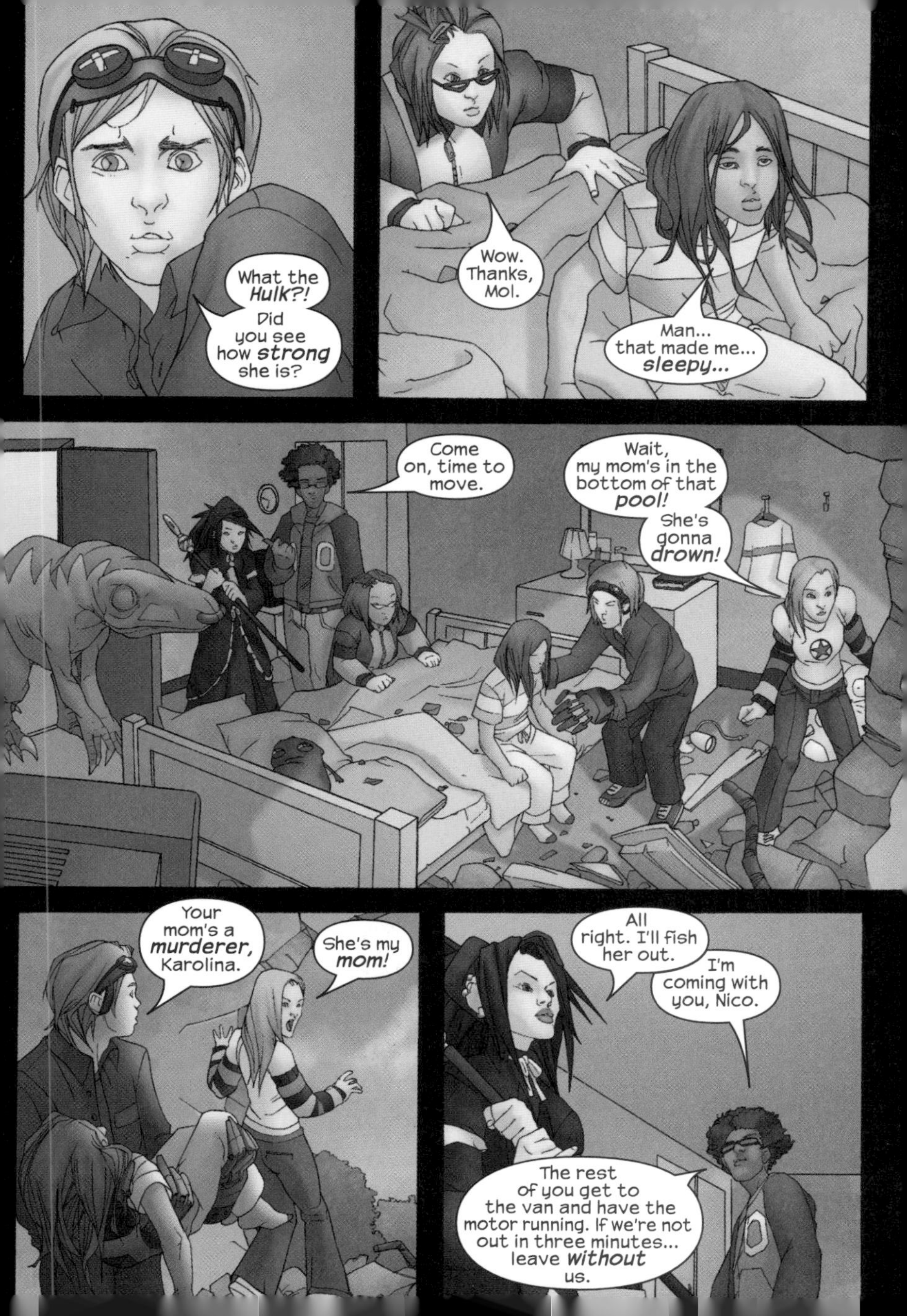
What the Hulk?!
Did you see how strong she is?
Wow. Thanks, Mol.
Man... that made me... sleepy...
Come on, time to move.
Wait, my mom's in the bottom of that pool!
She's gonna drown!
Your mom's a murderer, Karolina.
She's my mom!
All right. I'll fish her out.
I'm coming with you, Nico.
The rest of you get to the van and have the motor running. If we're not out in three minutes... leave without us.

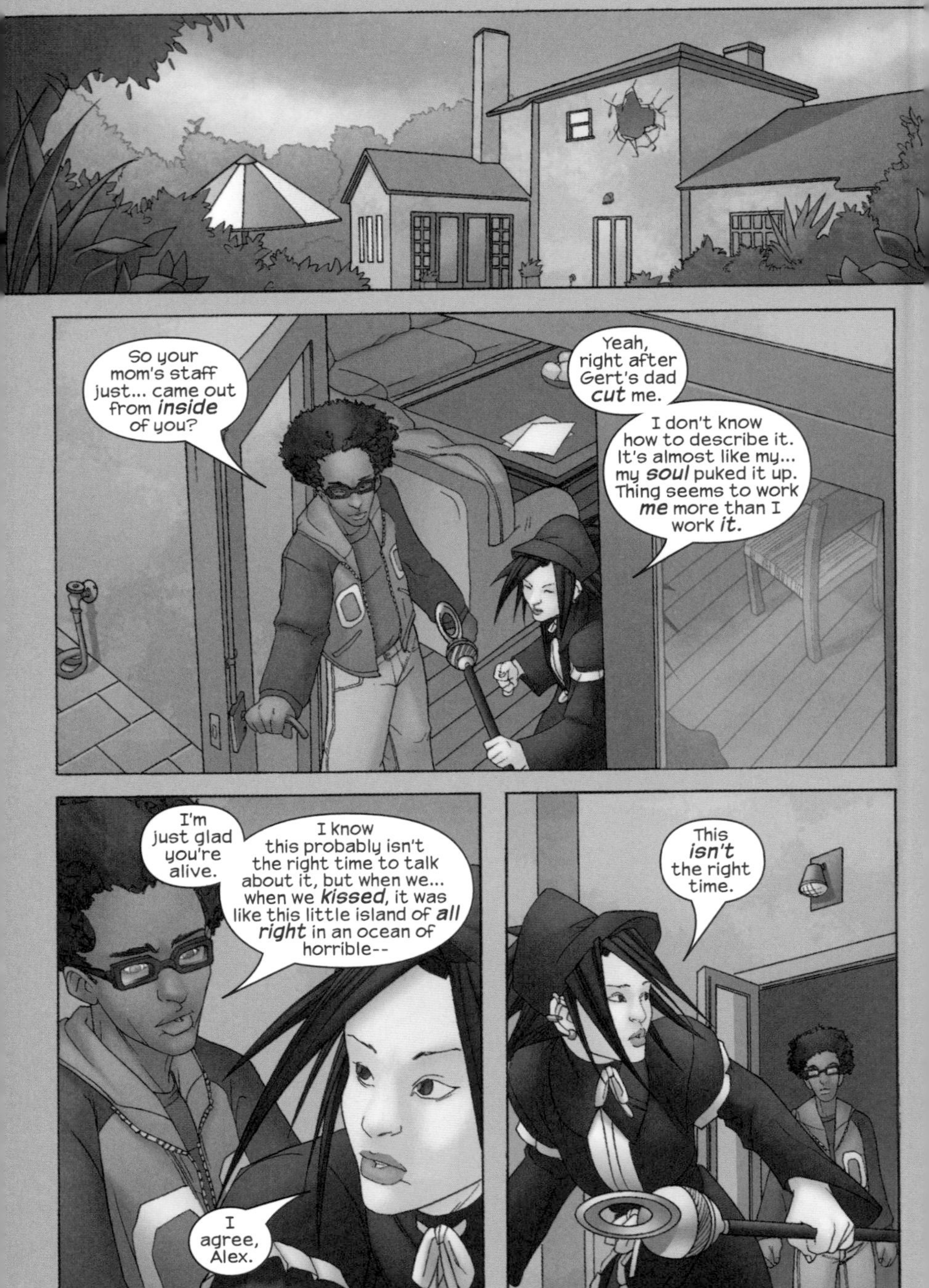
So your mom's staff just... came out from inside of you?
Yeah, right after Gert's dad cut me.
I don't know how to describe it. It's almost like my... my soul puked it up. Thing seems to work me more than I work it.
I'm just glad you're alive.
I know this probably isn't the right time to talk about it, but when we... when we kissed, it was like this little island of all right in an ocean of horrible--
I agree, Alex.
This isn't the right time.

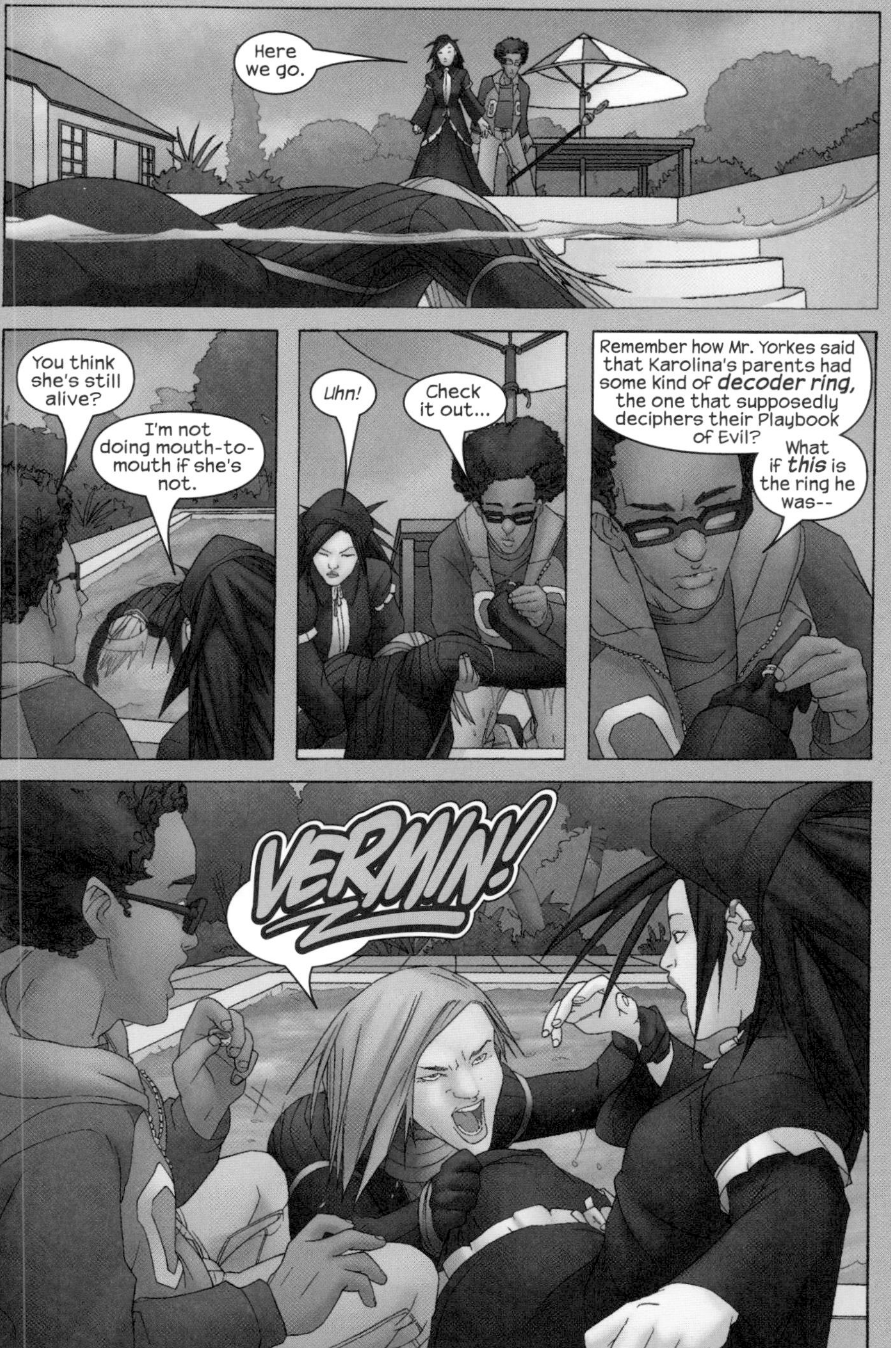
Here we go.
You think she's still alive?
I'm not doing mouth-to-mouth if she's not.
Uhn!
Check it out...
Remember how Mr. Yorkes said that Karolina's parents had some kind of decoder ring, the one that supposedly deciphers their Playbook of Evil?
What if this is the ring he was--
VERMIN!

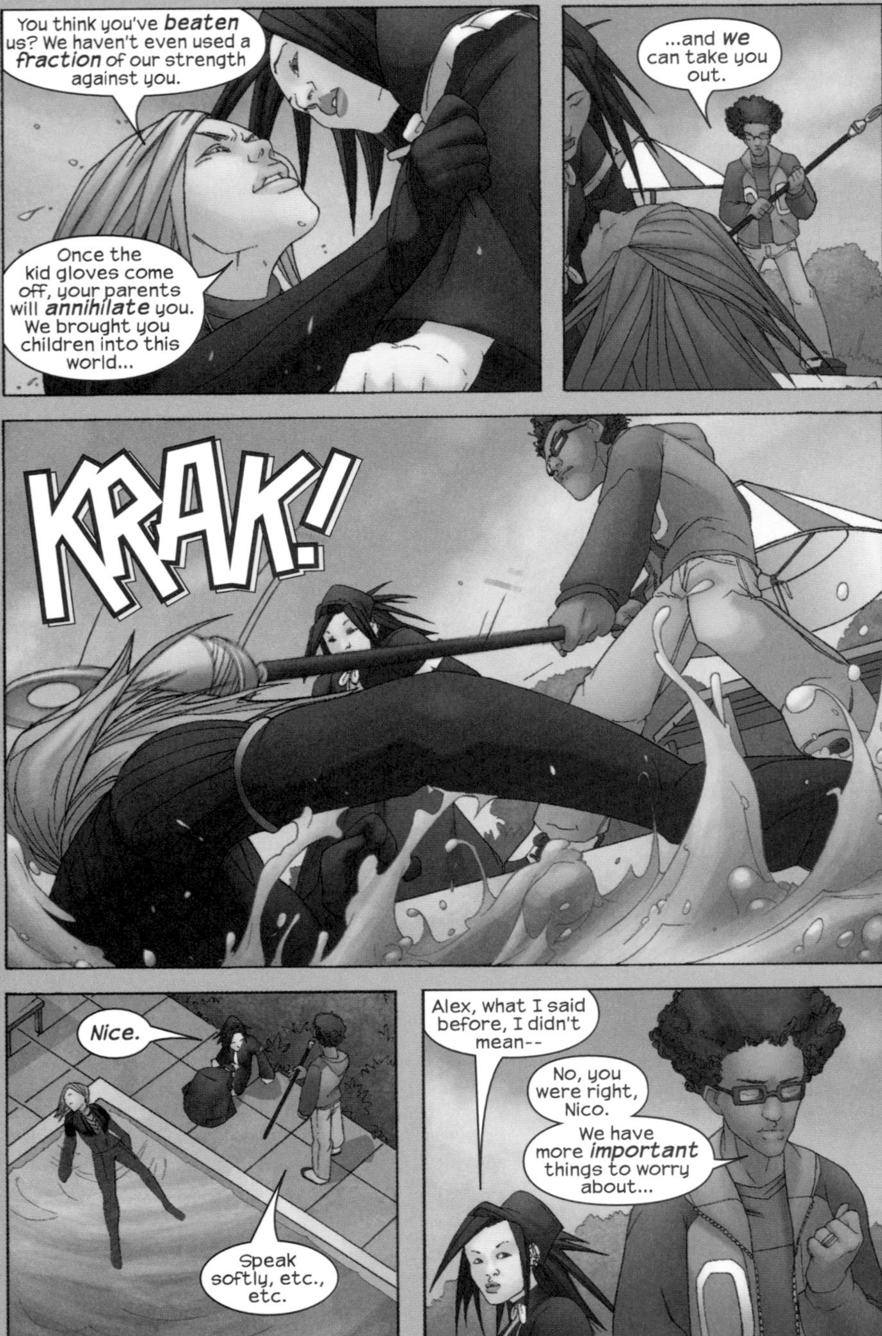
You think you've beaten us? We haven't even used a fraction of our strength against you.
Once the kid gloves come off, your parents will annihilate you. We brought you children into this world...
...and we can take you out.
KRAK!
Nice.
Speak softly, etc., etc.
Alex, what I said before, I didn't mean--
No, you were right, Nico.
We have more important things to worry about...

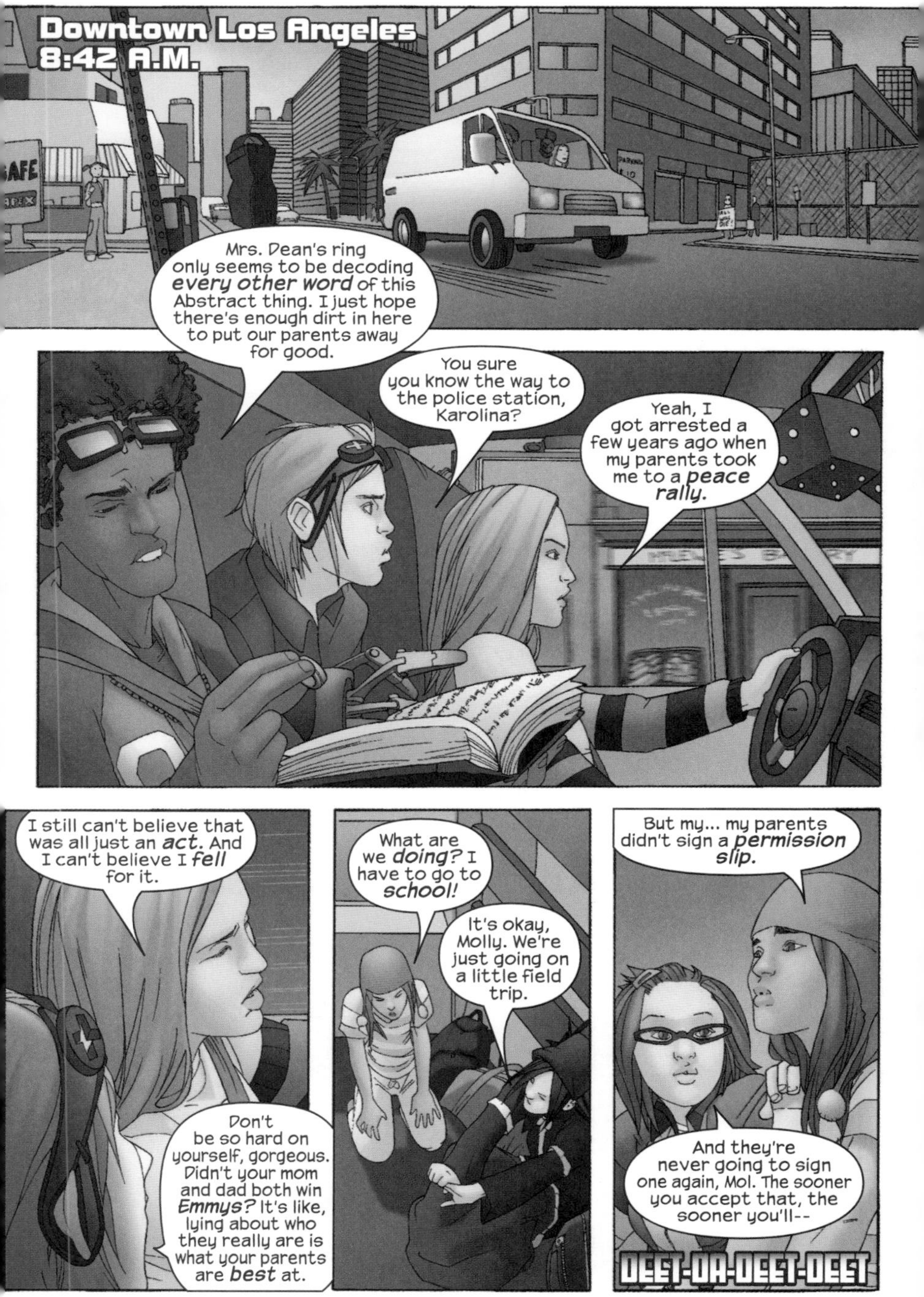
Downtown Los Angeles
8:42 A.M.
Mrs. Dean's ring only seems to be decoding every other word of this Abstract thing. I just hope there's enough dirt in here to put our parents away for good.
You sure you know the way to the police station, Karolina?
Yeah, I got arrested a few years ago when my parents took me to a peace rally.
I still can't believe that was all just an act. And I can't believe I fell for it.
Don't be so hard on yourself, gorgeous. Didn't your mom and dad both win Emmys? It's like, lying about who they really are is what your parents are best at.
What are we doing? I have to go to school!
It's okay, Molly. We're just going on a little field trip.
But my... my parents didn't sign a permission slip.
And they're never going to sign one again, Mol. The sooner you accept that, the sooner you'll--
DEET-DA-DEET-DEET

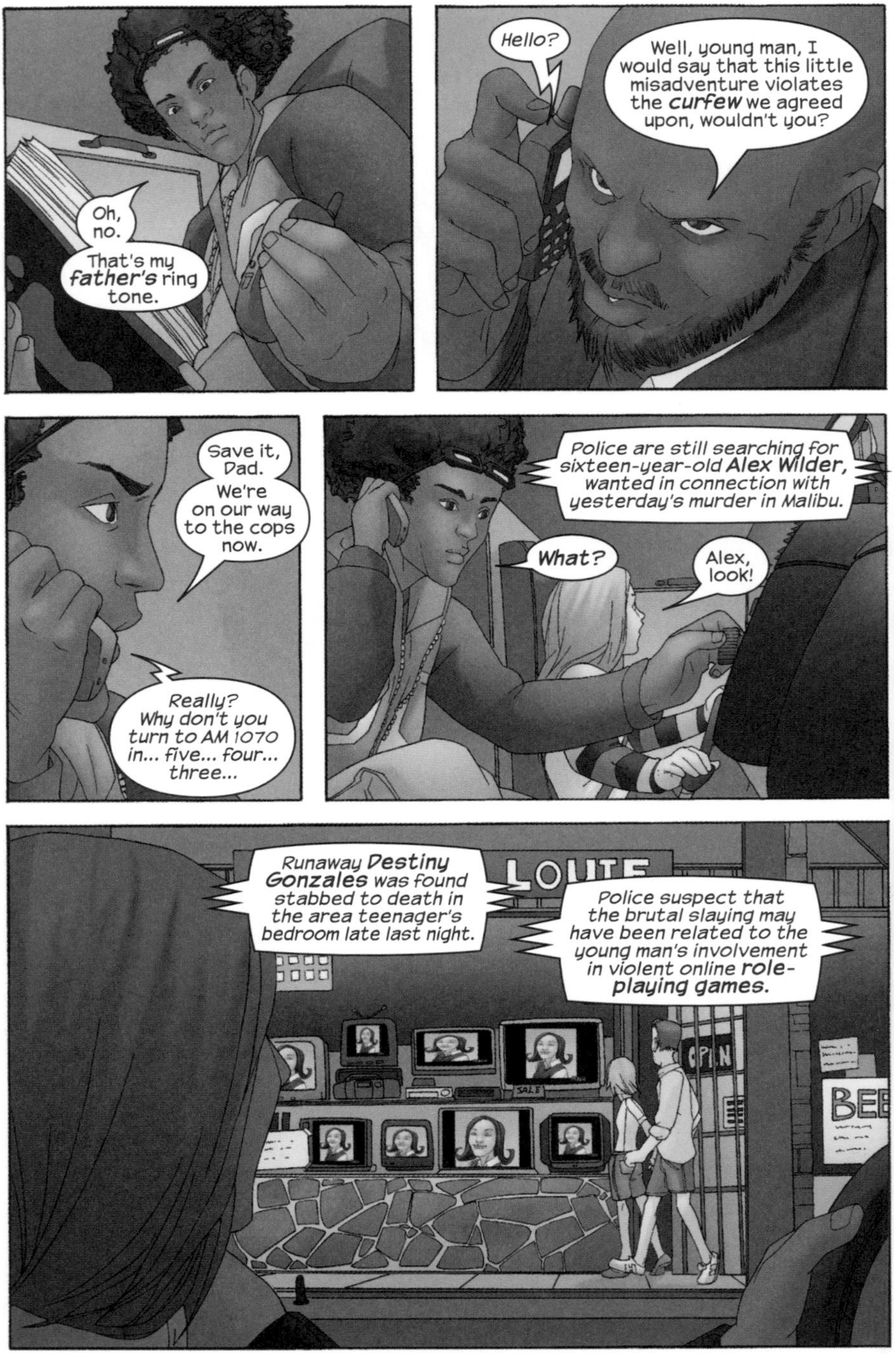
Oh, no.
That's my **father's** ring tone.
Hello?
Well, young man, I would say that this little misadventure violates the **curfew** we agreed upon, wouldn't you?
Save it, Dad.
We're on our way to the cops now.
Really? Why don't you turn to AM 1070 in... five... four... three...
Police are still searching for sixteen-year-old **Alex Wilder,** wanted in connection with yesterday's murder in Malibu.
What?
Alex, look!
Runaway **Destiny Gonzales** was found stabbed to death in the area teenager's bedroom late last night.
Police suspect that the brutal slaying may have been related to the young man's involvement in violent online **role-playing games.**
LOUTE
OPEN
SALE
BEE

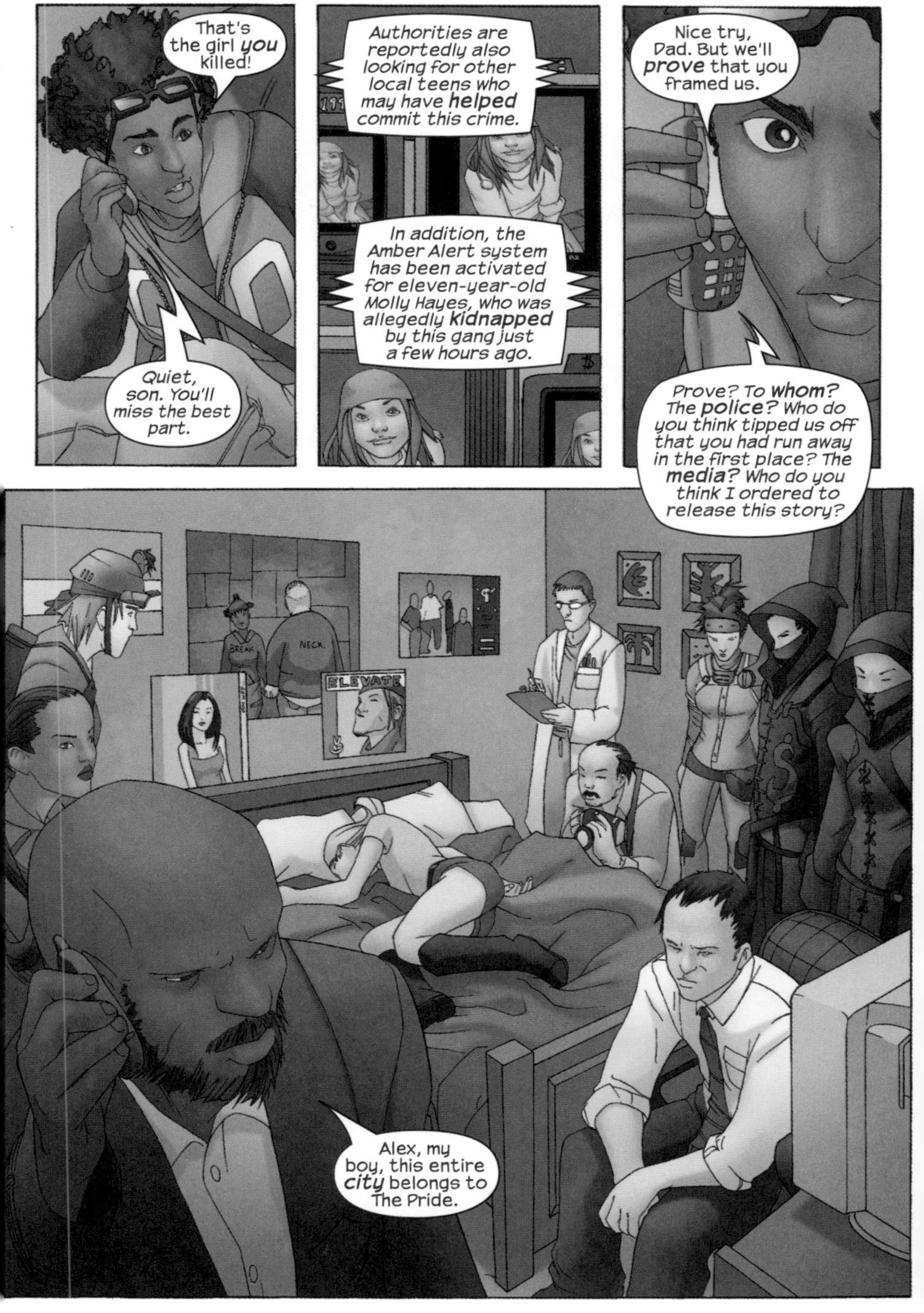
That's the girl you killed!
Quiet, son. You'll miss the best part.
Authorities are reportedly also looking for other local teens who may have helped commit this crime.
In addition, the Amber Alert system has been activated for eleven-year-old Molly Hayes, who was allegedly kidnapped by this gang just a few hours ago.
Nice try, Dad. But we'll prove that you framed us.
Prove? To whom? The police? Who do you think tipped us off that you had run away in the first place? The media? Who do you think I ordered to release this story?
BREAK
NECK
ELEVATE
Alex, my boy, this entire city belongs to The Pride.

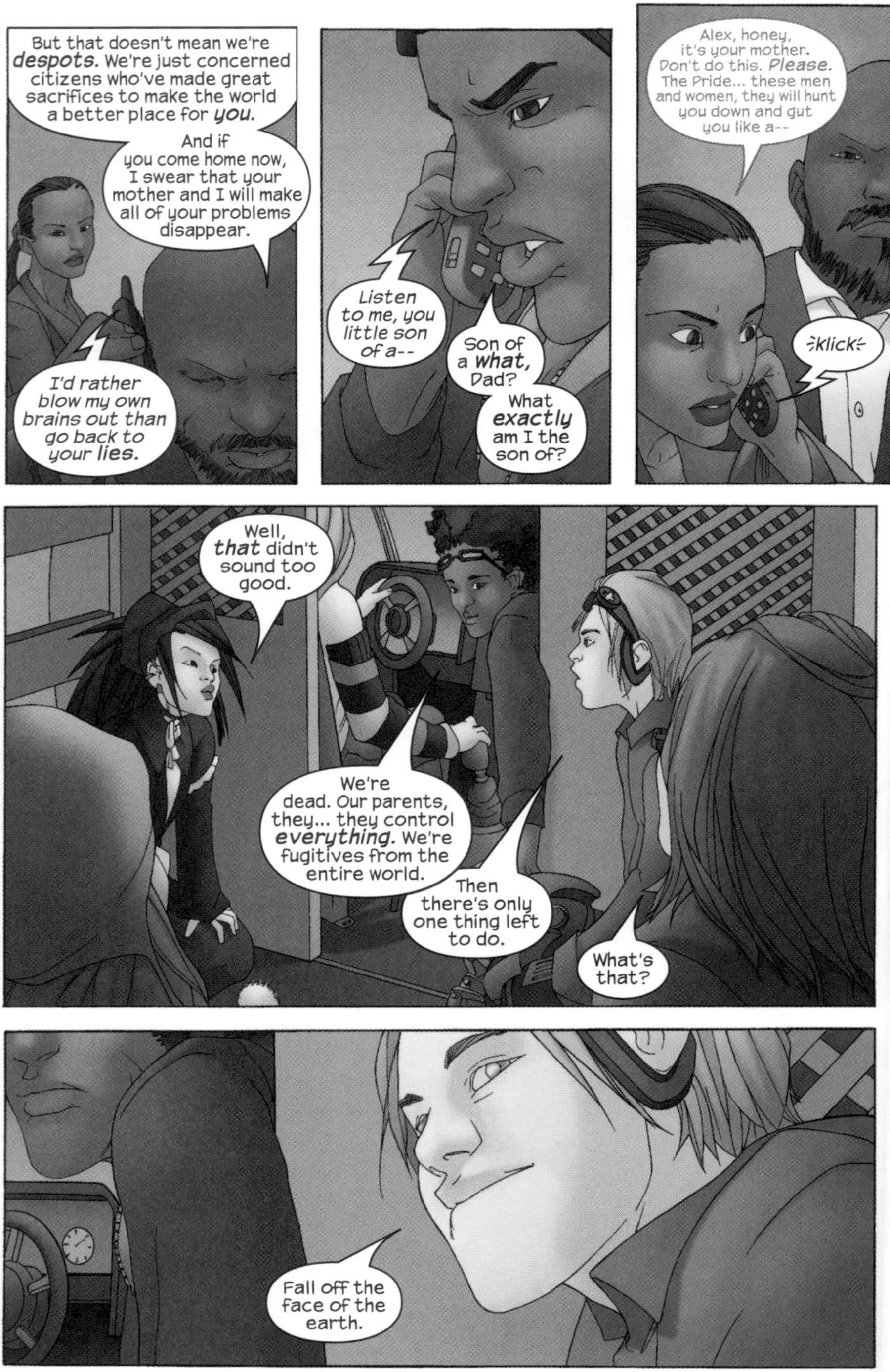
But that doesn't mean we're despots. We're just concerned citizens who've made great sacrifices to make the world a better place for you.
And if you come home now, I swear that your mother and I will make all of your problems disappear.
I'd rather blow my own brains out than go back to your lies.
Listen to me, you little son of a--
Son of a what, Dad?
What exactly am I the son of?
Alex, honey, it's your mother. Don't do this. Please. The Pride... these men and women, they will hunt you down and gut you like a--
klick
Well, that didn't sound too good.
We're dead. Our parents, they... they control everything. We're fugitives from the entire world.
Then there's only one thing left to do.
What's that?
Fall off the face of the earth.

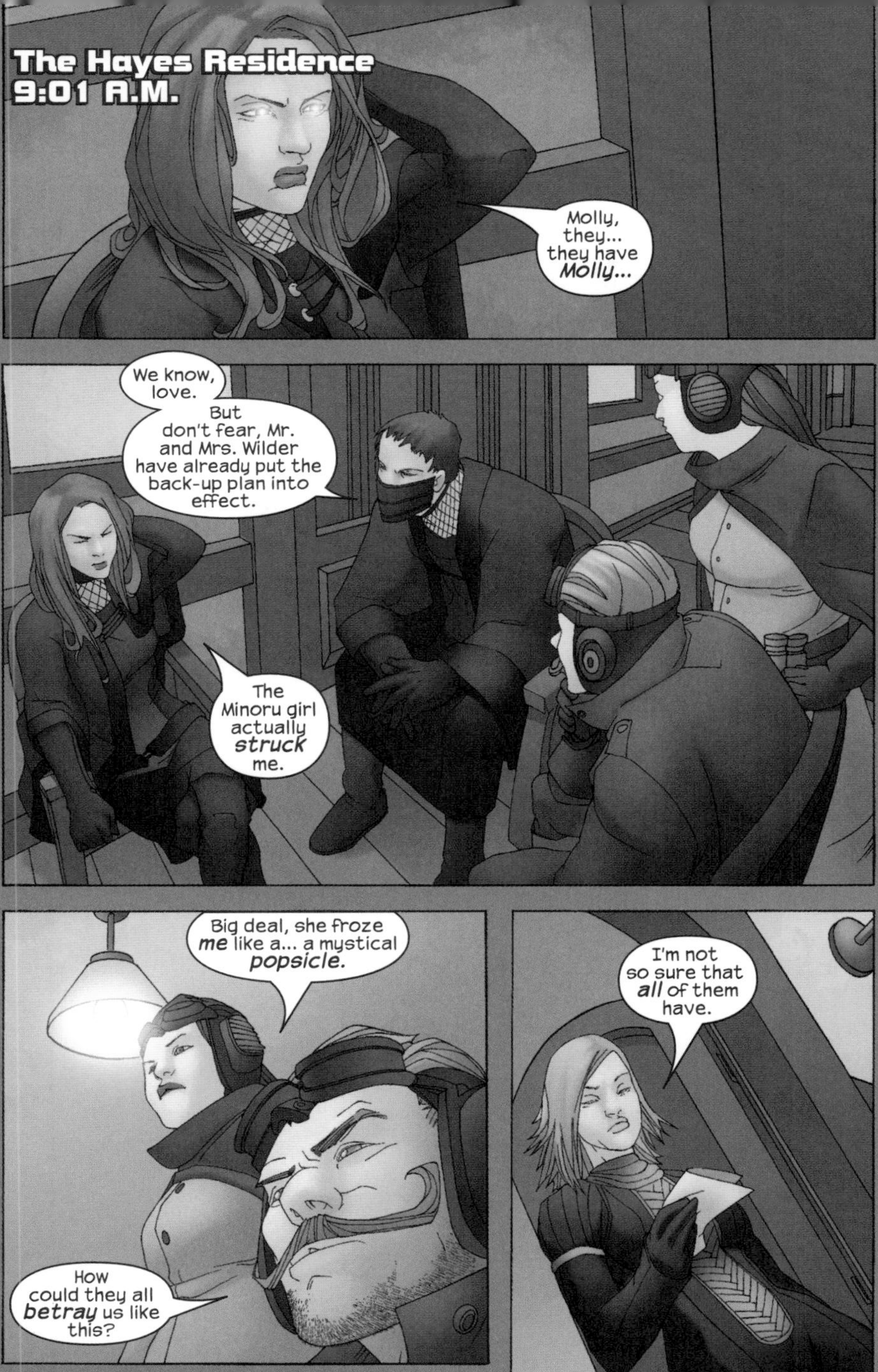
The Hayes Residence
9:01 A.M.
Molly, they... they have Molly...
We know, love.
But don't fear, Mr. and Mrs. Wilder have already put the back-up plan into effect.
The Minoru girl actually struck me.
Big deal, she froze me like a... a mystical popsicle.
How could they all betray us like this?
I'm not so sure that all of them have.

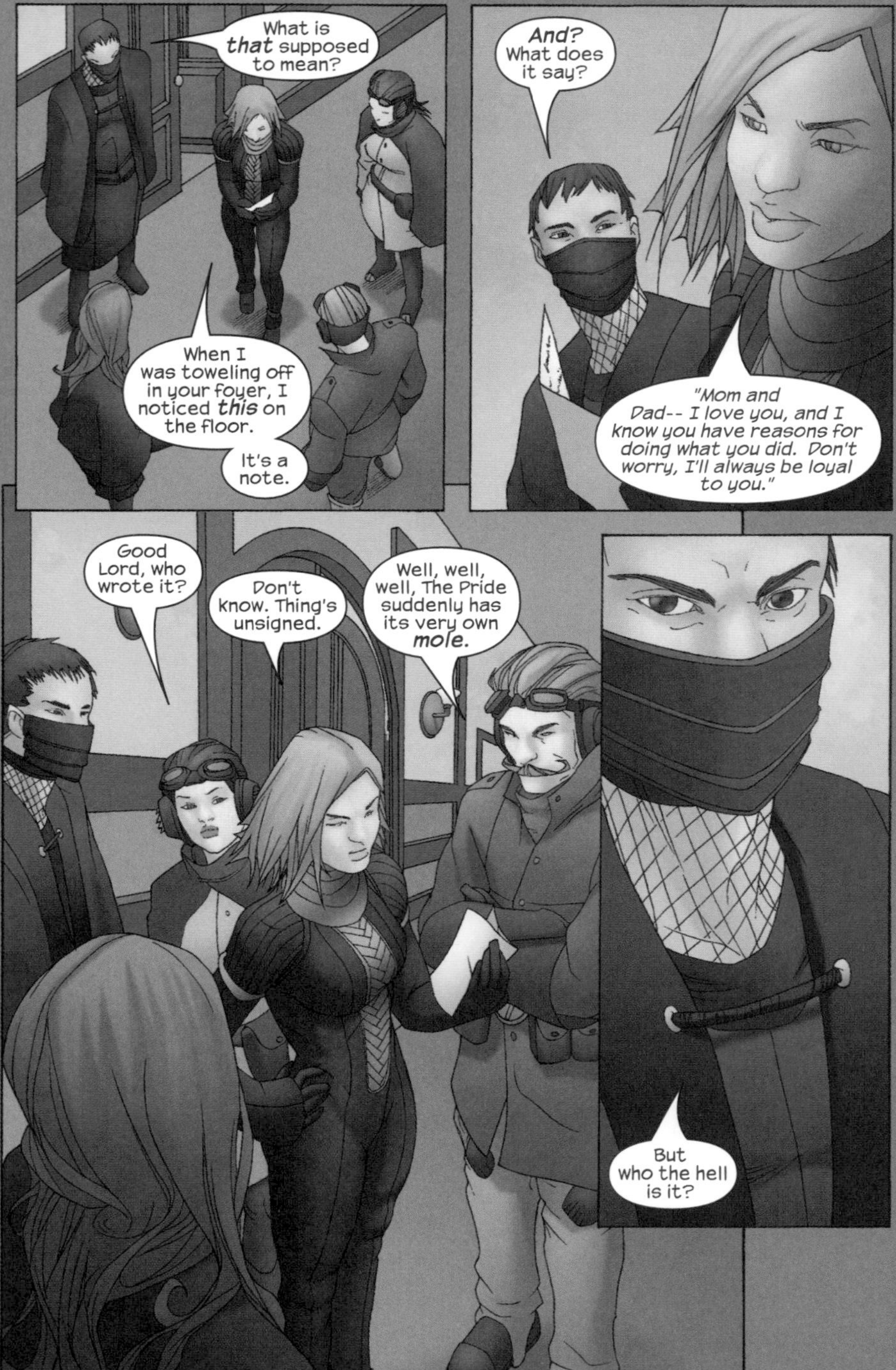
What is *that* supposed to mean?
When I was toweling off in your foyer, I noticed *this* on the floor.
It's a note.
And? What does it say?
"Mom and Dad-- I love you, and I know you have reasons for doing what you did. Don't worry, I'll always be loyal to you."
Good Lord, who wrote it?
Don't know. Thing's unsigned.
Well, well, well, The Pride suddenly has its very own *mole.*
But who the hell is it?

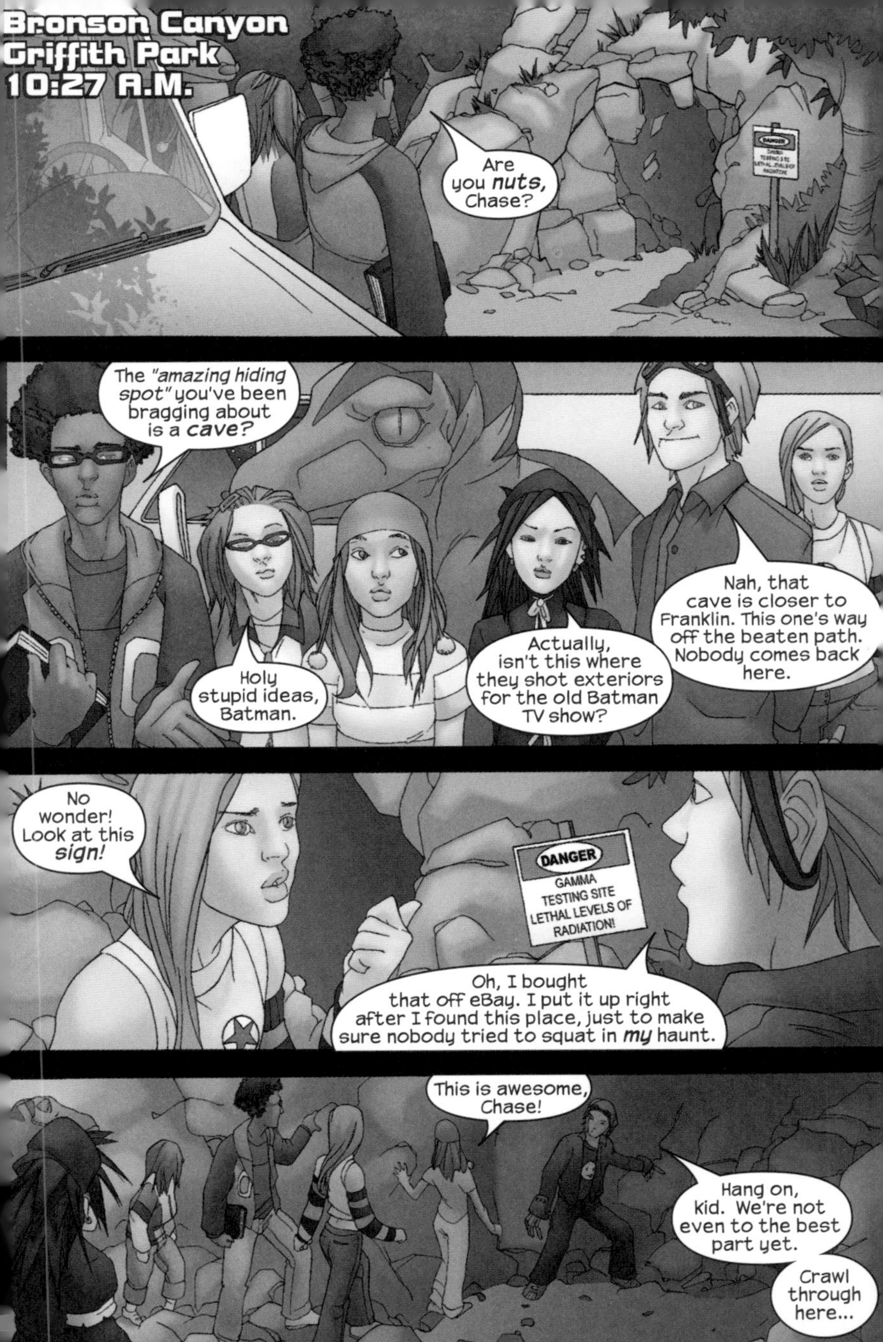
Bronson Canyon Griffith Park 10:27 A.M.
Are you *nuts,* Chase?
The *"amazing hiding spot"* you've been bragging about is a *cave?*
Holy stupid ideas, Batman.
Actually, isn't this where they shot exteriors for the old Batman TV show?
Nah, that cave is closer to Franklin. This one's way off the beaten path. Nobody comes back here.
No wonder! Look at this *sign!*
DANGER
GAMMA TESTING SITE
LETHAL LEVELS OF RADIATION!
Oh, I bought that off eBay. I put it up right after I found this place, just to make sure nobody tried to squat in *my* haunt.
This is awesome, Chase!
Hang on, kid. We're not even to the best part yet.
Crawl through here...

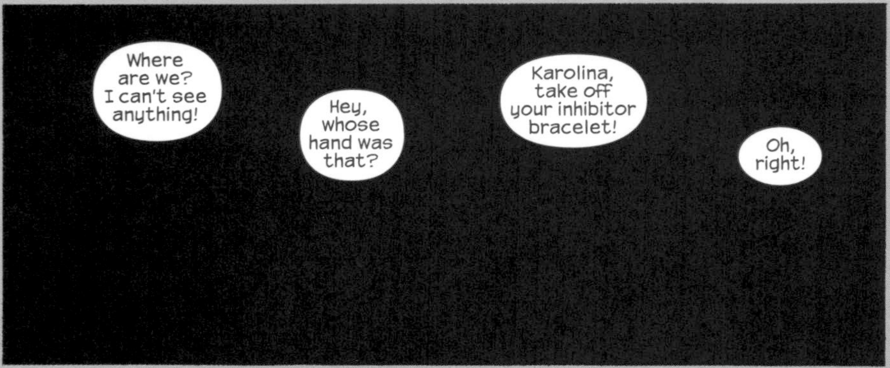
Where are we? I can't see anything!
Hey, whose hand was that?
Karolina, take off your inhibitor bracelet!
Oh, right!

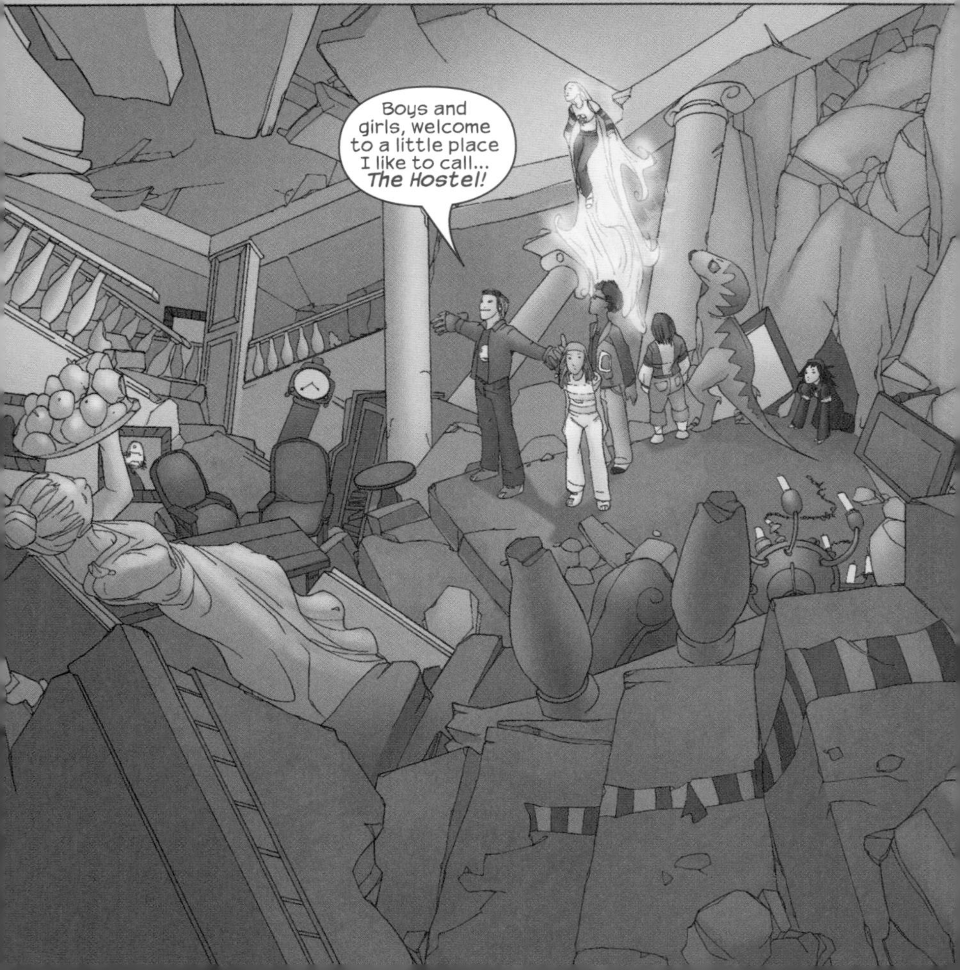
Boys and girls, welcome to a little place I like to call... *The Hostel!*

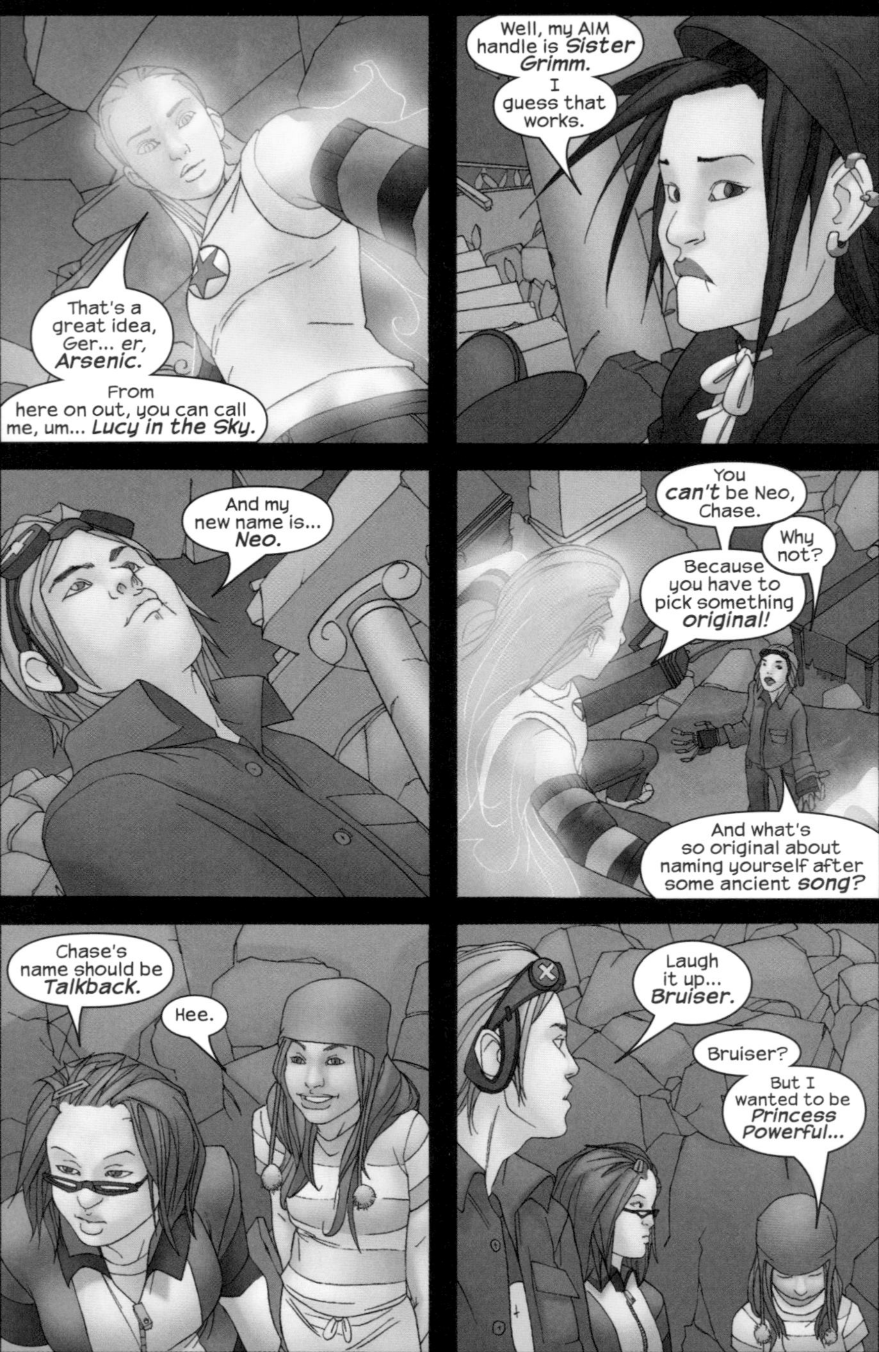
That's a great idea, Ger... er, Arsenic.
From here on out, you can call me, um... Lucy in the Sky.
Well, my AIM handle is Sister Grimm.
I guess that works.
And my new name is... Neo.
You can't be Neo, Chase.
Why not?
Because you have to pick something original!
And what's so original about naming yourself after some ancient song?
Chase's name should be Talkback.
Hee.
Laugh it up... Bruiser.
Bruiser?
But I wanted to be Princess Powerful...

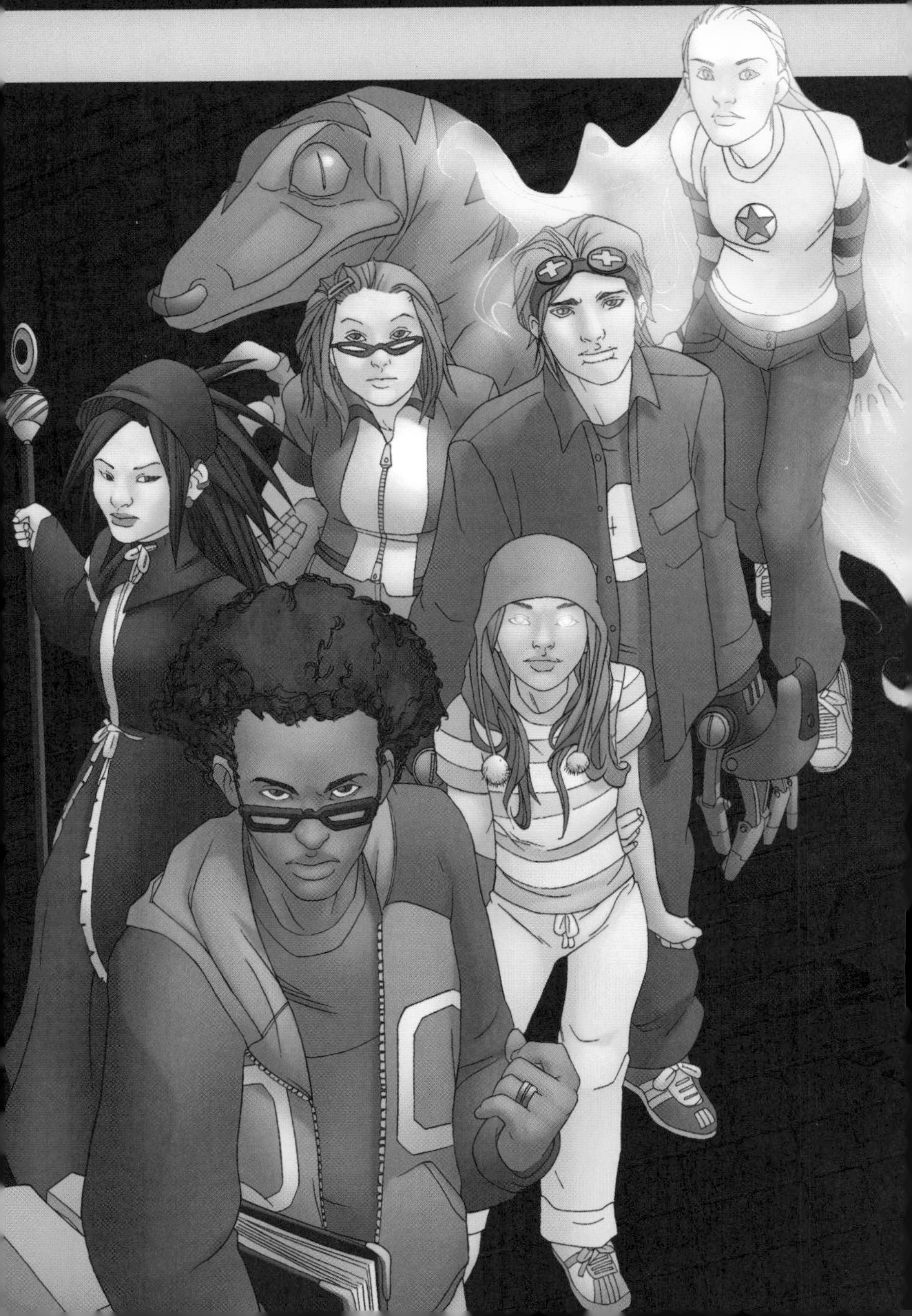

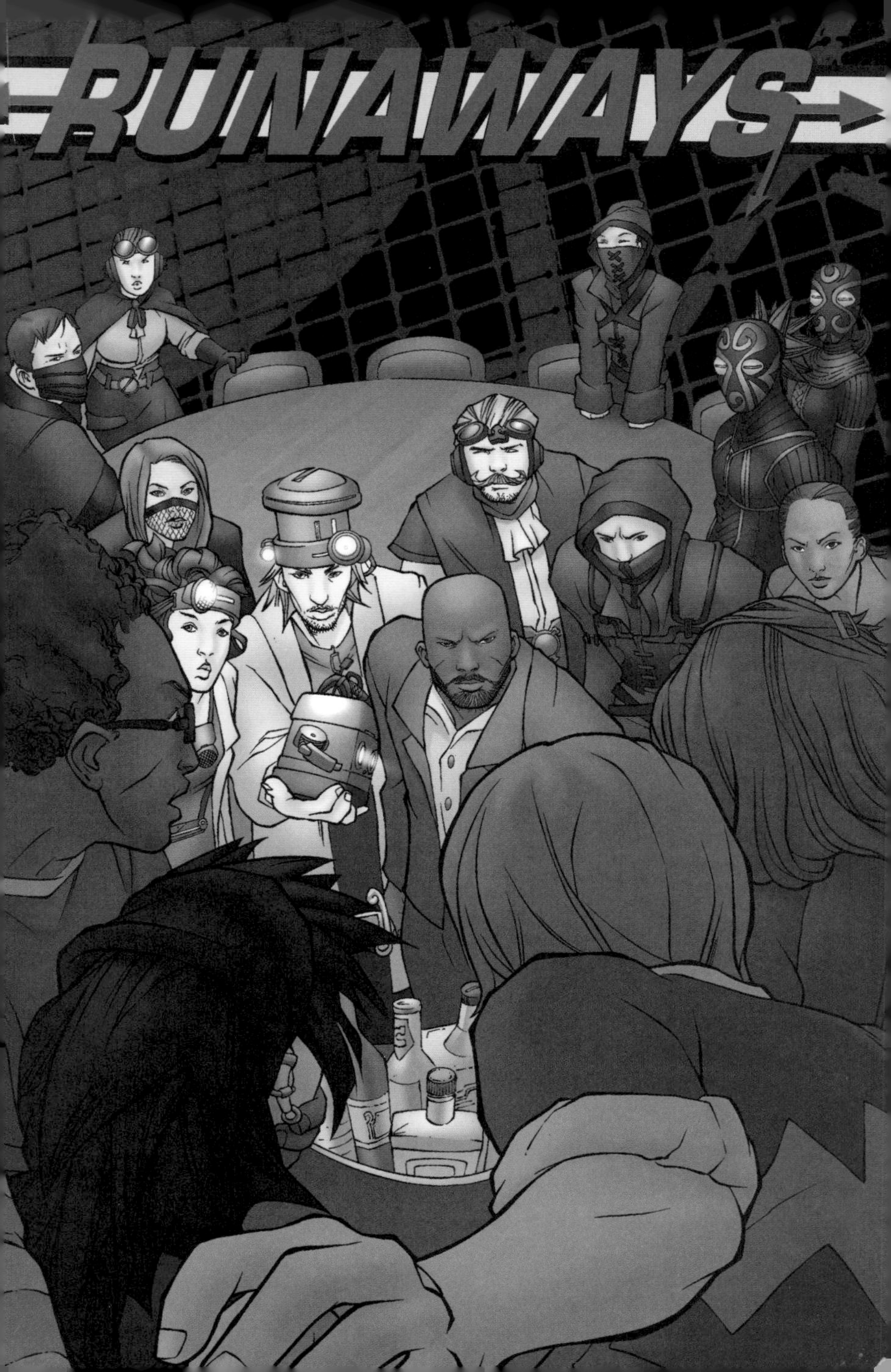
RUNAWAYS